SO-AYT-892

Student Science Opportunities

Student Science Opportunities

Your Guide to Over 300 Exciting National Programs,
Competitions, Internships, and Scholarships

Gail L. Grand

John Wiley & Sons, Inc.

New York • Chichester • Brisbane • Toronto • Singapore

Copyright © 1994 by Gail L. Grand
Published by John Wiley & Sons, Inc.

Library of Congress Cataloging-in-Publication Data:

Grand, Gail L., 1943—
    Student science opportunities : your guide to over 300 exciting
national programs, competitions, internships, and scholarships /
Gail L. Grand.
        p.   cm.
    Includes index.
    ISBN 0-471-31088-3 (pbk.)
    1. Science—Study and teaching (Secondary)—United States—
Handbooks, manuals, etc. 2. Science—Study and teaching
(Higher)—United States—Handbooks, manuals, etc. [1. Science—
Study and teaching. 2. Science—Competitions.]   I. Title.
Q183.3.A1G73   1994
507'.1'273—dc20   93-23412

Printed in the United States of America

10 9 8 7 6 5 4 3 2 1

To Harry, Alissa, Paul, and Tracy . . . With Love

Preface

At its core, this book is about opportunity—over 300 opportunities, actually—for people like you who are interested in science. Each opportunity may be considered an individual invitation to increase your knowledge, expand your world, and influence your choice of career. These opportunities are disguised as program descriptions, each telling you a bit about what awaits you if you choose to take part in that specific program. Most of the opportunities are directed toward high school and middle school students, while a few are open to younger or older students. However, any individual with an interest in learning more about science may find this guide a useful source of information.

Summer offerings range from wilderness adventures and science-oriented camps to intense study of a specific field of science or immersion in a research program or field experience. Summer programs might take you to a glacier in Alaska, a university campus in Colorado, a rain forest in Ecuador, an environmental center in the Poconos, a biological research facility in Maine, or a research vessel in the Pacific.

The school year presents you with additional opportunities. Research programs, distance-learning opportunities, school-break adventures and workshops, and specialized science schools all offer you a chance for hands-on, intensive, science experiences. Those of you who enjoy challenge will find descriptions of numerous contests and competitions that provide opportunities to test your knowledge and creativity.

Participation carries added rewards. There are intrinsic benefits gained through participation in a science program; students learn both about themselves and their world. In addition, scholarships and grants are offered to encourage capable young people to consider careers in the sciences and engineering.

Teachers serve on the front lines as providers of information, as mentors, and as advisors. Educators are encouraged to use this book as a resource in guiding their interested students to appropriate programs.

I encourage you to browse through the book, spending more time on those areas that inspire interest. Look over the appendixes and indexes that are provided to lead you to programs by subject, state, and program type. There is a separate index of programs for special populations such as women, minority students, the disabled, and the gifted.

Contact the programs that are of interest to you and consider their offerings carefully. All material presented has been drawn from the programs' informational publications and is as up-to-date as possible. However, course offerings sometimes change, or there may be revisions in program or application dates, length, or cost. Most of the offerings listed are sponsored or hosted by universities and science centers or are administered or funded by governmental agencies or private industry. Many of the science camps are accredited by the American Camping Association. Students and their parents are advised to investigate and evaluate the suitability of the specific programs they choose; the author does not endorse or evaluate any of the programs in this book.

Through the writing and publication of this resource guide, I have sought to reach out to our nation's most capable students and to make them aware of the opportunities available to those interested in the sciences. The National Science Foundation predicts severe shortages of scientists and engineers by the year 2005. Data has shown that students who participate in intensive science experiences before college are more likely to major in science or engineering while in college. Perhaps this book will have an impact on the expected shortfalls in technical areas.

Your involvement in one or more of these opportunities will make you more suited to life in a technological society, and you may decide to choose a rewarding career in the sciences or engineering. Perhaps, you may even be responsible for a discovery that makes the world a better place.

Acknowledgments

I gratefully acknowledge the many people who helped me to prepare this book. Numerous state science supervisors, program directors, and project coordinators supplied the program information described; in addition to information on their own programs, many also offered source advice and encouragement. My colleagues and students supplied both interest and ideas. I'm especially grateful for the input of both Linda Baumel and Donald Brott.

Family and friends were very supportive as I made my way through the process of readying this book for publication. Paul and Beverly Feldman and Alan and Ethel Pinkwasser contributed encouragement and moral support; Alan generously added his legal expertise and input. My parents, Helen Levin and Robert Grand, showed continued interest.

Finally, my heartfelt thanks go to my children. Alissa and Tracy supplied the enthusiasm that kept me researching and writing, while Paul gave willingly of both his time and considerable technical ability to help me organize the volume of information that arrived. Lastly, my gratitude goes to my husband, Harry, who supported my efforts, listened, offered ideas, edited text, and generally put up with me throughout. Thank you all.

Contents

Chapter 1   **"What I Did on My Summer Vacation":**
          A Guide to Summer Study Programs   **1**
          Aerospace   6
          Archaeology   13
          Astronomy   15
          Biological Science   17
          Engineering   31
          Environmental Science   57
          Health Science   71
          Marine Science   81
          Physical Science   95
          General Science   104

Chapter 2   **Academic-Year Adventures**   **201**

Chapter 3   **Challenge Yourself: Science Contests**
          and Competitions   **223**

Chapter 4   **Rewards for Young Scientists: Science**
          Scholarships   **245**

Appendix A   **Resources for Women and Minorities**   **263**

Appendix B   **National Agencies and Programs**   **269**

Indexes   **273**
          General Index   273
          State and Regional Index   280
          Index to Summer Programs by Subject   285
          Index to Field Experiences   288
          Index to Research Participation (Internship)
            Programs   289
          Index to Programs for Special Populations   291

"What I Did on My Summer Vacation":

A Guide to Summer Study Programs

Summer vacation—a time to hang out with friends, goof off, turn off your brain and vegetate, and work on your tan; perhaps a time to get a job, something exciting like bagging groceries, flipping burgers, or selling popcorn . . . . Why would anyone want to spend summer vacation studying? Actually, given the variety of summer programs available to high school and middle school students both in the United States and abroad and an understanding of all that a student might gain from these experiences, why *wouldn't* anyone want to spend summer vacation learning? Let's begin by looking at some of the benefits that you, the student, might obtain by investing a period of time, as little as five days to as much as the entire summer, in a summer program.

Summer programs can offer you experiences impossible to duplicate at your home school. You might find yourself involved in environmental studies on a glacier in the Juneau, Alaska, ice field or in a marine biology project in Santa Catalina, California. Perhaps you'll help with sea turtle research on a barrier island off the coast of Georgia or work on an archaeological dig excavating Anasazi Indian ruins in Colorado. You might spend your summer studying astronomy at an observatory in Arizona or using a supercomputer in Chicago. Whatever your interest in the fields of science and engineering, there is a program that will engage your time and challenge your imagination.

Summer programs allow you to take an early, realistic look at future career options. Unlike the little boy dreaming of being a fireman, high school students can explore careers and determine if their choice fits their abilities, interests, and personality characteristics. A program in engineering, or microbiology, or oceanography will give you a first-hand look at what the practicing engineer or scientist does. Time is provided for one-on-one conversations about the field with someone who does the work you're thinking about doing. You'll be able to put yourself in the picture and see how realistic the career choice is for you. In addition, many of the programs offer career counseling and presentations by scientists and engineers enthusiastic about their work and knowledgeable about future opportunities in their respective disciplines. Field trips to industrial sites and research facilities, often an integral part of the summer study programs, allow you to see science operating in the real world. You'll gain an accurate picture of what individuals engaged in the field actually do.

Summer study programs also provide participants with the opportunity to develop student-mentor relationships with faculty researchers and/or graduate students. You'll have the chance to work closely with someone who feels passionate about the work he or she does. These individuals serve as role models and advisors and may eventually become part of your professional network. If you do decide to pursue a scientific career, you'll be with people who can guide you in choosing an appropriate college and advise you about course selection.

Participation in a summer program also affords you the luxury of intensive study of a single discipline. During the school year, your day is fragmented as you take six or more different subjects; summer study can give you the opportunity to immerse yourself completely in a particular subject of interest to you. Here, too, you will find resources inaccessible to you during the school year: You'll be taught by professors knowledgeable in their fields; you'll have access to the university or program's libraries; you'll be able to use state-of-the-art laboratory equipment; and you'll have available computers and programs to speed data analysis.

Some of the other benefits of spending your summer learning are more intangible in nature. One is having a peer group of students who have similar interests and for whom it is "OK to be smart." One young man returned from a summer at Brandeis University elated to find that "there are other people like me." Formal and impromptu discussions are part of these programs; issues of current interest as well as topics such as scientific ethics are generally addressed. Summer study programs also have a social/recreational component. Students generally are encouraged to use the athletic facilities of the institution and have friends readily available when they want to play tennis, basketball, or go for a swim.

Still another benefit is the potential to get a taste of college life before you actually go to college. You'll learn about life in a dormitory, discover truisms about time and money management, and learn what it takes to be responsible for seeing to your own needs, such as laundry, or making time to study.

Finally, participation in a summer study program may give you an edge in the college admissions process. If you dream of attending a very selective institution, devoting your summer vacation to study demonstrates your serious commitment to education. Your experiences during the summer may become the focus of a required application essay or perhaps will evolve into a science project for a science fair or be incorporated into a research paper. You may also choose to have one of your summer college professors write a letter of recommendation for you to the college of your choice. The words of someone who is familiar with your ability to do college-level work carry a good deal of weight. Occasionally, participation in these programs affords students the opportunity to become eligible for college scholarships. Certainly, the summer will be like no other academic experience you have ever had. Sometimes, a summer experience may lend insight into a career that you will not want to pursue. Participation in a summer study program can affect the way you view education, challenge your ideas about your future, and perhaps even change the direction of your life.

PROGRAM TYPES

Part I of this book describes four major types of programs, categorized by academic intensity—summer study, internship, field experience, and science camp. *Summer study* is the largest group of programs and is the most academically rigorous. Participants in programs chosen from this group spend at least half their time in classroom lectures and science lab study. Programs of this type generally include field trips and both formal and informal discussions, but the focus is on academic study. Programs found in this group are the ones most likely to carry college credits.

The programs labeled *Internship* find participants spending the majority of their time in a research laboratory, pursuing answers to a scientific problem. The students generally work under the guidance of a faculty member, graduate student, or research scientist and are trained in research techniques, equipment use, and data analysis. Often, library research is a component to help the students become versed in the area being studied. Internship programs also may include field trips, discussion groups, and lectures, but their focus is on the research experience. Students often use results generated in this type of program as the basis for a science fair project. College credits may also be available.

Programs identified as *Field experience* place the participants at a research site; students learn about the topic being studied, are grounded in research techniques used to study the particular discipline, and participate in actual field research as part of a research team. Choosing a field experience program may lead to the student spending the summer on an archaeological dig, in a rain forest, on a glacier, or aboard a research vessel. College credits may also be available for field experiences.

The least academic of the summer programs is the *Science camp*. Campers may be involved in a wilderness camping experience, an ecological study, a sailing and navigation program, an archeology camp, or a marine biology program. The focus of science camps tends to be more recreational than academic, although learning definitely does take place, even if under the guise of fun.

USING THE LISTINGS

Each listing provides detailed information about the specific program, as well as a paragraph describing the experiences that are part of the program. You might simply want to browse through all of the programs, noting those that appeal to you most. If you are particularly interested in a specific scientific discipline, such as aerospace, marine science, engineering, or health sciences, you can begin your search in Part I, after checking the Contents listings or the Index by subject. Be sure to also look through listings under General Science for the more comprehensive programs that address a number of different areas of study. Within each area of study, the programs are grouped geographically by state, which are in alphabetical order. A special appendix at the end of the book will direct you to programs for minority students and women students. If you are limited to attending programs in a specific geographical area, you will find the index that lists programs by state helpful.

The program listings include the program name, which often indicates the program's focus, followed by host school when applicable.

Host School: Many of the programs are held on college campuses or at scientific institutes or research laboratories.

In addition, the listings include the following information:

Type: Describes the program's focus and academic intensity. Programs are categorized as summer study, internships, field experiences, or science camps.

Camper Level: Indicates the grade level or age of the campers (only for science camps).

Location: Indicates where the program is held.

Duration: Indicates length of program. Longer programs are more likely to offer college or high school credit.

Dates: Only approximate dates are listed. Specific dates vary from year to year. Contact the programs in which you are interested for this summer's dates.

Qualifications: The grade levels listed always refer to the grade in which the student will be the following fall. Occasionally, very qualified applicants one grade below those listed may be accepted. Ages refer to age at time of program unless otherwise specified.

Although all programs seek students who are interested in the program's focus, some programs have specific requirements. Some are limited to minority students, for example; others are for women only; some have academic qualifications (such as identification as "academically gifted"); while still others are limited to students residing in a particular state.

Housing: Although programs often include provision for commuter participants, programs usually provide residential housing options. On college campuses, this generally means living in a dormitory reserved for students of high school age. These dormitories are supervised by resident advisors or counselors associated with either the college or the program; more supervision is provided for younger students. Meals are provided in most cases, and supervised evening programs and weekend activities are an integral part of the program. Living with peers who have similar interests greatly enhances the summer experience; residential options should be chosen whenever possible. In addition to housing, students also have access to the university's athletic facilities, libraries, computer labs, and science laboratories. Living accommodations on field programs and at science camps are often Spartan. You might find yourself living in a group dorm or in a tent. However, some of the most rustic housing is found in the most spectacular natural settings.

Costs: Costs vary tremendously from program to program, depending upon duration, availability of college credits, and whether or not the program is subsidized by the college, private industry, or a governmental agency such as the National Science Foundation. In some cases, participants may receive full or partial scholarships to cover the cost of tuition, books, housing, and sometimes even transportation. A number of the internship programs pay the participants minimum wage as well as providing room and board. Generally, subsidized programs are limited to specific populations such as minority students or women. Need-based financial aid is usually available to assist students in paying the costs at unsubsidized programs. If you are applying for financial aid, be prepared to send copies of your parents' tax returns if requested by the program. Apply especially early to programs if you need financial aid to attend.

Credits Given: Indicates if college or high school credits are available. Science camp programs do not provide the opportunity to earn credits.

Contact: Write to (or phone) the contact listed for the programs in which you are interested. After reading the complete brochures, you will be able to determine which programs best suit you and can apply to the program(s) of your choice.

A descriptive paragraph concludes each listing, describing the program, listing areas of study and activity options, and providing a look at how the program is structured. Application deadlines are listed when available. If no deadline appears, a call to the program director will provide a closing date. Please note, however, that it is always better to complete your application as early as possible; many of the programs accept students on a rolling basis, filling places as qualified applicants apply. The later your application, the poorer your chance of acceptance. Occasionally, a program is not filled by the date listed; a phone call after that date will allow you to determine if space is still available.

LOCAL OPPORTUNITIES

If you cannot or do not wish to leave home this summer, how can you find out about local programs? If you are interested in a study program, call colleges, universities, or community colleges in your area and inquire about the availability of such programs. You might try contacting either the special program office or the office of continuing education. Even if no organized program exists, you may be able to take college-level courses as a special student. Also, check with your school guidance counselor. Your counselor may know of local opportunities, such as governor's programs or internships, that welcome commuter students. Call or write to your State Department of Education for additional options.

Another possibility is to check with local institutions such as science and nature museums and science institutes, the Department of Parks and Recreation, the National Park Service, or the local chapter of environmental groups such as Greenpeace or Earthwatch. These organizations often offer local students the opportunity to participate in summer courses or internships. If your interest is in research, you may be able to arrange your own laboratory experience. Try contacting the volunteer office or science research facilities at your area hospital and offer your services as an unpaid science intern. If your are interested in the health sciences, call your local veterinarian, optometrist, podiatrist, dentist, or medical doctor and ask if you can work as an apprentice. Spending your summer interning on a job may not provide you with funds, but the knowledge you gain about possible career options and the relationship you develop with a mentor may be far more rewarding than minimum wage. You will also gain insight into the applications of science and technology in the real world and begin to build a resume. Here's to a great, intellectually stimulating, and rewarding summer experience!

AEROSPACE

❖ Aviation Challenge

Type: Science camp
Camper Level: Basic: grades 7–9/Intermediate: grades 10–12
Location: Huntsville, AL
Duration: Five days
Dates: Late May through early September
Housing: Trainees are housed in an off-site, military-style facility on the campus of the University of Alabama in Huntsville, fully supervised at all times.
Costs: $650 covers all costs of the program. Scholarships are available based on financial need, ethnic background, and scholastic achievement.
Contact: Aviation Challenge
                  U.S. Space and Rocket Center
                  One Tranquility Base
                  Huntsville, AL 35807
                  (800) 63-SPACE

Aviation Challenge has been patterned on actual military jet-pilot programs; it encourages participants to meet physical and mental challenges in preparation for highly technical future study. Both levels focus instructionally on aerodynamics, flight systems, propulsion, maneuvering, emergency ejection, and land and water survival. In addition, trainees learn about civilian and military opportunities in aviation careers. Calisthenics and obstacle-course training help prepare participants for the rigors of aviation. In military-operations training, students study aircraft carrier operations and undergo training exercises. Tactical maneuvering and navigation are taught by former military pilots, and trainees practice skills on simulators. The program culminates in a networked flight simulation based on jet-fighter-pilot training.

❖ U.S. Space Academy

Type: Science camp
Camper Level: Level I: grades 7–9/Level II: grades 10–12
Location: Huntsville, AL
Duration: Five days for Level I; eight days for Level II
Dates: Throughout the year
Housing: Trainees are housed in the Space Habitat Complex in Huntsville and take their meals at the Training Center.
Costs: The program costs depend upon dates chosen. Level I price ranges from $525 for winter and spring programs to $650 for June through August. Level II program fee of $725 covers all costs. Scholarships are available based on scholastic achievement, ethnic background, and need.
Contact: U.S. Space Academy
                  U.S. Space and Rocket Center
                  One Tranquility Base
                  Huntsville, AL 35807
                  (800) 63-SPACE

The U.S. Space Academy program provides trainees with hands-on experience and academic training and allows them to participate in simulated space shuttle missions. Level I emphasizes shuttle crew activities, mission control, and space station simulations. Each camper is assigned to a team and trains for his or her mission assignment as a member of the shuttle crew, mission control, or space station team. The teams conduct two simulated shuttle flights, providing members the opportunity to experience mission control, space station, and orbital flight. Level II, for older students serious about careers in aerospace, provides more than 90 hours of instruction and training. Participants choose one of three tracks of study: technology, engineering, or aerospace. Technology and engineering trainees participate in entry-level scuba activities along with selected instruction in their field. The aerospace track trains students in mission control and space shuttle piloting.

❖ Sun Flight

Host School:	Embry-Riddle Aeronautical University
Type:	Summer study
Location:	Daytona Beach, FL, and Prescott, AZ
Duration:	Two weeks
Dates:	Late June to mid-July in Florida; end of July to early August in Arizona
Qualifications:	Ages 16 to 21 Students should have a strong interest in aviation.
Housing:	Sun Flight students are housed in Embry-Riddle dormitories and are supervised by live-in chaperones. Meals are provided on campus.
Costs:	$2,500 includes all flight, room, food, instruction, books and materials, simulator time, and tours. Sun Flight II option for additional instruction is $900.
Credits Given:	None
Contact:	Ms. Phyllis Gagnon Sun Flight Embry-Riddle Aeronautical University Center for Professional Programs 600 South Clyde Morris Boulevard Daytona Beach, FL 32114 (904) 226-6187; FAX (904) 226-6299

Sun Flight provides participants with the opportunity to fly and to explore career opportunities in the field of aviation. Students spend their weekday mornings in the cockpit of an airplane learning to fly; a goal of Sun Flight is for students to solo by the end of the two-week program. The flight phase includes 14 hours of observation time, 14 hours of hands-on, dual flight instruction, 4 hours of preflight and postflight instruction, and one-half hour of solo time if ready. Afternoons are spent in field trips and career exploration. Evenings are devoted to ground instruction, which consists of 22 hours of training in regulations, basic aerodynamics, navigation, and basic flight maneuvers, and studying. A second phase (six more days) is also available, and prepares students to take the Federal Aviation Administration (FAA) Private Pilot Written Test. Application deadline: contact program for information.

❖ Careers in Aerospace Summer Camp

Type:	Science camp
Camper Level:	Grades 10–12
Location:	Cahokia, IL
Duration:	Eight days
Dates:	Two sessions: mid-June and mid-July
Housing:	Students are housed in the dormitories of Parks College.
Costs:	$500 includes flight and simulator time, instruction, lodging and meals for seven days, and field trips.
Contact:	Mr. Paul McLaughlin
	Careers in Aerospace Summer Camp
	Director, Summer Aerospace Camp
	Parks College of St. Louis University
	Cahokia, IL 62206
	(618) 337-7575 ext. 364; (800) 851-3048

Students interested in exploring career opportunities in aerospace and aviation can spend eight exciting days totally involved in this world. The program is held at Parks College of St. Louis University, an institution known for the quality of its aerospace education program. Orientation sessions are held exploring fields such as aeronautical administration, aerospace engineering, aviation science, aircraft maintenance, computer science, electrical engineering, and meteorology. Aerospace activities include ground training, instruction in a flight simulator, flying time in a Mooney aircraft with a flight instructor, and model rocketry construction and launch. Field trips to Air Force bases and airports are included.

❖ Illinois Aerospace Institute

Host School:	University of Illinois
Type:	Summer study
Location:	Urbana, IL
Duration:	One week
Dates:	Early July
Qualifications:	Grades 9-12
	Students should be interested in aerospace as a possible career choice.
Housing:	Students live in a campus residence hall, eat meals with team members, and are supervised by live-in counselors. Students have access to the university library and all sports facilities.
Costs:	$650 includes all instructional costs, lodging, and meals.
Credits Given:	None
Contact:	Ms. Diana Jeffers
	Illinois Aerospace Institute
	University of Illinois
	308 Talbot Lab
	104 South Wright Street
	Urbana, IL 61801
	(217) 244-8048

The program seeks to introduce participants to the excitement and opportunities of aerospace science and engineering. The students are divided into 10-member "design teams" and rotate through a curriculum that includes aeronautical engineering: exploring aerodynamics and principles of aircraft design through a visit to a wind tunnel and hands-on experiments with model planes and jet- and rocket-propulsion systems, and experiments with model rockets. Astronautical engineering explores space flight from launch through reentry, while communications in space and the electronic systems needed are explored. A course in aviation technology explores navigation and air traffic control and enables students to fly in a simulator and in a small airplane. Application deadline: March 15.

❖ Space Science Activities Workshop

Host School:	University of Northern Iowa
Type:	Summer study
Location:	Cedar Falls, IA
Duration:	Two weeks
Dates:	Middle through late June
Qualifications:	Grades 10-12
	Students should have a demonstrated interest in science and at least a 2.0 grade point average.
Housing:	Students are provided with housing and meals at the university.
Costs:	There is no cost to the student for this workshop. Travel expenses are also provided. This program is sponsored by the Iowa Space Grant Consortium and the University of Northern Iowa.
Credits Given:	None
Contact:	Space Science Activities Workshop
	University of Northern Iowa
	Physics Department
	Cedar Falls, IA 50614-0150

This unusual program provides students interested in space science with an opportunity to learn about the field, perform experiments that are associated with space science, and explore career opportunities in this area. The workshop presents space through an interdisciplinary study of related sciences and presents numerous opportunities for students to take part in hands-on discovery activities. Some of the activities include experiments at an amusement park, others involving hot air balloons, and microgravity simulations in a swimming pool. Field trips, equipment construction, use of NASA materials and computer software are supplemented by evening observational astronomy and scuba diving. Secondary school science teachers team with students to test materials for use in their home schools. Application deadline: April 27.

❖ Future Astronaut Training Program (Space Camp) at The Kansas Cosmosphere & Space Center

Type:	Science camp
Camper Level:	Grades 7–9
Location:	Hutchinson, KS
Duration:	Five days

Dates:	Multiple sessions from beginning of June through early August
Housing:	Campers live in the Hutchinson Community College dormitory with adult counselors.
Costs:	$495 for Level I; $545 for Level II. Fee includes room, board, flight jacket, model rocket, and all materials.
Contact:	Future Astronaut Training Program (Space Camp) Kansas Cosmosphere and Space Center 1100 North Plum Hutchinson, KS 67501-1499 (800) 397-0330

Two levels of programs are offered introducing campers to the world of space. Level I campers become part of a space shuttle crew, learning to work together to successfully launch a payload into orbit. Participants learn about life in space, explore spacecraft design, train on simulators, examine rocket engines, build and launch their own model rockets, study in the KCSC planetarium, use telescopes, and "fly" the Falcon—launch through landing. Level II students continue training begun in Level I, learn about careers in America's space program, and spend two days at the Johnson Space Center with NASA personnel.

❖ Epoch Pilot: Private Pilot Training for High School Students

Host School:	University of North Dakota, Aerospace
Type:	Summer study
Location:	Grand Forks, ND
Duration:	Two months
Dates:	Summer
Qualifications:	Grade 12 and at least age 17 by August 1
Housing:	Participants live in one of UND's modern residence halls. Shuttle buses provide transportation around campus and to the airport. Meals are provided in the dining halls.
Costs:	Average cost is about $5,600, which includes $4,700 flight costs, $700 for room and board, $60 for tuition, and $150 for books and supplies. There is an additional cost for students choosing to take other classes.
Credits Given:	5 college credits for the aviation classes. Students can also earn additional college credits.
Contact:	Epoch Pilot: Private Pilot Training for High School Students University of North Dakota, Aerospace University and Tulane Grand Forks, ND 58202-8216 (701) 777-2791; (800) 258-1525; FAX (701) 777-3016

The Epoch Pilot Program is designed to teach students how to fly and to earn their Private Pilot Certificate during summer break. Along with university students, participants in this program learn to fly in new Piper Cadets and Aerospatiale Tampicos, taught by university instructors. Ground-school training and UND-developed computer software, along with practice in the Frasca flight simulators, provide the training to make students competent pilots. UND Aerospace is recognized as a leader in aviation education and is endorsed by both Northwest Airlines and Airbus for their pilot programs. Participants can also take additional UND college courses while learning to fly, getting a jump start on their college education. Application deadline: contact program for information.

❖ International Aerospace Camp

Host School:	University of North Dakota
Type:	Summer study
Location:	Grand Forks, ND
Duration:	Ten days
Dates:	Two sessions: Middle to late July and late July through early August.
Qualifications:	Ages 14 to 16 Students should have an interest in aviation and a desire to explore career opportunities in aerospace science.
Housing:	Students are housed in double rooms at Walsh Hall, a dormitory on the University of North Dakota campus, and are supervised by Aerospace Camp staff during the day and by university housing staff in the evening. Meals are provided.
Costs:	$995 includes flight time, advanced ground training time, instruction, T-shirt, 11 nights lodging, and meals.
Credits Given:	None
Contact:	Mr. Ken Polovitz International Aerospace Camp University of North Dakota Center for Aerospace Sciences Box 8216 University Station Grand Forks, ND 58202-8216 (701) 777-2791; (800) 258-1525; FAX (701) 777-3016

The word *camp* in the name of the program is a misnomer; this program is actually a 10-day educational seminar in which students get to log flight time, build rockets, and learn about the past, present, and future of aerospace. Classes in aerodynamics and labs involving model aircraft combined with student flights (with an instructor) in a fixed-wing simulator and five different aircraft all help give participants a firsthand look at aviation. Numerous trips and tours, aircraft design competitions, and a full range of athletic activities round out this program. Application deadline: rolling admissions.

❖ Oklahoma Aerospace Academy

Host School:	University of Oklahoma
Type:	Summer study/Science camp
Location:	Norman, OK
Duration:	Five days
Dates:	Mid-June through early August, depending upon level
Qualifications:	Ages 11 to 14 and 15 to 18 Participants should be interested in exploring aerospace technology.
Housing:	Cadets are housed in the university dormitories adjacent to the Academy. All meals are provided.
Costs:	$445 includes housing, meals, instruction, flight suit, and squadron photo. A discount is available for early registration (by March 15).

Credits Given: None
Contact: Oklahoma Aerospace Academy
University of Oklahoma
1600 S. Jenkins
Norman, OK 73037-0008
(405) 325-1635

The emphasis of this interdisciplinary, hands-on program is on problem solving through cooperative learning and team activities. The program focuses on the growing field of aerospace science and actively involves the participants in learning by doing. Cadets at the Aerospace Academy take classes in space architecture, rocketry, aviation, and robotics while training for a simulated space shuttle mission. Students are grouped by age and experience level. All participants gain an expanded knowledge of aviation, aerospace, science, and engineering while having fun. Advanced camps are held for cadets who have previously attended other sessions of the Academy. Application deadline: rolling admissions.

❖ Summer Space Academy at the Penn State National Space Grant College

Host School: Penn State University
Type: Internship
Location: University Park, PA
Duration: Two weeks
Dates: Late June through early July
Qualifications: Grades 11 or 12
High-achieving and high-potential students are eligible. Students should have strong grades and have completed a course in Algebra II. Female, minority, and disabled students are strongly encouraged to apply.
Housing: Students are housed in supervised campus residence halls and are provided with meals.
Costs: The program is free. Tuition, housing, meals, and research materials are provided by grants from sponsoring organizations. Students are responsible only for personal expenses and travel costs.
Credits Given: None
Contact: Dr. Richard Devon
Summer Space Academy
Penn State University
245 Hammond Building
University Park, PA 16802
(814) 865-2952; FAX (814) 863-7229

Students interested in space-related topics can spend an exciting two weeks working with engineers and scientists in their laboratories at Penn State. Participants engage in research in challenging areas that include studies on black holes, the origins of the universe, the effects of weightlessness, and changing patterns of the world's ecosystems. Daily discussions about research and careers are led by practicing scientists, engineers, and mathematicians. Students tour laboratories conducting space-related research and use the libraries to read up on the newest advances. Free time may be spent using Penn State's athletic facilities (including both the swimming pool and ice rink), and taking part in informal discussions. Application deadline: March 26.

ARCHAEOLOGY

❖ Crow Canyon Archaeological Center High School Field School

Host School:	Crow Canyon Archaeological Center
Type:	Field experience
Location:	Cortez, CO
Duration:	Four weeks
Dates:	End of June through end of July
Qualifications:	Grades 9-12 and at least age 14 by March 1
	Students should have an interest in archaeology
Housing:	Housing accommodations are in comfortable log hogans or in the Crow Canyon Lodge.
Costs:	$2,200 for the four-week program. High school students may also participate in one-week adult research programs.
Credits Given:	High school credit is available.
Contact:	Ms. Dottie Sanders
	Crow Canyon Archaeological Center High School Field School
	Crow Canyon Archaeological Center
	23390 County Road K
	Department DU
	Cortez, CO 81321
	(303) 565-8975; (800) 422-8975

Participants in Crow Canyon's High School Field School gain hands-on excavation experience and an early look at archaeology as a career option. Students become part of the Crow Canyon research team and make real contributions to the excavation and field work. The program begins with an introduction to Southwestern prehistory and archaeology, visiting excavation sites and participating in the digs. Time is spent with archaeologists both in the field and in the lab analyzing artifacts. Two weekend camping trips take place in the mountains and/or the desert. Participants also tour Mesa Verde. Evening programs further the learning experiences. Days are warm and the sun is bright; nights are cool. Application deadline: contact program for information.

❖ Center for American Archaeology: One Week Field School

Host School:	Center for American Archaeology
Type:	Field experience
Location:	Kampsville, IL
Duration:	One week
Dates:	Early June through early July
Qualifications:	High school or college student or adult
	Participants should have an interest in archaeology.
Housing:	Students are housed in separate men's and women's dormitories with live-in college- and graduate-student chaperones. Meals are served at the Center.

Costs:	$400 for high school students
Credits Given:	None
Contact:	Center for American Archaeology: One Week Field School
	Center for American Archaeology
	Box 366
	Kampsville, IL 62053
	(618) 653-4316

High school students may participate along with college students and adults in one or more field schools at a working archaeological dig in Kampsville, Illinois. Participants excavate and participate in a variety of archaeological experiences. Daytime hours are split between work on the dig and work in the laboratory, while evenings are devoted to study and lectures. The cultural history of the region is investigated in a hands-on manner using data and artifacts from the Center's collections. Students also learn to use experimental archaeology to reconstruct ceramics, stone tools, and prehistoric dwellings. Application deadline: contact program for information.

❖ NSF's Young Scholars Program: Archaeology and the Natural Sciences Center for American Archaeology

Host School:	Center for American Archaeology
Type:	Field experience
Location:	Kampsville, IL
Duration:	Five or six weeks
Dates:	Early June through mid-July; mid-July through end of August
Qualifications:	Grades 11 or 12
	Students should have an interest in archaeology.
Housing:	Students live in separate men's and women's dormitories where they are supervised by college- and graduate-student chaperones. Meals are provided except during weekends.
Costs:	$1,750 for the five-week program; limited financial aid is available. The six-week program is funded by NSF and offers full tuition scholarships. Room and board fee is $90 per week. Some need-based aid is available for the six-week program to offset expenses.
Credits Given:	High school credit in world history.
Contact:	NSF's Young Scholars Program: Archaeology and the Natural Sciences
	Center for American Archaeology
	Box 366
	Kampsville, IL 62053
	(618) 653-4316

During this field school program, students get extensive training in the various aspects of archaeology, including excavation, analysis, geomorphology, botany, zoology, and stone-tool analysis. Students spend much of the day on the dig and some of their time assisting in the laboratory. Participants work closely with professional researchers to design independent research projects that increase the world's body of knowledge. Each student also participates in a series of lectures on the prehistory of the Midwest, and attends guest lectures on current research and excavations going on in the Midwest. Special seminars explore the ethical issues that face contemporary archaeologists. Weekends are devoted to individual research projects and field trips. Application deadline: contact program for information.

❖ Young Scholars Research Participation Program in Paleontology/Geology

Host School:	Oregon Museum of Science and Industry (OMSI)
Type:	Field experience
Location:	Portland, OR
Duration:	Six weeks
Dates:	Early July through mid-August
Qualifications:	Grades 10-12 Students should demonstrate interest in science and especially paleontology.
Housing:	At Hancock Field Station, students live in A-frame cabins and eat in the dining hall. Wilderness camping is part of the field experience portion of the program.
Costs:	The program is completely funded by a grant from the Young Scholars Program of the National Science Foundation. Students have personal expenses only.
Credits Given:	None
Contact:	Dr. Jeffry Gottfried Young Scholars Research Participation Program in Paleontology/Geology Oregon Museum of Science and Industry (OMSI) 1945 S.E. Water Avenue Portland, OR 97214-3354 (503) 797-4571

Participants have a unique opportunity to live the life of a paleontologist for the summer. For three weeks, students work in two field environments collecting and studying fossil plants and animals near Hancock Station in central Oregon and from the Ochoco Mountains in eastern Oregon. After work in the field, participants return to the lab near Portland for analysis of fossil finds, fossil preparation, library research, and presentations of individual research projects. For the six weeks of this program, students engage in hands-on research activities under the direction of outstanding researchers, participate in numerous field trips and wilderness camping experiences, and are introduced to the world of the professional scientist while interacting with other talented high school students. Application deadline: April 1.

ASTRONOMY

❖ The Astronomy Camp of Steward Observatory and the University of Arizona

Type:	Science camp
Camper Level:	Ages 12 to 19
Location:	Tucson, AZ
Duration:	One week

Dates:	Beginning camp: early June/ Advanced camp: mid-June
Housing:	Participants are housed in the residence hall on the University of Arizona campus and/or in the astronomer's dormitory on Mt. Lemmon.
Costs:	$485 includes all costs at the program site. Financial aid is available.
Contacts:	Don McCarthy
	The Astronomy Camp of Steward Observatory and the University of Arizona
	Steward Observatory
	Tucson, AZ 85721
	(602) 621-4079

Campers spend most of their program time atop Mt. Lemmon, a mountain located about an hour away from the University of Arizona. Here, the participants operate large telescopes to explore planets, stars, and galaxies. During the daytime, campers explore the diverse ecology and geology of the area and hear talks by internationally known researchers speaking about their work. Students learn about computers, optics, and engineering by using the tools of professional astronomers and through interaction with both professors and astronomy students. Teams of campers at the advanced camp complete a research project for presentation to the group. Application deadline: May 30.

✦ The Thacher School Summer Science Program

Host School:	The Thacher School
Type:	Summer study
Location:	Ojai, CA
Duration:	Six weeks
Dates:	End of June through early August
Qualifications:	Grade 12 (Some exceptional 11th-grade students may be admitted.) Applicants must have taken three years of mathematics (precalculus preferred) and one year of laboratory science (physics preferred)
Housing:	Students are housed in dormitories of the Thacher School.
Costs:	$2,200 for tuition, room, and board. Financial aid, travel grants, and funds for personal expenses are available for students with demonstrated need.
Credits Given:	None; this is an enrichment program.
Contact:	Mr. Roger Klausler
	The Thacher School Summer Science Program
	The Thacher School
	5025 Thacher Road
	Ojai, CA 93023
	(805) 646-4377; FAX (805) 640-1033

The Summer Science Program held at the Thacher School and sponsored by the National Science Foundation and California State University along with a number of other California colleges offesr to 36 highly motivated students 30 hours of intense classroom instruction focused on astronomical study. Class topics include studies in math, physics, computer science, and observational astronomy and are linked to a central, hands-on research problem. Students work in teams, using professional telescopes, to add to the body of knowledge of the central topic. This program seeks students who enjoy cooperative rather than competitive learning. Applications are reviewed beginning April 17. Program is normally filled by mid-May.

❖ Young Scholars Program

Host School:	Massachusetts Institute of Technology (at Haystack Observatory)
Type:	Summer study
Location:	Westford, MA
Duration:	Three weeks
Dates:	Middle to end of July
Qualifications:	Grades 7-9
	Students are chosen from schools located within 15 miles of Haystack Observatory in Westford, MA. Participants must be interested in learning about science.
Housing:	This is a nonresidential program. Students should live within 15 miles of the observatory.
Costs:	None; for their participation, participants receive $50 per week plus materials, including a calculator, science book, and a one-year journal subscription.
Credits Given:	None
Contact:	Dr. Joseph Salah
	Young Scholars Program
	Massachusetts Institute of Technology (at Haystack Observatory)
	Haystack Observatory
	Route 40
	Westford, MA 01886
	(508) 692-4764; FAX (617) 981-0590

This commuter-only program introduces students to the fundamentals of radio astronomy, geodesy, and atmospheric science and is taught by Massachusetts Institute of Technology (MIT) staff. Students spend from 9 AM to 3 PM at Haystack Observatory and also participate in several field trips. In addition to instruction, participants tour the facilities and get a look at how scientists function in a working environment dedicated to scientific research. Hands-on activities using computers and scientific equipment at the observatory allow the participants to experience science firsthand. All students must participate in follow-up activities during the school year. These activities, which take a few hours per month, include special projects, astronomical observations, and a conference. Application deadline: May 1.

BIOLOGICAL SCIENCE

❖ Interdisciplinary Program in Biological Science with an Emphasis on Research

Host School:	University of California Davis
Type:	Internship/Summer study
Location:	Davis, CA
Duration:	Six weeks
Dates:	End of June through early August

Qualifications:	Grades 11 and 12
	The program is open to high-ability students who have a strong interest in science and desire more experience in research science.
Housing:	Students are housed in specially reserved sections of the campus dormitories, supervised by dormitory counselors. Meals are served in the dining commons. Students have access to all recreational facilities at the university.
Costs:	$1,200 for room and meals for the six weeks. The Program's instructional fees and some remaining costs are supported by grants from the National Science Foundation. University Extension credits are available for $20 per credit. Limited need-based financial aid is available.
Credits Given:	Up to 4 University Extension credits are available.
Contact:	Dr. Victor Perkes
	Interdisciplinary Program in Biological Science with an Emphasis on Research
	University of California Davis
	Division of Education—Science
	College of Letters and Science
	Davis, CA 95616
	(916) 752-0757 or 752-2622

This program is strongly laboratory and field oriented with student participation in ongoing research at the university. Students gain knowledge along with laboratory and research skills. Approximately 85 percent of the student's program time is devoted to laboratory activities, choosing from research in agricultural engineering, agronomy, genetics, nutrition, crop and animal science, human and veterinary medicine, epidemiology, and physiology, among others. During the early part of the program, morning lectures and activities establish a conceptual base, and students begin to work one-on-one with university researchers. Weekend excursions take students to the Sierra Nevada, Pacific Coast, and San Francisco Bay areas. Other recreational and athletic activities are also planned. Application deadline: March 15.

❖ Project YES (Young Exceptional Scholars)

Host School:	University of California/Los Angeles
Type:	Summer study
Location:	Torrance, CA
Duration:	Four weeks
Dates:	Summer
Qualifications:	Grades 11 and 12
	Applicants must have physical, health, or learning disabilities, and be from Arizona, California, Nevada, or Oregon. Students must demonstrate interest in science and/or math and have the intellectual capacity for college. High school grades will not disqualify a student from the program.
Housing:	Students live in UCLA dormitories supervised by specially trained graduate-student counselors. Meals are provided.
Costs:	Estimated costs are approximately $1,500 for room, board, and

transportation to UCLA. Tuition and other program costs are paid by a grant from NSF. Scholarships are available on a need basis.

Credits Given: None
Contact: Maria Silva
Project YES (Young Exceptional Scholars)
University of California/Los Angeles
The Foundation on Employment & Disability, Inc.
3820 Del Amo Boulevard, Suite 201
Torrance, CA 90503
(310) 214-3430; FAX (310) 214-4153

Project YES is a unique joint venture between the Department of Microbiology at UCLA and the Foundation on Employment & Disability, Inc. The goal of the program is to help students with disabilities overcome attitudinal and educational barriers to academic success and enable them to pursue an interest in scientific careers. Half of each day is spent in a hands-on biology program that emphasizes laboratory and field work in microbiology, physiology, and marine science. Students are also involved in college- and career-awareness activities that seek to improve skills in goal setting, career planning, and independent living. More than half the professional staff is composed of individuals with disabilities who serve as role models. Students participate in campus and Project YES social activities. Application deadline: June 1.

❖ Young Scientist Program: A Research Experience in Biology

Host School: Colorado State University
Type: Summer study/Internship
Location: Fort Collins, CO
Duration: Four weeks
Dates: Late June to late July
Qualifications: Grades 11 and 12 and first year of college
High-ability or high-potential students interested in plant, soil, or natural resource research.
Housing: Students are housed in dormitories on the campus of Colorado State and are provided with meals. The campus health center and recreational facilities are available for student use.
Costs: $2,000 covers all expenses related to the program, including tuition, room and board, field trips, and fees.
Credits Given: None
Contact: Dr. Jack Fenwick
Young Scientist Program: A Research Experience in Biology
Colorado State University
Department of Agronomy
Fort Collins, CO 80521-9984
(303) 491-6517; FAX (303) 491-0564

Participants in this Young Scientist Program have an opportunity to conduct their own research in the laboratory of and under the guidance of university scientists. Lectures on the genetic engineering of plants, the effects of climate changes on ecosystems, and the environmental factors that affect plant-soil interactions are part of the topics addressed.

Students participate also in field trips to Rocky Mountain National Park and the Pawnee Grasslands. The program provides both an understanding of plant, soil, and natural resources science along with the opportunity to conduct research on a topic of interest to the individual student. Application deadline: April 1.

✦ DOE High School Life Sciences Honors Program

Host School:	Lawrence Berkeley Laboratory
Type:	Internship
Location:	Berkeley, CA
Duration:	Two weeks
Dates:	Late July through early August
Qualifications:	Grade 12 or first year of college
	Students must show superior academic achievement and recognition in the sciences. Advanced classes in the life sciences and chemistry will be helpful. One student from each state is selected for this program; contact individual State Department of Education for information.
Housing:	Students are housed in approved facilities arranged by the laboratory.
Costs:	None. All expenses are paid by the sponsoring agencies, including transportation for the student to and from the laboratory.
Credits Given:	None
Contact:	Mr. Richard Stephens
	DOE High School Life Sciences Honors Program
	Lawrence Berkeley Laboratory
	ER-80
	U.S. Department of Energy
	Washington, DC 20585
	(202) 586-8949

Sponsored by the U.S. Department of Energy (DOE) and the Lawrence Berkeley Laboratory, this program offers summer research opportunities for outstanding high school students interested in the life sciences. Participants are associated with members of the scientific staff in an intensive two-week training program designed to provide research experience in biomedical research, biotechnology, chemical biodynamics, and biology. The program also features lectures by scientists, including Nobel Laureates, tutorial instruction, tours of the University of California, Berkeley, and use of its library, and access to the facilities of the laboratory. Application deadline: contact State Department of Education for information.

✦ Caretta Research Project

Host School:	Savannah Science Museum
Type:	Field experience
Location:	Savannah, GA
Duration:	One week
Dates:	Weekly sessions: mid-May through mid-September
Qualifications:	Age 15 to adult
	Participants must be able to meet physical demands of walking several miles and have good night vision and an upbeat attitude.

Housing:	Participants live in a dormitory cabin divided into two rooms each containing four bunks and having both an indoor bath and an indoor shower. There is a separate kitchen/dining cabin; team members share in housekeeping and meal chores.
Costs:	$395 for weeks before mid-August; $350 for weeks mid-August to mid-September. Covers costs of boat transportation between Wassaw Island and the Savannah Science Museum, housing, and food.
Credits Given:	Credits may be available through individual schools and colleges.
Contact:	Ms. Patti Mouchet
	Caretta Research Project
	Savannah Science Museum
	4405 Paulsen Street
	Savannah, GA 31405
	(912) 355-6705

The Caretta Research Project gives participants a rare opportunity to take part in hands-on work with an endangered species. Teams of eight volunteers working with an Island Leader study the threatened loggerhead sea turtle on Wassaw Island, an uninhabited barrier island near Savannah, GA. Members work either with the female turtles that come ashore to lay eggs or with the baby loggerheads in the protected nests, depending upon week chosen. Loggerhead research takes place mainly at night; during the day, team members can hike the island's oak-lined trails, explore the six miles of beach, fish, read, and relax. Places in the program fill on an ongoing basis. Call for more information. Applications deadline: rolling admissions.

❖ Molecular Biology Enrichment for Youth

Host School:	Iowa State University
Type:	Summer study
Location:	Ames, IA
Duration:	Four weeks
Dates:	Mid-June through mid-July
Qualifications:	Grades 8 and 9
	High-ability and high-potential students are eligible for the program.
Housing:	Participants live in residence halls on the Iowa State campus, supervised by program assistants. Meals are provided.
Costs:	$550 covers room and board. Grants from the National Science Foundation and Eli Lilly & Company cover all tuition costs. Need-based financial aid is available.
Credits Given:	None
Contact:	Dr. Bernard White
	Molecular Biology Enrichment for Youth
	Iowa State University
	Department of Biochemistry and Biophysics
	4210 Molecular Biology Building
	Ames, IA 50011
	(515) 294-7713; FAX (515) 294-0453

This exciting, demanding academic program introduces participants to the world of microbiology through lectures and laboratory studies. Morning lectures in chemistry, biochemistry, biotechnology, and cellular and molecular biology provide the background for further studies. At least four hours each day are spent in the laboratory, developing skills and lab techniques and performing experiments such as chemical analyses and DNA characterization. Visits to research centers and a commercial biotechnology company, as well as an overnight laboratory experience at the Springbrook Conservation Center, provide looks into real-world science. Career-planning activities are part of the program. An academic-year extension assists students with planning and performing independent research under the guidance of a mentor. Application deadline: May 1.

❖ Training for Research: The Summer Student Program

Host School:	The Jackson Laboratory
Type:	Internship
Location:	Bar Harbor, ME
Duration:	Ten to twelve weeks
Dates:	Mid-June through mid-August
Qualifications:	Grade 12 and college
	The program is open to highly qualified students interested in scientific research in the fields of genetics, developmental biology, molecular biology, biochemistry, biochemistry, physiology, or immunology. Selection is competitive.
Housing:	Students are housed, generally, in three-person rooms, at Highseas, a 32-room house overlooking Frenchman Bay. Meals are provided during the week by a professional cook and on weekends by a student kitchen crew. Supervision is provided by the residence staff.
Costs:	$1,800 covers room, board, supplies, and services for high school students. Need-based scholarships and stipends are available. College undergraduates receive full scholarships plus stipends of $1,500.
Credits Given:	None
Contact:	Training for Research: The Summer Student Program The Jackson Laboratory Training and Education Office 600 Main Street Bar Harbor, ME 04609-0800 (207) 288-3371 ext. 1253

One of the Jackson Laboratory's three missions is the sharing of knowledge through training. To this end, the Laboratory provides research training for more than 50 students each year. The students learn through participation in the ongoing research under the direct guidance of a researcher sponsor. Participants learn research skills by personal involvement; knowledge is gained while emphasis is put on methods of discovery and communication of new knowledge. Working in their sponsors' laboratories, students learn about project design, implementation, data analysis, and reporting of research results. The program concludes with a symposium. Recreational activities are arranged by the residence staff. Application deadline: February 21.

❖ Summer Science Institute: Gene Cloning

Host School:	Western Maryland College
Type:	Summer study
Location:	Westminster, MD
Duration:	Five days
Dates:	Two sessions: late July and first week in August
Qualifications:	Grades 10-12
	The program is open to students interested in careers in the natural sciences or in health-related fields. Applicants should have completed at least one year of biology, physics, or chemistry and have at least a B average.
Housing:	Students live in the college dormitory supervised by college-student dormitory counselors who help Institute participants adjust to college life.
Costs:	$295 covers room, board, and instruction. Financial aid is not available.
Credits Given:	1 college credit
Contact:	Dr. Michael Brown
	Summer Science Institute
	Western Maryland College
	Lewis Hall of Science, Room 205
	2 College Hill
	Westminster, MD 21157-4390
	(301) 857-2401

Western Maryland College offers to interested students a class that introduces the principles of DNA science. A small group of students (enrollment limited to 14) performs state-of-the-art recombinant DNA procedures including plasmid DNA isolation, genetic transformation of *E. coli*, and Agarose gel electrophoresis. Participants gain an understanding of recombinant DNA science and discuss the principles of cloning and its implications for society. Students attend class from 9 AM to 4:30 PM each day, participating in discussions, laboratories, and field trips. Living in the college dormitory and interacting with other students helps provide participants with a picture of college life. Application deadline: May 14.

❖ Summer Scholars Program—Biotechnology and Human Reproduction: Tinkering with Nature

Host School:	University of Minnesota, Morris
Type:	Summer study
Location:	Morris, MN
Duration:	Two weeks
Dates:	Early to middle July
Qualifications:	Grade 12
	Academically talented students who rank in the upper 20 percent of their class and who have completed one year of high school biology are eligible for the program.
Housing:	Students live in a campus residence hall supervised by residence hall staff. Meals are provided in the campus dining hall.

Students have access to the university's libraries, Student Center, and Physical Education Complex.

Costs: $300 is paid by students for half of the program tuition and fees. The university pays complete room and board for two weeks and subsidizes the remaining tuition and fees. A limited amount of need-based financial aid is available for qualified students to pay student cost.

Credits Given: 4 college credits

Contact: Thomas McRoberts
Summer Scholars Program
University of Minnesota, Morris
Continuing Education and Summer Session
231 Community Services Building
Morris, MN 56267-2114
(612) 589-2211 ext. 6450; (800) 842-0030; FAX (612) 589-1661

This exciting program takes a close look at the new techniques that are being employed to influence human reproduction. With topics like *in vitro* fertilization, fetal tissue transplants, eugenics, and genetic engineering currently in the news, students study the physiology of reproductive systems, learn about techniques used to control reproduction, and discuss the biological consequences of those controls. Ethical issues and the social implications of using biotechnology are considered through discussions with guest lecturers, faculty researchers, and academic study. Planned social and recreational activities complement the program. Application deadline: March 1.

❖ Itasca Field Biology and Enrichment Program

Host School: University of Minnesota, Twin Cities

Type: Field experience/Summer study

Location: Lake Itasca State Park, MN

Duration: Two weeks

Dates: Mid-June through beginning of July

Qualifications: Grades 11 and 12 and first year of college
Students must have an interest in science and a grade point average of 3.0 or higher and have had a high school biology course.

Housing: Students are housed at the field station. Meals are provided.

Costs: $565 covers tuition, room, and board. Need-based financial aid is available to Minnesota residents.

Credits Given: None

Contact: Dr. Bill Ganzlin
Itasca Field Biology and Enrichment Program
University of Minnesota, Twin Cities
College of Biological Sciences
223 Snyder Hall, 1475 Gortner Avenue
St. Paul, MN 55108
(612) 624-9717

Conducted at the University of Minnesota Forestry and Biological Station at Lake Itasca State Park in northern Minnesota, this field program places its emphasis on the life sciences. Participants are involved with a wide range of hands-on experiences with plants and animals as they attend class six hours a day along with occasional evening and Saturday seminars. University faculty members present subjects including aquatic biology, animal behavior, plant biology, field biology photography, forest and prairie ecology, ornithology, and mammology. The program allows students to experience firsthand the life of a research field biologist. Application deadline: May 14.

❖ Biology Career Workshop

Host School:	University of Nebraska, Lincoln
Type:	Summer study
Location:	Lincoln, NE
Duration:	One week
Dates:	End of July
Qualifications:	Grades 11 and 12
	Students must have completed at least one year of high school biology and be interested in the life sciences.
Housing:	Students are housed in Burr Residence Hall, supervised by program assistants. Meals are provided.
Costs:	$130 is paid by each student toward program fees, tuition, room, and board. The remaining $800 program cost is provided in the form of a scholarship from the college. Limited financial aid is available on a need basis. Students are responsible for their own transportation to campus.
Credits Given:	None
Contact:	Biology Career Workshop
	University of Nebraska, Lincoln
	103 Agricultural Hall
	PO Box 830702
	Lincoln, NE 68583-0702
	(402) 472-2541; (800) 742-8800 ext. 2541

Through hands-on experiences, participants in the Biology Career Workshop explore disciplines that include biotechnology, horticulture, environmental science, plant and animal science, food science, and other related subject areas. Half-day field projects and laboratory activities provide students with an understanding of current issues in applied biology. Career workshops allow students to explore career alternatives available in the applied biological sciences. Other seminars address college admissions and financial aid. The recreational and athletic facilities of the University of Nebraska are available to participants. A full program of evening recreation and entertainment is planned. Application deadline: April 30.

❖ Hughes High School Research Scholars

Host School:	University of Nevada, Reno
Type:	Internship
Location:	Reno, NV
Duration:	Ten weeks
Dates:	Mid-June through late August
Qualifications:	Grade 12 or first year of college
	Applicants must be U.S. citizens or permanent residents, high

achieving students with an overall grade point average of B or better. Prerequisites include at least one year of high school biology, algebra, and geometry. Selection is competitive; at least half the positions are awarded to women and/or minorities.

Housing:	Students are housed in the University dormitories.
Costs:	None. The program is supported by a grant from the Howard Hughes Medical Institute.
Credits Given:	None
Contact:	Dr. Robert Mead
	Hughes High School Research Scholars
	University of Nevada, Reno
	College of Arts and Sciences—086
	Reno, NV 89557
	(702) 784-6155

This program seeks to encourage early entry of talented students into the scientific community by providing them with realistic research experiences. Students are paired with faculty mentors who integrate them into an ongoing research team. Participants choose from a wide variety of research projects related to the biological or medical sciences and spend their summer working on problems appropriate for their developing skills. In addition to the laboratory research, students attend an orientation session and participate in seminars and informal discussions that deal with ethical and political issues in science, career opportunities, college selection, and financial aid. Application deadline: February 19.

❖ Howard Hughes Trainee Program

Host School:	University of Nevada (UNV), Reno
Type:	Summer study/Internship
Location:	Reno, NV
Duration:	Seven weeks
Dates:	Mid-June through end of July.
Qualifications:	The program is open to grade 12 Reno-area students or students who will enter the University of Nevada, Reno, in the fall, who have a strong interest in the biological sciences, but who have experienced difficulty in mathematics courses. Applicants must be U.S. citizens or permanent residents. Women, minorities, and physically disabled students are especially encouraged to apply.
Housing:	Housing is provided for students who will be entering the University of Nevada, Reno, in the fall. High-school-age trainees may attend as commuters.
Costs:	None. Students selected for this program will receive a stipend of $2,000 for the seven-week period.
Credits Given:	1 college credit in bioloby, chemistry, or biochemistry
Contact:	Dr. Robert Mead
	Howard Hughes Trainee Program
	University of Nevada, Reno
	College of Arts and Sciences—086
	Reno, NV 89557
	(702) 784-6155

A unique feature of this program is the awareness that some students intensely interested in the biological sciences may not have developed the mathematical skills needed for success in scientific study. Students selected for this program are given the opportunity to improve their mathematical abilities through intensive skills classes and tutoring sessions. Participants are taught to tutor others and are encouraged to use these skills as paid tutors during the coming school year. Besides attending the math skills classes, a student spends part of each day working as a member of an ongoing research team in an area of the student's interest, chosen from a variety of biological and medical research projects. Selection is competitive; at least half the positions are given to women and/or minorities. Application deadline: February 19.

❖ The Research Participation Program in Science

Host School:	Roswell Park Cancer Institute
Type:	Internship
Location:	Buffalo, NY
Duration:	Eight weeks
Dates:	Late June to mid-August
Qualifications:	Grade 12 and above
	Students should be gifted in the area of science and interested in pursuing a career in science and/or medical research.
Housing:	Students are housed in a residence hall on the State University of New York at Buffalo campus, supervised by resident advisors.
Costs:	$60 activity fee. Scholarships are awarded to all students in the program that cover room and board charges. Students receive stipends of $100 per week for the eight weeks of the program. The program is funded by the National Science Foundation, the U.S. Department of Education, and others.
Credits Given:	None
Contact:	Dr. Edwin Mirand
	The Research Participation Program in Science
	Roswell Park Cancer Institute
	Elm and Carlton Streets
	Buffalo, NY 14203-9963
	(716) 845-5706

The Research Participation Program seeks to introduce participants to a research science atmosphere in which they are encouraged to develop their own philosophy of science and to discover their own scientific creativity. Based on the students' own interests, participants are assigned to departments such as molecular biology, cell physiology, biophysics, immunology, and pharmacology where they work under the direct supervision of a staff scientist. In addition to working at least 40 hours per week in their assigned labs, students attend seminars presented by visiting scientists and Roswell Park researchers on a variety of scientific topics. Students write weekly progress reports about their own research and present summer-project results at a culminating seminar. Application deadline: March 1.

❖ Governor's Summer Institute in Biology and Psychology

Host School:	Wittenberg University
Type:	Summer study

Location:	Springfield, OH
Duration:	One week
Dates:	Two sessions: psychology in late June to early July; biology in early through mid-July.
Qualifications:	Grades 10 and 11
	Students must show a record of superior academic achievement and must be Ohio residents.
Housing:	Students live in a residence hall on the campus and have meals in the Student Center dining room. Wittenberg undergraduates, supervised by a professional counselor, serve as residence hall staff. Recreational facilities of the university are available for the students' use.
Costs:	$162 for room and board. All tuition for the program is covered by a state grant. A number of need-based scholarships are available. Request a financial aid application if needed.
Credits Given:	None
Contact:	Governor's Summer Institute
	Wittenberg University
	School of Community Education
	PO Box 720
	Springfield, OH 45501
	(513) 327-7012; FAX (513) 327-6340

The Governor's Summer Institute seeks to provide the participants with the chance to master challenging concepts and the opportunity to work independently and engage in serious inquiry in a college setting. An important part of the experience is simply being with other bright peers for whom it is fine to show interest and curiosity and to ask "why." Students are involved in classroom discussions, lectures, readings, and numerous field and laboratory activities. All-day field trips, followed by work in the chemistry and biology laboratories, are further supplemented by experiences in the microcomputer lab analyzing data and performing computer simulations. A separate session focuses on psychology. Informal discussions, social events, and recreational activities complete the program. Application deadline: April 5.

❖ Field Studies in Multidisciplinary Biology

Host School:	University of Oklahoma
Type:	Summer study
Location:	Norman, OK
Duration:	Three weeks
Dates:	Mid-June through early July
Qualifications:	Grades 11 and 12
	The program is limited to Oklahoma residents who demonstrate above-average interest in science and mathematics. Selection is competitive.
Housing:	Students are housed in the Biological Station residence hall and have their meals in the cafeteria. Adult counselors supervise the students when they are not in classes. Weekend residence is optional; supervision is provided for students who choose to remain at the Biological Station over the weekends.

Costs:	All expenses, including room, board, supplies, books, and field-trip expenses, are provided by grants from the Oklahoma State Regents for Higher Education. Students are responsible for travel and incidental personal expenses. A small stipend given at the end helps to defray costs.
Credits Given:	None.
Contact:	Field Studies in Multidisciplinary Biology University of Oklahoma Precollegiate Programs: Summer Academy 1700 Asp Avenue Norman, OK 73037-0001 (405) 325-6897

Students who participate in this summer academy program have an opportunity to study and research organisms in their natural environment. Monday through Friday, participants live and work at the Biological Station on Lake Texoma. There, they learn to classify organisms and study the grasses, plants, trees, insects, fish, reptiles, birds, and mammals found in Oklahoma. The goal of the program is to aid students in developing investigative laboratory and communication skills by providing learning experiences that cannot be found in the students' home schools. This is a fast-paced, intensive program, requiring commitment from the participants. Application deadline: March 1.

❖ Pennsylvania Governor's School for the Agricultural Sciences

Host School:	Penn State University
Type:	Summer study
Location:	University Park, PA
Duration:	Five weeks
Dates:	Early July through early August
Qualifications:	Grades 11 and 12 Students must have demonstrated ability and interest in science, food, agriculture, or natural resources. Parents or guardians of applicants must be Pennsylvania taxpayers. Students may not have previously attended one of the six Governor's Schools.
Housing:	Students are housed in Penn State's residence halls with college-student counselors. Meals are provided at the residence hall. Students have access to the university athletic and recreational facilities.
Costs:	Full scholarships are provided to all participants covering room and board, books, activities, and all fees. Students are responsible for transportation costs to and from University Park and for incidental expenses.
Credits Given:	None
Contact:	Dr. Marianne Houser Pennsylvania Governor's School for the Agricultural Sciences Penn State University 101 Agricultural Administration Building University Park, PA 16802 (814) 865-7521

Because agricultural research and policy are so important to today's global economy, the Pennsylvania Department of Education, along with Penn State University, offers high-ability students the opportunity to explore the world of agricultural science. Participants attend classes in agricultural science and technology. With faculty members, students engage in study and research in their choice of such areas as nutrition, animal biochemistry, wildlife management, land-use planning, and computer monitoring systems. Seminars on current issues, field trips to agricultural agencies and industries, hands-on sessions in labs, greenhouses, and farms, along with college and career counseling, complete the program. Students also participate in social and recreational activities. Application deadline: February 24.

❖ Minority High School Students Research Apprentice Program

Host School: Texas A&M University, College of Agriculture and Life Sciences
Type: Internship
Location: College Station, TX
Duration: Six weeks
Dates: Late June through the beginning of August
Qualifications: Grades 11 and 12

College-bound, disadvantaged, high school students interested in the life sciences or in health-related careers are eligible for the program. Special consideration is given to students who identify themselves as being Black, Hispanic, American Indian, Alaskan native, or Pacific Islander/Asian. Applicants must be U.S. citizens or have permanent visas.

Housing: Students are housed in the campus residence halls and eat in the dining facilities.
Costs: The only cost to participants is transportation to and from the university. Students receive modest wages of approximately $1,000 for their work. Room and board are provided for minority students.
Contact: Edward Funkhouser
Minority High School Students Research Apprentice Program
Texas A&M University
Department of Biochemistry and Biophysics
College Station, TX 77843-2128
(409) 845-1012 or 845-8271

This six-week, summer research-oriented program is designed to introduce its participants to life-science-related research and career opportunities. It is appropriate for students interested in majoring in biochemistry, biology, chemistry, or genetics or in preprofessional health majors leading to medicine and veterinary medicine. Students apprentice in the laboratories of the university, learning about laboratory procedure and scientific techniques that are commonly used in scientific research. In addition, weekly seminars are held that provide instruction in the life sciences, and presentations are made by speakers engaged in current research at the university. A two-day science symposium completes the experience. A similar program entitled "Lab Start" is offered to nonminority, commuter students. Application deadline: Mid-April.

ENGINEERING

❖ Minority Introduction to Engineering (MITE)

(Similar programs are held at a number of universities. Please see the listing that follows this one.)

Host School:	Tuskegee University
Type:	Summer study
Location:	Tuskegee Institute, AL
Duration:	One week
Dates:	Mid-June
Qualifications:	Grade 12
	Minority students considering careers in engineering are eligible for the program.
Housing:	Students are housed in supervised dormitories and are provided with three meals a day.
Costs:	No cost to the participants for tuition, housing, or meals, Students are expected to provide their own transportation to and from the college and are responsible for personal expenses.
Credits Given:	None
Contact:	Dr. Shaik Jeelani
	Minority Introduction to Engineering (MITE)
	Tuskegee University
	Associate Dean
	School of Engineering and Architecture
	Tuskegee Institute, AL 36088
	(205) 727-8970 or 727-8430

MITE (Minority Introduction to Engineering) is a rigorous summer program that seeks to introduce minority students to the field of engineering through an in-depth exposure to the various engineering disciplines. During this week, students are totally immersed in campus life. In the classroom, students develop skills needed for success in college classes; work focuses on chemistry, mathematics, physics, and engineering theory. Laboratory experiments provide hands-on learning. Presentations by both engineering faculty and practicing engineers and field trips to industrial and laboratory facilities provide students with a close look at careers in engineering. Students have access to campus facilities including the libraries, athletic complex, and health services. Application deadline: April 30.

❖ Minority Introduction to Engineering (MITE) Programs

Summer programs similar to the MITE program at Tuskegee University are held at campuses across the United States. Most are provided at little or no cost to the participants and are designed to encourage members of minority groups to consider careers in science and/or engineering. Each of the following programs is one week in length and targets students entering grades 10 through 12. Contact individual programs for more information.

MITE
U.S. Coast Guard Academy
c/o Director of Admissions
15 Mohegan Avenue
New London, CT 06320
(203) 447-2897

MITE
Dr. Lytia Howard
Georgia Institute of Technology
College of Engineering
Atlanta, GA 30332-0362
(404) 894-3354

Summer Engineering Academy (SEA)
University of Michigan
Minority Engineering Program Office
1301 Beal Avenue, 2316 EECS Building
Ann Arbor, MI 48109-2116
(313) 764-6497

MITE
Michigan Technological University
Youth Programs Office
1400 Townsend Drive
Houghton, MI 49931-1295
(906) 487-2219

Summer Enrichment Experience (SEE) in Engineering Program
Texas A&M University
204 Zachry Engineering Center
College Station, TX 77843-3127
(409) 845-7200

MITE
University of Virginia
School of Engineering and Applied Science
A 127 Thornton Hall
Charlottesville, VA 22901
(804) 924-3518

Two-week MITE programs are also available. Contact those listed below for more information.

MITE
Dr. David Powell
University of Illinois, Urbana-Champaign
College of Engineering
1308 West Green Street, Room 207
Urbana, IL 61801-2982
(217) 244-4974; (800) 843-5410

MITE
Purdue University
1286 Enad, Room 214
West Lafayette, IN 47907–1286
(317) 494–3974; FAX (317) 494–5819

Summer Engineering Academy MITE
University of Michigan
Minority Engineering Program Office
1301 Beal Avenue, 2316 EECS Building
Ann Arbor, MI 48109–2116
(313) 764–6497

Institute for PreCollege Enrichment MITE
Prairie View A&M University
PO Box 66
Prairie View, TX 77446–0066
(409) 857–2055; (800) 622–9643

❖ Engineering Summer Residency Program (ESRP)

Host School:	University of California, Davis
Type:	Summer study
Location:	Davis, CA
Duration:	One week
Dates:	Late June
Qualifications:	Grades 11 and 12
	The program is open to students interested in learning about possible career opportunities in the field of engineering. Program is limited to population groups that have been traditionally underrepresented in engineering (women, minorities, the disadvantaged).
Housing:	Participants are housed in the dormitories at UCD with junior and senior engineering students serving as resident advisors. Meals are served at the residence halls.
Costs:	There is no program cost to the students; the program is funded by grants from industry. Participants are responsible only for transportation to and from the university and personal expenses.
Credits Given:	None
Contact:	Ms. Jane Elliot
	Engineering Summer Residency Program (ESRP)
	University of California, Davis
	College of Engineering
	Davis, CA 95616
	(916) 752-7761

This program seeks to introduce students to the world of engineering and to career opportunities in this field. The daily schedule is similar to that of college students and includes lectures, laboratories, demonstrations, and a field trip. Computer science as well as engineering activities are explored. Through this program, it is hoped that the participants discover how the sciences, math, computer knowledge, and English are all impor-

tant tools of the professional engineer and that students learn about the academic prepa-
rations they should make if they wish to become engineers. Students also get a taste of
college life as well as an opportunity to interact with University of California, Davis,
faculty, engineering students, and professionals in the field. Evenings are filled with
group projects and recreational and social activities. Application deadline: April 2.

❖ Early Experience Program: The Making of an Engineer

Host School:	University of Denver
Type:	Internship/Summer study
Location:	Denver, CO
Duration:	Three weeks
Dates:	Mid-June through early July
Qualifications:	Grades 11 and 12 and first year of college
	Students should have a working knowledge of high school algebra.
Housing:	Students share double-occupancy rooms in supervised dormitories on the University of Denver's campus.
Costs:	$50 for tuition, $700 room and board. Most of the tuition cost is covered by a grant from the National Science Foundation. Need-based scholarships are available.
Credits Given:	4 quarter hours of university credit are available upon payment of $50 tuition
Contact:	Ms. Pamela Campbell
	Early Experience Program: The Making of an Engineer
	University of Denver
	Bureau of Educational Services
	Wesley Hall, #203
	Denver, CO 80208
	(303) 871-2663

This program is designed for high school students with a strong interest in science and
technology. The goal of the program is to stimulate interest in engineering as a profession. Towards this goal, students meet individually with several professors to work on
individualized honors projects including areas such as X-ray diffraction, robotics, super-
conductors, bioengineering, and computer-aided design, among other areas of study.
Participants learn to use the tools of the engineer and to perform analysis, design, and
other engineering tasks. College-level demonstrations, experiments, and design exercises
allow students to do hands-on engineering. Application deadline: May 1.

❖ Engineering 2000

Host School:	Catholic University of America
Type:	Summer study
Location:	Washington, DC
Duration:	Six days
Dates:	Mid-July
Qualifications:	Grade 12
	The program is open to high achievers in science and mathematics interested in exploring career opportunities in engineering.
Housing:	Students are housed in the university's Centennial Village

	Residence Hall and have access to the 40-acre athletic complex. Tennis and racquetball tournaments are planned.
Costs:	$150 registration fee. This fee can be waived if financial need is certified by the student's high school principal. Scholarships cover all other costs.
Credits Given:	None
Contact:	Dr. John Gilheany
	Engineering 2000
	Catholic University of America
	School of Engineering and Architecture
	Room 131—Pangborn Hall
	Washington, DC 20064-0001
	(202) 319-5160

Engineering 2000 seeks to educate rising high school seniors about what professional engineers do and how they are educated and to help students decide if work in engineering is their future. The program consists of educational, experimental, social, and recreational components. The educational component includes speakers on new technologies, counseling discussions about choosing colleges and careers, and discussions about ethical issues. The experimental component allows the student to participate in two projects chosen from selections including robotics, computer-aided design, cellular biomechanics, rehabilitation devices, and others. Sports programs, discussion groups, and the social-groups part of living in a college dormitory comprise the social and recreational components. Application deadline: May 1.

❖ Pre-College Engineering Program (PREP)

Host School:	Georgia Institute of Technology
Type:	Summer study
Location:	Atlanta, GA
Duration:	One week
Dates:	End of June
Qualifications:	Grades 11 and 12
	Students should have PSAT scores of at least 50 verbal and 55 math or SAT scores of at least 500 verbal and 550 math.
Housing:	Participants are housed in university residence halls and take their meals in the dining halls.
Costs:	$300. Scholarships are not available.
Credits Given:	None
Contact:	Dr. Lytia Howard
	Pre-College Engineering Program (PREP)
	Georgia Institute of Technology
	College of Engineering
	Atlanta, GA 30332-0362
	(404) 894-3354

The PREP (Pre-College Engineering Program) program seeks to introduce interested students to careers in engineering. The program includes presentations from the various engineering disciplines, meetings with industry representatives, and tours of area industries and of the engineering facilities at Georgia Tech. Participants take part in engineering experiments and go on field trips to local sites. Application deadline: May 1.

❖ Junior Engineering Technical Society Summer Workshop (JETS)

Host School:	University of Idaho
Type:	Summer study
Location:	Moscow, ID
Duration:	Two weeks
Dates:	Middle to late July
Qualifications:	Grades 11 and 12
	Students need to have a 3.0 or better grade point average, have taken three years of mathematics with grades of B or better, and have some knowledge of a computer language.
Housing:	Students are housed in a university dormitory under counselor supervision. Meals are provided in the dining hall. Participants have access to the recreational and cultural facilities of the university.
Costs:	$350 to cover tuition, food, housing, and supplies. A limited amount of need-based financial aid is available.
Credits Given:	2 college credits
Contact:	Jean Teasdale
	Junior Engineering Technical Society Summer Workshop: JETS
	University of Idaho
	College of Engineering
	Moscow, ID 83843
	(208) 885-6438

JETS is a pre-engineering program in which participants learn about the application of engineering principles with an emphasis on the use of computers. Topics covered in this workshop include computer programming and graphics, computer-aided design and drafting, engineering economics, statistics, and problem solving. The approach is to solve a real-world problem by applying what has been learned. Students participating in this program will gain an appreciation of the course material covered in typical engineering programs and an awareness of career opportunities in engineering. Field trips to surrounding industrial facilities along with recreational and cultural activities round out the program. Application deadline: May 24.

❖ JETS Summer Program in Engineering

Host School:	University of Illinois, Urbana-Champaign
Type:	Summer study
Location:	Urbana, IL
Duration:	Two weeks
Dates:	Late June through early July
Qualifications:	Grade 12
	Students should have an interest in engineering and applied science and have demonstrated ability to pursue a college education.
Housing:	Participants live and take their meals in university residence halls or in university-approved housing.

Costs:	$400 covers room and board, supplies, and insurance. No tuition fee is charged. A limited number of scholarships are available.
Credits Given:	None
Contact:	David Powell
	JETS Summer Program in Engineering
	University of Illinois, Urbana-Champaign
	1308 West Green Street, Room 207
	Urbana, IL 61801-2982
	(217) 244-4974; (800) 843-5410

This Junior Engineering Technical Society (JETS) program seeks to familiarize students with the various fields of engineering and to help them get a clear picture of the demands placed upon practicing engineers. The program consists of lectures by faculty members working in the various engineering disciplines, small-group performance of engineering laboratory experiments, 10 hours of computer aided design lab training, and a team project (led by a graduate student advisor) related to current ongoing research in engineering. College and career related issues are addressed through roundtable discussions with other students, faculty, and practicing engineers, and by lectures covering scientific research topics as well as college preparation. The program also includes intramural sports and a dance. Application deadline: April 1.

❖ Exploring Engineering & Science Women in Engineering (WIE) and Men in Engineering (MIE)

Host School:	Tri-State University
Type:	Summer study
Location:	Angola, IN
Duration:	One week
Dates:	Mid-June and late June sessions for MIE; mid-July and late July sessions for WIE
Qualifications:	Grades 10-12
	The program is open to young women and young men interested in exploring engineering as a possible career choice.
Housing:	Housing and meals are provided at Tri-State University.
Costs:	$195 covers fees for room and board. The remainder of the costs of the program are provided by business and industry sponsors.
Credits Given:	None
Contact:	Dr. Frank Swenson
	Exploring Engineering & Science
	Tri-State University
	Dean of Engineering Office
	Angola, IN 46703
	(219) 665-4188; (800) 347-4878

Two separate programs, Women in Engineering and Men in Engineering, introduce their participants to the job of an engineer as a way of helping young people decide if engineering is an appropriate career choice for them. Participants use laboratory equipment such as wind tunnels and analog and digital computers, visit engineers at work, view films of engineering projects, and interact with practicing engineers. All of this is designed to provide students with a clear understanding of opportunities for women and for men in the engineering disciplines and an awareness of the kinds of projects on which engineers work. Participants discover how engineers apply mathematics, science, and technology to improve today's living. Application deadline: June 11 for MIE and July 7 for WIE.

❖ PREFACE

Host School:	Purdue University
Type:	Summer study
Location:	West Lafayette, IN
Duration:	One week
Dates:	Mid-July
Qualifications:	Grades 10 and 11
	The program is open to minority students interested in exploring career opportunities in engineering and is limited to African American, American Indian, Mexican American, and Puerto Rican students.
Housing;	Students are housed in McCutcheon Hall, one of Purdue's newest residence halls. Meals are also served in the residence hall.
Costs:	The program is provided through industrial support that covers most costs. Students are responsible only for a $100 administrative fee and for travel and personal expenses.
Credits Given:	None
Contact:	PREFACE
	Purdue University
	Minority Engineering Program
	1286 Enad #214A
	West Lafayette, IN 47907-1286
	(317) 494-3974; FAX (317) 494-5819

Participants spend an enjoyable week on Purdue's campus while exploring the career opportunities that exist in the field of engineering. Students learn about the importance of high school preparation, develop better study skills and learning techniques, and engage in discussions about college and life planning. The field of engineering is explored through discussions with practicing engineers and engineering students, through tours, and by hands-on activities. Each participant designs and builds at least one engineering-related project during the week. Special sessions focus on engineering as a career choice for minority students. PREFACE students also have use of the Recreational Gymnasium, which provides facilities for a number of sports activities, and participate in other leisure-time activities. Application deadline: May 27.

❖ Engineering Ahead!

Host School:	University of Kentucky
Type:	Summer study
Location:	Lexington, KY
Duration:	Three weeks
Dates:	Early through late June
Qualifications:	Grades 11 and 12
	Participants are high-achieving students who enjoy using

mathematics and scientific principles to solve problems and must be residents of Kentucky, West Virginia, Ohio, Indiana, or Tennessee. Chemistry and Algebra II are prerequisites.

Housing: Students are housed in university residence halls, supervised by undergraduate students. Meals are served in the campus dining areas. Recreational activities are also provided.

Costs: All expenses, including tuition, room, and meals, are provided at no cost to the students. Participants are expected to pay only for transportation to and from campus and for personal expenses.

Credits Given: None

Contact: Dr. S.T. Wang
Engineering Ahead!
University of Kentucky
College of Engineering
242 Anderson Hall
Lexington, KY 40506-0046
(606) 257-4916

Engineering Ahead!, supported through grants from the National Science Foundation and the Alcoa Foundation, is designed to acquaint young people with the challenges and rewards to be found in engineering. Classroom activities, involving extensive use of computers, introduce students to disciplines that include agricultural, chemical, civil, electrical, mechanical, and mining engineering, as well as materials science. Students use engineering physics to solve real-world problems. Field trips to manufacturing plants and a mining operation provide participants with the opportunity to "shadow" a practicing engineer. Workshops on ethics, cooperative education, college admissions, and financial aid are also part of program. An independent project during the school year completes the cycle. Application deadline: April 15.

❖ Recruitment into Engineering of High Ability Minority Students (REHAMS)

Host School: Louisiana State University

Type: Summer study

Location: Baton Rouge, LA

Duration: Four weeks

Dates: Early June through early July

Qualifications: Grade 12
The program is open to minority students who have outstanding high school grades in math and science and high achievement test scores.

Housing: Participants live in double rooms in a university residence hall. Counselors selected from advanced engineering students live in the residence halls and serve as advisors. Meals are provided Monday through Friday.

Costs: Room and board, books and instructional supplies, health insurance, and field-trip expenses are provided at no cost to the participant. The participant is responsible for transportation to and from home, personal expenses, and weekend meals.

Credits Given:	None
Contact:	Mr. Forest Smith
	Recruitment into Engineering of High Ability Minority Students (REHAMS)
	Louisiana State University
	3304 CEBA
	College of Engineering
	Baton Rouge, LA 70803-6401
	(504) 388-5731

This program seeks to offer academically talented minority students a chance to experience the activities and thought patterns characteristic of engineering. This enrichment program includes classes in math, computer usage, and oral and written communication skills. Methods of solving engineering problems are presented. Participants are introduced to the various engineering disciplines by faculty members working in each of eight fields. Engineers from industry and government also talk to students about engineering opportunities for minorities. Field trips to area facilities are planned for once a week. Participants will also be involved in projects that require the application of engineering principles and individual innovations. Application deadline: March 31.

❖ Engineering Summer Institute

Host School:	Southern University and A&M College
Type:	Summer study
Location:	Baton Rouge, LA
Duration:	Four weeks
Dates:	Mid-June through mid-July
Qualifications:	Grades 9-12
	The program is open to high school students interested in exploring career opportunities in science and engineering. Students must have at least a 3.0 GPA (on a 4.0 scale).
Housing:	Participants are housed in double-occupancy rooms in the university's air-conditioned dormitories. Three meals per day are provided.
Costs:	$200 registration fee. The university and supporters of the Institute will pay all other expenses for participants, with the exception of transportation to and from the Institute and personal expenses.
Credits Given:	None
Contact:	Dr. Thomas Henderson
	Engineering Summer Institute
	Southern University and A&M College
	Baton Rouge, LA 70813-9552
	(504) 771-3798

The Engineering Summer Institute seeks to expose students to possible career opportunities in engineering and science. Classes offering enrichment activities in math, computers, and engineering science are held Monday through Thursday. Each of these afternoons is devoted to project work in engineering. Fridays are reserved for field trips to industrial facilities in the area including visits to companies such as Dow Chemical, Gulf States Utilities, and Procter & Gamble. This schedule allows participants to get a firsthand look at commercial engineering opportunities. Through participation in the program, it is hoped that students will have the necessary information for making informed career decisions. Application deadline: April 1.

❖ Summer Study in Engineering Program for High School Women

Host School:	University of Maryland
Type:	Summer study
Location:	College Park, MD
Duration:	Six weeks
Dates:	Mid-July through late August
Qualifications:	Grade 12
	Students must be women with an interest in engineering as a possible career choice.
Housing:	Students are strongly encouraged to live in university housing on campus so that they can conveniently participate in all of the cultural, social, and recreational programs offered on the campus.
Costs:	Students are responsible for the cost of meals. Tuition and housing fees are paid by a University of Maryland fund established for this purpose.
Credits Given:	6 college credits
Contact:	Summer Study in Engineering Program for High School Women University of Maryland Student Affairs Office, College of Engineering 1131 Engineering Classroom Building College Park, MD 20742 (301) 405-3855

The program seeks to expose young women to a program of college-level engineering study so that they will have the knowledge needed to make an informed choice about a possible career in engineering. The sponsors also hope to provide the students with the confidence to know that they can be successful in engineering study. Participants take two courses: Introductory Engineering Science provides an introduction to engineering science and design, including the use of computers to solve engineering problems. Computer applications are stressed, and the students work as a group to design, manufacture, and assemble a project. The World of Engineering serves as an introduction to the various engineering disciplines. Field trips and visits complement this experience. Application deadline: June 1.

❖ Summer Study in Engineering: Young Scholars Program

Host School:	University of Maryland
Type:	Summer study
Location:	College Park, MD
Duration:	Six weeks
Dates:	Mid-July through late August
Qualifications:	Grade 12
	The program is open to academically talented, Maryland high school students interested in exploring career opportunities in science and engineering.

Housing:	Participants have the option of living on campus in the university dormitories. Commuter students must be on campus from 8:30 AM to 3:00 PM. Lunch is provided by the program.
Costs:	About $450 for tuition and fees. Participants receive a generous stipend, part of which is to be used to meet this cost. Students who choose to live on campus will pay $520 for housing.
Credits Given:	3 college credits
Contact:	Mr. James Newton
	Summer Study in Engineering: Young Scholars Program
	University of Maryland
	College of Engineering
	College Park, MD 20742
	(301) 405-6608

The Young Scholars Program at the University of Maryland provides a balance of classwork in a college setting with research projects, laboratory experiments, field activities, and career workshops. Participants will take an Introductory Engineering Science course and learn to use computers and the computer language Quick Basic, which will enable them to solve engineering problems using the computer. Students will also learn engineering drawing and will be assigned to group research projects. Seminars on career exploration, including resume writing and interview techniques, as well as ethics in the sciences, will be offered. Application deadline: May 1.

❖ Minority Scholars in Computer Science and Engineering

Host School:	University of Maryland
Type:	Summer study
Location:	College Park, MD
Duration:	Six weeks
Dates:	Mid-July through late August
Qualifications:	Grade 12
	The program is limited to African-American, Hispanic, and Native American students. Selection will be based on academic ability; GPA, PSAT, or SAT scores (minimum 1000 combined, 550 Math), and recommendations.
Housing:	Students live in university housing.
Costs:	Students are responsible for the cost of their meals and transportation to and from the campus. Tuition, fees, and housing are paid by the program sponsors.
Credits Given:	6 college credits
Contact:	Ms. Rosemary Parker
	Minority Scholars in Computer Science and Engineering
	University of Maryland
	Center for Minorities in Science and Engineering
	College Park, MD 20742
	(301) 405-3878

This six-week program is an exploration of the educational and career opportunities to be found in the fields of computer science and engineering. Students take two courses: Introductory Engineering Science covers the languages of the engineer and graphics, while Introduction to Math II provides students with an introduction to logic, Boolean algebra, and probability. Application deadline: contact program for information.

❖ Engineering Career Orientation (ECO)

Host School:	University of Massachusetts
Type:	Summer study
Location:	Amherst, MA
Duration:	Two weeks
Dates:	Two sessions held during July
Qualifications:	Grades 8 through 12
	The program is open to minority students (Black, Hispanic, and Native American) who are U.S. citizens. Students should be interested in possible careers in science, engineering, or math and have demonstrated high potential.
Housing:	Students live in the university residence halls, supervised by full-time counselors, and eat at on-campus dining facilities.
Costs:	$100 registration fee. All other costs are covered by the Minority Engineering Program. Financial aid for students who are unable to meet the registration fee is available on a case-by-case basis.
Credits Given:	None
Contact:	Dwight Tavada
	Engineering Career Orientation (ECO)
	University of Massachusetts
	Minority Engineering Program
	128 Marston Hall
	Amherst, MA 01003
	(413) 545-2030

The ECO program seeks to stimulate interest in careers in science and engineering among minority students and to provide practical hands-on experiences in academic areas related to these fields. Students take five hour-long classes each day in such subjects as pre-calculus math, chemistry, introduction to computers, and writing. One of the goals of the program is to teach students how to learn. Evening presentations by minority represen-tatives from private industry and university personnel provide role models for the stu-dents along with familiarizing them with opportunities for careers in the engineering disciplines. Application deadline: May 15.

❖ Summer Engineering Academy (SEA): Summer Apprenticeship Program (SAP)

Host School:	University of Michigan
Type:	Internship
Location:	Ann Arbor, MI
Duration:	Eight weeks
Dates:	Late June through mid-August
Qualifications:	Grades 11 and 12
	The program is limited to minority students (African-American, Hispanic, and Native-American) interested in practical experience in engineering and is nonresidential; only students

able to commute to and from the UM campus each day are considered.

Housing:	Housing is not available.
Costs:	None. Students may either receive a stipend for their work or may earn high school credit.
Credits Given:	High school credit may be available.
Contact:	Summer Engineering Academy (SEA): Summer Apprenticeship Program (SAP)
	University of Michigan
	Minority Engineering Program office (MEPO)
	1301 Beal Avenue, 2316 EECS Building
	Ann Arbor, MI 48109-2116
	(313) 764-6497

The Summer Apprenticeship Program places interested students with engineering faculty and graduate-level assistants who are conducting research projects in one of the engineering disciplines. SAP allows students to get hands-on experience while they develop research skills and gives students an in-depth practical view of the field of engineering. A Student Technical Symposium, at which students present the results of their research experience, is held at the end of the apprenticeship program. Application deadline: April 30.

❖ High School Engineering Institute

Host School:	Michigan State University
Type:	Summer study
Location:	East Lansing, MI
Duration:	Six days
Dates:	Late June
Qualifications:	Grades 11 and 12
	Students must be interested in mathematics and science and rank in the top 30 percent of their high school class.
Housing:	Students are housed in a university dormitory supervised by resident assistants who live with the students. Meals are provided. University recreational facilities are available to Institute members.
Costs:	$350 covers instructional fees, supplies, computer time, and room and board. A limited amount of need-based financial aid is available.
Credits Given:	None
Contact:	High School Engineering Institute
	Michigan State University
	College of Engineering
	G 65 Wilson Hall
	East Lansing, MI 48824-1226
	(517) 355-6616

The High School Engineering Institute is designed to stimulate interest in science and engineering by providing experiences leading to a better understanding of the work that engineers do. Students are involved in projects that illustrate the challenges that face today's engineers. Projects in agricultural, chemical, civil, electrical, and mechanical engineering as well as bioengineering, mechanics, and computer and materials sciences are included. Classroom and discussion groups, along with laboratory experiments and interaction with engineers, help students gain an understanding of engineering. A session related to preparing for college admissions and scholarship opportunities is also part of the program. Cultural and athletic events are planned for participants. Application deadline: April 30.

❖ Women in Engineering Program

Host School:	Michigan Technological University
Type:	Summer study
Location:	Houghton, MI
Duration:	One week
Dates:	Two sessions: middle to late June and late June to early July
Qualifications:	Grades 10-12
	The program is open to young women with a strong science and math background. Participants should have taken two years of high school mathematics and a year of chemistry.
Housing:	Students are housed in the university's residents hall and have their meals in the dining hall.
Costs:	The only cost to participants is a $25 registration fee, personal expenses, and transportation to and from the university. Room, board, and tuition costs are paid by the program's sponsors.
Credits Given:	None
Contact:	Ms. Shalini Rudak
	Women in Engineering Program
	Michigan Technological University
	Youth Programs Office
	1400 Townsend Drive
	Houghton, MI 49931-1295
	(906) 487-2219

❖ Fundamentals of Engineering (A Week in Engineering School)

Host School:	University of Missouri, Rolla
Type:	Summer study
Location:	Rolla, MO
Duration:	One week
Dates:	Three sessions: Mid-June, early August, mid-August
Qualifications:	Grade 12 and first year of college
	Applicants should be interested in engineering as a career option and rank in the top 25 percent of their class.
Housing:	Students are housed in the Thomas Jefferson Residence Hall. Meals are provided.
Costs:	About $300, which includes registration and instruction, room, and board.
Credits Given:	1 college credit available for those who later enroll at the University of Missouri, Rolla.

Contact: Walter Ries
Fundamentals of Engineering
University of Missouri, Rolla
103 Mechanical Engineering Annex
Rolla, MO 65401-4132
(314) 341-4132; (800) 752-5057

Fundamentals of Engineering seeks to introduce students to the various engineering disciplines and to the tools engineers use to do their work. As a result of taking this course, participants should better understand what engineers do, how math and science relate to engineering, and whether engineering is an appropriate career choice for them. Through lectures and demonstrations, combined with practical exercises, students experience the basic laws of engineering, while visits to selected engineering departments provide a familiarity with job experiences and opportunities in disciplines such as ceramic, chemical, geological, petroleum, nuclear, and mining engineering, as well as computer science and engineering management. Recreational activities and experience in campus living are also provided. Application deadline: contact program for information.

❖ The Engineering Experience for Minorities: TEEM

Host School: Rutgers University
Type: Summer study
Location: Piscataway, NJ
Duration: Three weeks
Dates: Middle to end of July
Qualifications: Grade 12
　　　　　　The program is limited to Black, Hispanic, or Native American students interested in exploring career options in engineering.
Housing: Students live in the university residence halls and take meals in the dining facilities.
Costs: No program cost to participants; sponsoring companies pay all fees relating to tuition, room, and board. Students are only responsible for transportation to and from campus and for personal expenses.
Credits Given: None
Contact: Ms. Ilene Rosen
The Engineering Experience for Minorities: TEEM
Rutgers University
College of Engineering, Room B-110
PO Box 909
Piscataway, NJ 08855-0909
(908) 932-2687

The Engineering Experience for Minorities: TEEM introduces minority students to opportunities available in the field of engineering while exposing them to the intellectual challenges found in college-level study. The program includes academic study through hands-on laboratory activities, computer work, library research, and engineering projects. Students solve real problems using the methods of practicing engineers. Computer sessions focus on BASIC and computer graphics. Laboratory tours and informational discussions with engineers and educators provide a look at opportunities in engineering today. College planning workshops are also part of the program. An additional feature of this program is its emphasis on improving communication skills, an area necessary for professional success. Sports and recreational activities are planned. Application deadline: March 31.

❖ Exploration in Engineering

Host School:	Cornell University
Type:	Summer study
Location:	Ithaca, NY
Duration:	Six weeks
Dates:	Late June through early August.
Qualifications:	Grade 12 or first year college
	Students must be of superior academic ability as reflected in high school record and PSAT/SAT scores.
Housing:	Participants live in Cornell dormitories with other Summer College students. The dorms are supervised by resident advisors and program assistants. Students have access to a wide variety of athletic facilities.
Costs:	$3,800 covers tuition, room and board, and fees but does not include transportation, books, and supplies. A limited number of full and partial scholarships are available for needy gifted students. A number of minority scholarships are also offered.
Credits Given:	6 to 8 college credits
Contact:	Exploration in Engineering
	Cornell University
	Cornell University Summer College
	B 12 Ives Hall Box 158
	Ithaca, NY 14853-3901
	(607) 255-62031; FAX (607) 255-8942

Exploration in Engineering provides interested students with firsthand experience in the field of engineering. A daily seminar investigates disciplines such as bioengineering, civil and mechanical engineering, operations research, and computer-aided design. Discussions are held with practicing engineers and with Cornell faculty members. Field trips to area facilities, both on and off campus, round out the career experience. Students also complete several engineering design projects. Participants also take a college-level course in math or computers and another course of their choice. With other members of the Summer College, students participate in workshops on college admission, study skills, stress, and time management and have available a full range of sports and cultural activities. Application deadline: April 17.

❖ Summer College Engineering Program

Host School:	Syracuse University
Type:	Summer study
Location:	Syracuse, NY
Duration:	Six weeks
Dates:	Early July through mid-August
Qualifications:	The program is open to high school students, including graduating seniors, who are mature, motivated, and in good academic standing.

Housing: Students are housed with other high school students taking
                    precollege programs at Syracuse in a supervised undergraduate
                    dormitory. Meals are provided in the dining hall. Special
                    weekend recreational and social activities and informational
                    seminars are provided.

Costs: Resident students pay $2,850, which covers the cost of tuition,
                    room and board, accident insurance, and selected activities.
                    Commuting students pay $1,995. A limited number of partial
                    tuition scholarships are available on the basis of academic merit
                    and perceived need. Deadline for scholarship applications: May
                    3.

Credits Given: 6–7 college credits

Contact: Summer College Engineering Program
                    Syracuse University
                    Division of Summer Sessions
                    111 Waverly Avenue, Suite 230
                    Syracuse, NY 13244-2320
                    (315) 443-5297

Participants learn about the various engineering disciplines offered at Syracuse while
becoming acquainted with the work of practicing engineers. Through laboratory experiments, lectures, and field trips, students discover how their own interests in science and
mathematics can be applied to a future career in engineering. Each student takes two
undergraduate courses for credit. The Survey of Engineering course provides a look at the
profession of engineering and allows participants to understand how engineers solve
problems. Numerous laboratory experiences, field trips, and guest lectures contribute to
the scope of this class. Students may choose any liberal arts course for their second class,
but enrollment in a mathematics, computer, physics, or chemistry class is strongly
recommended. Application deadline: June 1.

❖ Preface Program

Host School: Rensselaer Polytechnic Institute
Type: Summer study
Location: Troy, NY
Duration: Two weeks
Dates: Middle to end of July
Qualifications: Grade 12
                    The program is open to academically talented minority and women
                    students who are interested in exploring careers in engineering
                    and who are U.S. citizens or permanent residents.

Housing: Housing is provided in the university dormitories supervised by
                    undergraduate counselors. Meals are provided in the dining hall.
                    Students have access to the campus recreational, sports, and
                    social events.

Costs: No cost to participants. Funding for this program is provided by the
                    Office of Naval Research and by Rensselaer. Scholarships
                    include tuition, fees, room, board, and round-trip transportation.

Credits Given: None

Contact: Mark Smith
                    Preface Program
                    Rensselaer Polytechnic Institute
                    Office of Minority Student Affairs
                    Troy Building
                    Troy, NY 12180-3590
                    (518) 276-8197

The Preface Program is designed to provide women and minority students, traditionally underrepresented in science and engineering, an opportunity to explore possible career opportunities in the field of engineering. Participants experience problem solving on a college level and do intensive work in interactive computer graphics and computing. Lectures, laboratory experimentation, field trips, and discussions all combine to give participants a realistic look at the challenges that are part of engineering study. Career-exploration activities provide a look at a future as an engineer. Evening workshops address topics that include academic planning, assessment of strengths and weaknesses, and college admissions and financial aid. Application deadline: Mid-March.

❖ Student Introduction to Engineering (SITE)

Host School: North Carolina State University
Type: Summer study
Location: Raleigh, NC
Duration: One week
Dates: Two sessions: mid-June and late June
Qualifications: Grades 11 and 12
                    Students should have a minimum 3.0 grade point average and be
                        enrolled in advanced math and science classes. Interested
                        minority and female students are especially welcome.
Housing: Students are housed in the university dormitories and eat at the
                        dining hall.
Costs: $225 covers room, board, and tuition. Some need-based financial
                        aid is available.
Credits Given: None
Contact: Kathy Lambert
                    Student Introduction to Engineering (SITE)
                    North Carolina State University
                    Box 7904
                    Raleigh, NC 27695-7904
                    (919) 515-3264

The Student Introduction to Engineering (SITE) program seeks to help students prepare for careers in engineering by helping them to understand the background needed for the profession, by providing a realistic look at the life-styles and working environments of engineers, and by showing students the challenging nature of engineering studies. The program includes demonstrations, lectures, and laboratory experiments and features many hands-on activities in the engineering labs. Career-awareness activities, such as presentations by practicing engineers, career exploration sessions, and interaction with engineering students, are also part of the program. Workshops on college admissions and financial aid are held. Application deadline: April 15.

❖ Women in Engineering Program (WIE)

Host School:	University of Dayton
Type:	Summer study
Location:	Dayton, OH
Duration:	Six days
Dates:	Mid-July
Qualifications:	Grades 10-12
	The program is open to female high school students who wish to explore career options in engineering.
Housing:	Students are housed in the university's residence halls with staff from the WIE program. Meals are served through the university's food service.
Costs:	$275 covers the student's portion and includes all expenses except for transportation to and from the university. Additional costs are covered by professional societies and the program.
Credits Given:	None
Contact:	Ms. Susan Pekarek
	Women in Engineering Program (WIE)
	University of Dayton
	School of Engineering
	Dayton, OH 45469-0230
	(513) 229-4645

Women in Engineering (WIE) is a career-awareness program designed to give young women the opportunity to experience and explore a number of the disciplines in engineering and engineering technology. Morning and afternoon sessions offer classroom instruction and laboratory experiments, including sessions such as computer-aided design labs. Among the special features of the program are a career fair with representatives from various companies offering insights into careers in engineering and technology, a dinner with women engineers from the Engineers Club who discuss educational goals and opportunities for women as they share their own experiences, a panel discussion presented by the Society of Women Engineers, and a day spent visiting industrial sites and labs. Application deadline: May 31.

❖ Chemical Engineering Summer Workshop

Host School:	University of Toledo
Type:	Summer study
Location:	Toledo, OH
Duration:	Three weeks
Dates:	Early July through late July
Qualifications:	Grades 11 and 12
	High achieving students who are interested in exploring careers in chemical engineering and who are U.S. citizens may attend.
Housing:	Students are housed at the University of Toledo. Optional weekend activities are planned.
Costs:	Program costs, including instruction, room and board, and lab fees, are met by the sponsors. Incidental costs to students are approximately $50. Students are paid a stipend of $200.

Credits Given:	None
Contact:	Mrs. Gale Mentzer
	Chemical Engineering Summer Workshop
	University of Toledo
	Academic Coordinator
	Department of Chemical Engineering
	Toledo, OH 43606
	(419) 537-4400

The Chemical Engineering Summer Workshop introduces participants to the field of chemical engineering through study of mathematics, chemistry, and physics and through discussions about the fundamentals of chemical engineering. Laboratory research, computer use and applications, and creative problem solving, as well as independent research projects, complete the program. Application deadline: March 30.

❖ Young Scholars Program: Introduction to Engineering and Computers Workshop

Host School:	Tennessee Technological University
Type:	Summer study
Location:	Cookeville, TN
Duration:	Four weeks
Dates:	Mid-June through mid-July
Qualifications:	Grade 12
	Students should rank in the top 20 percent of their class in science and mathematics.
Housing:	The 45 students live together in a university dormitory with four full-time counselors. Meals are provided at the University Center.
Costs:	Almost all costs (including tuition, room and board, and fees) are covered by grants from the National Science Foundation and other sponsors. Participants pay a $25 registration fee, transportation costs to and from Tennessee Tech, and personal expenses.
Credits Given:	None
Contact:	Mr. Tony Marable
	Introduction to Engineering and Computers Workshop
	Tennessee Technological University
	College of Engineering, PO Box 5005
	Cookeville, TN 38505
	(615) 372-3172

The Young Scholars Program at Tennessee Tech has been designed to provide high school students with science experiences unavailable at their home schools; the program is centered on engineering. Goals are to make students aware of career options in engineering, to stimulate creativity and problem-solving ability, and to help students gain an understanding of the interrelationships between energy production and the environment. The program includes lectures on engineering and on current concerns, computer programming (using FORTRAN), and engineering design. Each participant conducts a research project. Field trips and individual career and financial counseling are provided.

Recreational activities are scheduled in the evenings and on some weekends. Application deadline: May 7.

✦ Early Identification Program

Host School:	Christian Brothers University
Type:	Summer study
Location:	Memphis, TN
Duration:	Five weeks
Dates:	Early July through early August
Qualifications:	Grade 12 or first year of college
	The program is limited to students from groups underrepresented in engineering; that is, minority students, including African Americans, Asian Americans, American Indians, and others, and women. Program is for above average students with ACT composite scores of 20+.
Housing;	Students are housed in dormitories on campus. Meals are taken in the dining hall.
Costs:	There is no cost to the participants for tuition, books, and lodging. Meals and travel expenses are the responsibility of the students.
Credits Given:	Up to 6 college credits
Contact:	Dean Ray Brown
	Early Identification Program
	Christian Brothers University
	School of Engineering
	650 East Parkway South
	Memphis, TN 38104
	(901) 722-0405

This program is designed to open doors for underrepresented students who are considering careers in engineering. The program's academic component consists of college-level classes. Most participants take a precalculus course, while those with excellent mathematical backgrounds may opt for a class in discrete math. Students also take a class entitled Introduction to Engineering Design. Nonacademic components of the program include seminars addressing topics that include time and stress management, working with groups, study skills, career opportunities in engineering, and the ins and outs of college life. Some students may choose to return for a second year of this program. Application deadline: April 21.

✦ Minority Engineering Summer Research Program

Host School:	Vanderbilt University
Type:	Summer study/Internship
Location:	Nashville, TN
Duration:	Five weeks
Dates:	Early July through early August
Qualifications:	Grade 12 or first year of college at Vanderbilt in the fall
	The program is open to minority students. Most of the places are for students who will be matriculating at Vanderbilt in the fall, but some spaces are available for qualified high school seniors.

Housing:	Students live in the Vanderbilt dormitories and eat on campus.
Costs:	There is no cost to the students for this program. The university provides participating students with room, board, and transportation to Nashville. Because students will be unable to work for this five-week period, a stipend is provided for each selected student.
Credits Given:	College credits are available
Contact:	Dr. Carolyn Williams
	Minority Engineering Summer Research Program
	Vanderbilt University
	Vanderbilt University School of Engineering, Office of the Dean
	Box 6006, Station B
	Nashville, TN 37235
	(615) 322-2724

This program, sponsored in part by industrial companies, is designed to give participants a chance to experience college life and the demands of an engineering curriculum while introducing them to a variety of career options available in the field of engineering. Weekday mornings are spent in the classroom; students explore the mathematics and science aspects of engineering and participate in a regular summer school course. Special lectures by industrial leaders and field trips to local industrial sites provide a look at engineering as practiced today. Afternoons are spent working with a Vanderbilt professor on a research project. Application deadline: March 1.

❖ Young Scholars Program

Host School:	Texas A&M University
Type:	Summer study
Location:	College Station, TX
Duration:	Three weeks
Dates:	Early to late July
Qualifications:	Grades 8 and 9
	Responsible, self-motivated, and academically talented students who have an A or B average in math and science classes are eligible for the program.
Housing:	Students live in a dormitory at Texas A&M and are provided with a full meal plan.
Costs:	There is no cost to the participants; the program is funded by a grant from the National Science Foundation. In addition, students receive a stipend for travel to and from the university and a limited allowance for personal expenses.
Credits Given:	None
Contact:	Dan Turner
	Young Scholars Program
	Texas A&M University
	College of Engineering
	Engineering Experiment Station
	College Station, TX 77843-3124
	(409) 845-8986

This enrichment program for junior high school students interested in mathematics, science, and engineering gives participants a chance to discover what engineering is all about. Activities designed to introduce 10 of the engineering disciplines are combined with hands-on learning about methods of engineering inquiry, research, and problem solving. Students participate in a summer research project as part of a research team that includes a professor and an undergraduate engineering or science student. Field trips and tours of engineering laboratories help students discover engineering as it is practiced today. Students are also given instruction in communication skills, both oral and written, as well as library research and study techniques. Application deadline: May 20.

❖ Minority Enrichment Seminar in Engineering Training (MESET)

Host School:	University of Houston
Type:	Summer study
Location:	Houston, TX
Duration:	Two weeks
Dates:	Early to mid-June
Qualifications:	Grade 12
	Minority students planning to pursue a career in engineering and who have shown an aptitude for engineering study are eligible for the program.
Housing:	Students are housed in the air-conditioned university dormitories, supervised by counselors. Meals, except for weekend meals, are served in the university dining hall.
Costs:	There is no cost to the students for room, board, and instructional fees; the program is underwritten by grants from Exxon, JETS, and other sponsors. Personal expenses and weekend meals are the responsibility of the students.
Credits Given:	None
Contact:	Dr. G.F. Paskusz
	Minority Enrichment Seminar in Engineering Training (MESET)
	University of Houston
	PROMES
	4800 Calhoun Rd.
	Houston, TX 77204-4790
	(713) 743-4222

The Minority Enrichment Seminar in Engineering Training (MESET) program is intended to give gifted minority students the opportunity to become familiar with opportunities in the field of engineering and to experience life in a university environment. A number of short courses explore areas of study that include computers, chemistry, math, physics, problem solving, and engineering design. Field trips to industrial facilities on the Gulf Coast as well as tours of the college facilities give participants a firsthand look at the work done by practicing engineers. Guest lectures, sports, and social events along with weekend and evening programs round out the experience. Application deadline: April 15.

❖ Summer Pre-Engineering Program

Host School:	Texas A&I University

Type:	Summer study
Location:	Kingsville, TX
Duration:	Three weeks
Dates:	Early through late June
Qualifications:	Grades 10 and 11
	The program is open to students interested in exploring career opportunities in science and engineering who have at least an overall B average. Women and minority students are strongly encouraged to apply.
Housing:	Students are housed in double rooms in the air-conditioned campus dormitories and are supervised by dorm counselors. Three meals a day are provided during the week with brunch and dinner available on weekends.
Costs:	$600 covers housing, meals, and field-trip transportation. Sponsoring groups cover instructional costs. Students are also responsible for incidental expenses and transportation to and from the campus. A limited number of full and partial scholarships are available with preference given to Texas residents and minorities.
Credits Given:	None
Contact:	Ms. Jorja Kimball
	Summer Pre-Engineering Program
	Texas A&I University
	College of Engineering
	Campus Box 121
	Kingsville, TX 78363
	(512) 595-3028

This educational enrichment program emphasizes the improvement of math and science skills as students learn about careers in science and engineering. The program focuses on space and the environment. Academic instruction is complemented by hands-on laboratory experiences, speakers, field trips and project work. On Monday through Thursday, classes in physics, problem solving, and computer science are followed by afternoon laboratories in computers and engineering. Evening activities include recreational programming and time to work on independent projects. Fridays are reserved for industrial field trips and evening social events. Weekends are devoted to cultural trips and recreational activities. Application deadline: April 26.

❖ Electrical Engineering Program for High School Students

Host School:	Milwaukee School of Engineering
Type:	Summer study
Location:	Milwaukee, WI
Duration:	One week
Dates:	Three sessions: mid-June, early July, and mid-July
Qualifications:	Grades 10-12
	The program is open to students interested in exploring the possibility of a career in electrical engineering. No prior experience in computers or electronics is necessary.

Housing:	Students are housed in a university residence hall; all meals are provided.
Costs:	$365 includes tuition, room and board, and a ticket to the baseball game. Commuting students can be accommodated for $235, which includes tuition, lunches, and the baseball game.
Credits Given:	None
Contact:	Dr. Richard Born
	Electrical Engineering Program for High School Students
	Milwaukee School of Engineering
	1025 North Broadway
	Milwaukee, WI 53202-3109
	(414) 277-7200; (800) 332-6763; FAX (414) 227-7475

The Milwaukee School of Engineering offers high school students the opportunity to explore the field of electrical engineering. The program provides a hands-on introduction to electronics as well as to several areas of electrical engineering. Students work in teams of two or three, conducting laboratory experiments as a way of learning about the tools used by electrical engineers. The students receive an introduction to biomedical electronics, computers and digital electronics, communications and analog electronics, and power electronics. A recreational highlight of the program is an evening at a Milwaukee Brewers baseball game. Application deadline: May 31.

❖ Young Scholars Program: Engineering Summer Program

Host School:	University of Wyoming
Type:	Summer study
Location:	Laramie, WY
Duration:	Three weeks
Dates:	Mid-June to early July
Qualifications:	Grade 12
	Students should be interested in hands-on experience in the various fields of engineering. Selection is competitive.
Housing:	Students are housed on the campus of the University of Wyoming in a university residence hall. Meals are provided.
Costs:	Participants pay only a $25 activity fee. The University of Wyoming and the National Science Foundation provide the costs of room, board, and tuition. For students with unusual financial need, an additional stipend may be provided.
Credits Given:	None
Contact:	Susan McCormack
	Engineering Summer Program
	University of Wyoming
	College of Engineering Box 3295
	Laramie, WY 82071
	(307) 766-4254; FAX (307) 766-4444

Students selected for this Young Scholars Program explore the field of engineering through practical experiences. Participants can choose to build a digital circuit, to design building trusses, to test the aerodynamics of a tennis racket, or to study acid rain. The areas of materials science, image processing, composite materials, and environmental engineering issues are explored. Students work closely with faculty members to challenge their imagination and develop creative-thinking and problem-solving skills. Seminars on college admissions and career awareness expand the participants' knowledge. Field trips to engineering facilities, along with cultural, recreational, and social events, round out the program. Application deadline: April 15.

ENVIRONMENTAL SCIENCE

❖ Trailside Discovery's Alaskan Quest Programs, Alaska Center for the Environment

Type:	Science camp
Camper Level:	Teen program includes students ages 13–18
Location:	Anchorage, AK
Duration:	Six to fourteen days
Dates:	Numerous sessions held from mid-June through late August.
Housing:	Wilderness camping at various campsites.
Costs:	Program costs range from $300 to $590 depending upon trip chosen. A limited amount of need-based financial aid is available.
Contact:	Trailside Discovery's Alaskan Quest Programs
	Alaska Center for the Environment
	519 W. 8th Street, Suite 201
	Anchorage, AK 99501
	(907) 274-5437 or (907) 561-5437

The Alaska Center for the Environment offers a variety of outdoor education camps that focus on low-impact camping skills, cooperative activities, and learning about the effects of man on the land and on animal life. The Homer Marine Science Camps provide campout programs led by skilled naturalists on isolated beaches around Kachemak Bay. Other camps travel by sea kayak exploring the Kachemak Bay area and by raft down the Kenai River Canyon. Another offers participants a week of sea kayaking in Prince William Sound, followed by a week of backpacking in the spectacular Talkeetna Mountains. Still other options include bike and canoe trips as well as backpacking trips to specified regions. All trips are offered to limited age groups. Registration is on a first-come, first-served basis.

❖ Summer Glaciological and Arctic Studies Expeditionary Institute

Host School:	Foundation for Glacier and Environmental Research and the Universities of Alaska and Idaho
Type:	Field experience
Location:	Juneau, AL, and northern Canada
Duration:	Eight weeks
Dates:	Beginning of July through end of August
Qualifications:	Grades 11 and 12, college, and graduate school
	This is a physically demanding program. Experience in mountain and outdoor living is desirable, as are skills in cross-country skiing.
Housing:	Permanent housing is provided at the main field site, and temporary shelters and tents at trail sites.

Costs:	$2,500 plus travel expenses between participant's home and Juneau, Alaska, and back from Atlin, B.C. Scholarships are available through the National Science Foundation and other groups. Financial aid deadline: April 15.
Credits Given:	Up to 12 college credits through the University of Idaho and the University of Alaska.
Contact:	Dr. Maynard Miller
	Summer Glaciological and Arctic Studies Expeditionary Institute
	Foundation for Glacier and Environmental Research
	514 East First Street
	Moscow, ID 83843
	(208) 882-1237; (208) 885-6192

Spend the summer on an icefield, traveling between base and field camps by cross-country skis and dog-sled! This program combines academic and field training to provide an understanding of the total environment of arctic and mountain regions. It takes place in Juneau, Alaska, and in the Atlin Lake Region of northern British Columbia and Canada's Southwest Yukon Territory. The program's emphasis is on the expeditionary experience and on student participation in field research. Courses are offered in field geology, surveying, various environmental sciences, and glaciology, as well as in safety and survival training. Although most participants are of college age, highly motivated high school students are also included in this unique program held in a magnificent natural setting. Early application is encouraged. Application deadline: May 10.

❖ Breckenridge Outdoor Education Center (BOEC) Internships

Type:	Internship
Location:	Breckenridge, CO
Duration:	Three months
Dates:	Late May to end of August
Qualifications:	Interns must be at least high school graduates and should have a background in wilderness skills and/or a desire to work with people with disabilities. Enthusiasm, a desire to learn new skills, and a willingness to contribute are important qualities.
Housing:	Interns are housed at the center and provided with meals.
Costs:	Interns are responsible for their transportation costs and personal expenses. No stipend is given.
Contact:	Ms. Kate McNerny
	Breckenridge Outdoor Education Center Internships
	Breckenridge Outdoor Education Center (BOEC)
	PO Box 697
	Breckenridge, CO 80424
	(303) 453-6422

This is a program where a person can truly make a difference! The Breckenridge Outdoor Education Center provides year-round adventure-based wilderness programs for people with disabilities. The program focuses on empowering its participants to experience both physical and emotional success by encouraging participants to realize their full potential. The instructional staff, assisted by volunteer interns, are committed to these goals. Programs at the Center change by season and clientele, but have included sit and mono skiing, high ropes courses, backpacking, snowshoeing, rock climbing, cross-country skiing, and environmental awareness activities. Groups served include cancer patients, spinal-cord and head-injury patients, the hearing impaired, and the developmentally disabled, as well as people with multiple disabilities. Interns work with the center's professional staff, teaching disabled people to enjoy the outdoors. Application deadline: March for the summer session.

❖ Project Earth–Young Scholars

Host School:	Florida Institute of Technology
Type:	Summer study/Field experience
Location:	Melbourne, FL, and Tennessee
Duration:	Four weeks
Dates:	Late June through mid-July
Qualifications:	Grades 10-12
	The program is open to students from the Southeastern United States who have shown a strong interest in science, have a B+ average or better, and who have completed high school algebra and biology. The program is physically demanding.
Housing:	Students are housed on campus with chaperones in university residence halls. Meals are provided. While in the Smoky Mountains, participants will live in four-person tents in a commercial campground and will be responsible for cooking and cleanup under staff supervision.
Costs:	All accepted applicants receive full scholarships of approximately $3,000 to cover housing fees, food, field trips, and all instructional costs.
Credits Given:	5 quarter-hour college credits are available.
Contact:	Dr. Phillip Horton
	Project Earth-Young Scholars
	Florida Institute of Technology
	Science Education Department
	150 West University Boulevard
	Melbourne, FL 32901-6988
	(407) 768-8000 ext. 8126

A unique program that includes college-level instruction on the campus of the Florida Institute of Technology in Central Florida along with camping, hiking, and field work in the Great Smoky Mountains National Park in Tennessee. Program participants learn the basics of environmental science and terrestrial ecology in the classroom and then apply the learned concepts in the labs and in field studies. Participants learn to collect, analyze, and report data and then continue their studies at their home schools with the help of a sponsoring teacher. The program includes day-long hikes and mountain climbing, so participants need to be in good physical condition. Guest speakers and seminars focus on careers in science. Scientific and recreational field trips and activities complete the program. Application deadline: April 9.

❖ Summer Exploration of the Environment in Dubuque (SEED)

Host School:	University of Dubuque

Type:	Summer study
Location:	Dubuque, IA
Duration:	Three weeks
Dates:	Middle to end July
Qualifications:	Grades 11 and 12 and first year of college
	The program is open to students interested in exploring environmental topics.
Housing:	Students are housed in the dormitories at the University of Dubuque and take meals in the dining hall.
Costs:	$1,075 covers tuition, room and board, and field trips. A limited number of partial scholarships are available.
Credits Given:	3 college credits
Contact:	Dr. Rodney Foth
	Summer Exploration of the Environment in Dubuque (SEED)
	University of Dubuque
	Department of Biology
	2000 University Avenue
	Dubuque, IA 52001-5099
	(319) 589-3142

Two courses focusing on the Mississippi River are offered as part of the SEED program. Archaeological Studies provides an overview of 6,000 years of human interaction with the Upper Mississippi River environment. Participants are involved with artifact interpretation, pottery and bone-tool production, and rock-shelter testing. The course in River Studies centers on collection, examination, and analysis of living organisms and their Mississippi environment. Additional time is spent studying archaeology, forestry, geology, mining, soil conservation, and commercial use of the river. Students develop an awareness of the importance of the natural environment and learn to consider its interactions with modern society. Application deadline: May 31.

✦ Young Scholars Program in Coastal Erosion and Preservation

Host School:	McNeese State University
Type:	Summer study
Location:	Lake Charles, LA, and Holly Beach
Duration:	Three weeks
Dates:	Two sessions: middle to late June and early to late July
Qualifications:	Grades 10-12
	Students residing in the Gulf Coast states are eligible for this program. Selection is based on records, recommendations, and an essay.
Housing:	Students live in a dormitory on the McNeese State campus, supervised by dorm counselors. Most meals are taken in the McNeese cafeteria; students are provided with an $8-per-day meal allowance when off campus.
Costs:	No program cost to the participants. Students are responsible for personal and transportation expenses. Financial aid is available for students who need help with transportation expenses.
Credits Given:	None

Contact: Mary Richardson
            Young Scholars Program in Coastal Erosion and Preservation
            McNeese State University
            PO Box 90655
            Lake Charles, LA 70609
            (318) 475-5123

Students explore coastal erosion first-hand on a Gulf of Mexico beach and follow up their field discoveries with laboratory and classroom work. Each year, the U.S. coastline erodes still more; Louisiana loses 60 square miles of land to the ocean each year. Participants in this Young Scholars Program discover some of the reasons for this occurrence and learn about ways to use engineering technology to solve the problem. Participants spend time on Holly Beach, the site of an outdoor laboratory, studying erosion and attempts at coastal preservation. Work in the laboratories using wave tanks enables students to build and test their own coastal-protection devices. Classwork and a three-day field trip to one of the finest coastal engineering laboratories in the world complete the program. Application deadline: April 15.

❖ Student Conservation Association High School Work Groups (HSWG) Resource Management and Environmental Studies

Host School: Student Conservation Association Inc. (SCA)
Type: Internship
Location: National sites
Duration: Four to five weeks during the summer
Dates: June through August
Qualifications: The program is open to high school students and graduating seniors who will be at least 16 years old by the end of the program. Positions are offered on a competitive basis.
Housing: Interns are provided with housing or camping accommodations. Meals are provided.
Costs: No tuition costs. Food, lodging, and group equipment are provided by the SCA. Participants are responsible for personal gear and transportation to and from the program area. Financial aid is available on an as-needed basis.
Contact: Mr. Dean Klein
               Student Conservation Association High School Work Groups
               Student Conservation Association Inc. (SCA)
               Box 550
               Charlestown, NH 03603
               (603) 826-4301; FAX (603) 826-7755

High School Work Group (HSWG) participants spend four to five weeks completing outdoor work projects, such as trail construction, wildlife habitat improvement, construction of shelters, and archaeological field survey work, for government land management agencies, including the National Park Service, Fish and Wildlife Service, and the Bureau of Land Management. Informal educational activities, including field identification and geology, discussions of environmental issues and ecological principles, and low-impact camping techniques are part of the program. Recreational activities are available after work, and one week of each session is devoted to a recreational backpack or canoe trip. Participants have an opportunity to explore career opportunities in the natural resource field and are exposed to practical environmental education. Application deadline: March 1.

❖ The Governor's School on the Environment

Host School:	Stockton State College
Type:	Summer study
Location:	Pomona, NJ
Duration:	Four weeks
Dates:	July
Qualifications:	Grade 12
	The program is open to gifted students interested in exploring environmental challenges including not only those of the natural environment but also those of the social, economic, and political environments.
Housing:	Students are housed in supervised dormitories and take meals in the dining facilities.
Costs:	No cost to the participants for this program
Credits Given:	None
Contact:	The Governor's School on the Environment
	Stockton State College
	Pomona, NJ 08240-9988
	(609) 652-4924

This program offers students an intensive learning experience exploring the relationships between human beings and their impact on each other and on the environment. The program seeks to encourage students to develop into community leaders by providing them with both skills and knowledge. Another goal is to increase student sensitivity to our fragile ecosystems. The program is structured around an intensive course that focuses on specific areas such as environmental protection, global ecosystems, or the quality of urban life, along with small-group seminars that further explore issues. Frequent field trips provide experience with multiple habitats as well as opportunities for research. Evening programs, arts events, and social activities complete this stimulating program. Application deadline: January 4.

❖ New York State Summer Institute for Science and Mathematics– Environmental Sciences

Host School:	State University of New York at Stony Brook
Type:	Summer study
Location:	Stony Brook, NY
Duration:	Three weeks
Dates:	Early to late July
Qualifications:	Grades 11 and 12
	Participants must be outstanding science and mathematics students and New York State residents.
Housing:	Students live in the dormitories at Stony Brook and take their meals in the dining halls.
Costs:	$900 for tuition costs. Other program expenses are provided by the

N.Y. State Education Department. Need-based tuition assistance is also available.

Credits Given:	None
Contact:	New York State Summer Institute for Science and Mathematics
	State University of New York at Stony Brook
	Room 685 EBA
	State Education Department
	Albany, NY 12234
	(518) 474-8773

This program expands the participants' knowledge of the environmental sciences by challenging the students to develop an urbanization plan for Long Island, NY. Students must determine how to take advantage of the unique marine resources of the area with minimal impact on the environment. Five-member teams examine the problems and issues that confront modern environmental scientists as they develop their own plan for the island. This interdisciplinary program includes classwork, field trips, and individual research. Evening lectures on marine and environmental science, day cruises, and site visits, as well as social and recreational activities, round out the program. Application deadline: April 1.

❖ Cornell Environmental Sciences Interns Program

Host School:	Cornell University
Type:	Internship
Location:	Ithaca, NY
Duration:	Six weeks
Dates:	Late June through the beginning of August
Qualifications:	Students must be New York State residents and have a strong academic record and an interest in the environmental sciences. Students from underrepresented groups, including minority, rural, disabled, and low-income students, are encouraged to apply.
Housing:	Students are housed in the university dormitories, and take meals in the dining halls.
Cost:	None. Participants receive a stipend of $500.
Credits Given:	None
Contact:	Dr. Marianne Krasny
	Cornell Environmental Sciences Interns Program
	Cornell University
	Department of Natural Resources
	Fernow Hall
	Ithaca, NY 14853-3001
	(607) 255-2827

Cornell University sponsors this six-week research-and-career-exploration program for students interested in the environmental sciences. Interns experience "real" scientific research and increase their skills as they spend three days of each week working alongside Cornell researchers on field-based or laboratory research projects. The other two days are spent teaching science to economically disadvantaged children and contributing to their learning, exploring career opportunities in environmental science, and examining ethical issues. Application deadline: April 1.

❖ Duke Action: A Science Camp for Young Women

Type:	Science camp
Camper Level:	Grades 6–8
Location:	Durham, NC
Duration:	Three weeks
Dates:	Late July through mid-August
Housing:	Residential campers live in the campus dormitories under the supervision of residence counselors who live with campers and lead recreational activities. Meals are eaten in the Blue & White Cafeteria.
Costs:	$1,800 for residential campers; $940 for day campers. Fees include all instruction, classroom and lab materials, and field trips, as well as room and board for residential campers. Day campers have an optional lunch plan available for $50. The four-day trip is included for all campers. Limited financial aid is available.
Contact:	Ms. Cheri Sistek
	Duke Action
	Duke Continuing Education
	Box 90702
	Durham, NC 27708
	(919) 684-6259

Duke Action is an activity-intensive program that involves campers in hands-on field and laboratory work as they investigate forest and marine environments. Based on the Duke University campus and in the Duke Forest, campers engage in studies of ecology, such as predator-prey relationships and animal diversity, and of environmental science issues, including acid rain and endangered wildlife. Numerous field trips to sites such as the Duke Primate Center and the North Carolina Museum of Life and Science, as well as visits to university research laboratories, introduce the campers to careers in the sciences and give them a look at how modern scientists conduct research. The camp ends with a four-day trip to the coast of North Carolina for a first-hand study of the marine environment. Afternoons and evenings are devoted to recreational activities.

❖ Young Scholars Research Participation Programs in Aquatic Ecology and High Desert Ecology

Host School:	Oregon Museum of Science and Industry (OMSI)
Type:	Field experience
Location:	Various sites in Oregon
Duration:	Early July through mid-August
Qualifications:	Grades 10-12
	Students with a demonstrated interest in science and especially in freshwater and/or fisheries or in biology and/or ecology are eligible for the program.
Housing:	Students live in A-frame cabins and eat in the dining hall while at the Hancock Field Station. Wilderness camping is a part of the field experience.
Costs:	The program is completely funded by the Young Scholars Program of the National Science Foundation. Students pay only for personal expenses.

Credits Given:	None
Contact:	Dr. Jeffry Gottfried
	Young Scholars Research Participation Programs in Aquatic Ecology
	Oregon Museum of Science and Industry (OMSI)
	1945 SE Water Ave.
	Portland, OR 97214-3354
	(503) 797-4571

Participants in the Aquatic Ecology program become members of a research team working at a field site in the Mt. Hood National Forest. Beginning with a week at OMSI's Hancock Field Station, the students receive basic training in field techniques. Moving to a research site on the upper Clackamas River, under the direction of aquatic researchers, participants study the plants, animals, and ecology of the river, a beaver pond, and the wetlands region. The relationship between forest and aquatic resource management is explored through study of the salmon habitats in the region. Students choosing the High Desert Ecology program study the diverse plant and animal communities of the high desert region of Central Oregon. After basic training, the group moves to a base camp where participants conduct intensive ecological field studies in the John Day River Basin. Samples are analyzed in the laboratories of the Oregon Graduate Institute during the later part of the program. Students engage in hands-on field research while working closely with other talented peers under the guidance of professional scientists. Application deadline: April 1.

❖ DOE High School Honors Program in Environmental Science

Host School:	Oak Ridge National Laboratory
Type:	Internship
Location:	Oakridge, TN
Duration:	Two weeks
Dates:	Middle to late July
Qualifications:	Grade 12
	The program is open to students showing superior academic achievement and recognition in science. Students should have completed biology and chemistry; course work in environmental science, geology, or advanced life science is desirable. U.S. citizens only; interns selected by State Departments of Education.
Housing:	Students are housed in approved facilities arranged by the Laboratory.
Costs:	All expenses are paid by the sponsoring agencies, including transportation for the student to and from the facility.
Credits Given:	None
Contact:	Mr. Richard Stephens
	DOE High School Honors Program in Environmental Science
	Oak Ridge National Laboratory
	ER-80
	U.S. Department of Energy
	Washington, DC 20585
	(202) 586-8949

Sponsored by the U.S. Department of Energy (DOE) and the Oak Ridge National Laboratory (ORNL), this program's theme is identifying and solving environmental problems caused by conventional energy technologies. Studies focus on the analysis of aquatic and terrestrial ecosystems. At ORNL, interdisciplinary teams of researchers work together at one of the world's largest environmental research laboratories. The student participants form research teams and join scientists in investigation of environmental issues and problems. Students also attend lectures, visit laboratories, and take part in field trips. Applications deadline: contact program or State Department of Education for information.

✦ Camp Planet Earth

Host School:	College of Geosciences and Maritime Studies, Texas A&M University
Type:	Science camp
Camper Level:	Grades 8 and 9 (Limited to disadvantaged and/or Black or Hispanic students.)
Location:	College Station, TX, and Telluride, CO
Duration:	Two weeks
Dates:	Early to mid-July
Housing:	Students are housed in dormitories at Telluride and Texas A&M and also spend a few nights camping.
Costs:	There is no cost to the participants for tuition, food, housing, transportation, and materials.
Contact:	Dr. John Giardino
	Camp Planet Earth
	College of Geosciences and Maritime Studies
	Texas A&M University
	College Station, TX 77843-3147
	(409) 845-7141

Held in the town of Telluride, Colorado, Camp Planet Earth provides campers with an opportunity to gain an understanding of the importance of the environment and an appreciation for the environmental sciences. The goal of the program is to instill a respect for the environment and a desire to pursue careers in the geosciences. This unique program combines academic learning with "outward bound" type adventure programs. Students are asked to take on leadership roles during camp activities, are expected to help with camp chores, and learn to live in harmony with the environment. The program concludes with two days on the campus of Texas A&M at College Station, Texas. Application deadline: May 1.

✦ Aquatic Studies Camp

Type:	Science camp
Camper Level:	Ages 9 to 15
	Sessions are organized by age.
Location:	San Marcos, TX
Duration:	One week
Dates:	Six sessions mid-June through late July
Housing:	Campers are housed in the dormitories at Southwest Texas State University, the primary site of the Aquatic Studies Camp.

Costs:	$425 includes room, board, instruction, and all activities.
Contact:	Aquatic Studies Camp
	Southwest Texas State University, EARDC
	248 Freeman Building
	San Marcos, TX 78666-9989
	(512) 245-2329

At this unique camp, students can explore two aquatic habitats, the San Marcos River and the Edwards Aquifer. Mornings are spent investigating the subterranean inhabitants of the aquifer and the organisms that live in the river. Campers are taught sampling techniques to compare water quality of several rivers and learn about the physical characteristics of these bodies of water. Time is also spent exploring life in a pond. Afternoons are reserved for recreational aquatic activities including tubing on the San Marcos River, learning scuba-diving techniques, taking a raft trip on the Guadalupe River, swimming, and exploring Natural Bridge Caverns and Seaworld. Campers are supervised at all times by a trained professional staff. Enrollment is on a first-come, first-served basis, and limited to 26 campers per session.

❖ DOE High School Honors Program in Ecology

Host School:	Pacific Northwest Laboratory
Type:	Internship
Location:	Sites in Washington State
Duration:	Two weeks
Dates:	Beginning to mid-August
Qualifications:	Grade 12 and first year of college
	Students should show superior academic achievement and recognition in science and should be U.S. citizens. A background in field biology or chemistry is desirable. Participants are selected by state Departments of Education, one student per state.
Housing:	Students are housed in approved facilities arranged by the Laboratory.
Costs:	All expenses, including transportation to and from the Laboratory, are paid by the sponsoring agencies.
Credits Given:	None
Contact:	Mr. Richard Stephens
	DOE High School Honors Program in Ecology
	Pacific Northwest Laboratory
	ER-80
	U.S. Department of Energy
	Washington, DC 20585
	(202) 586-8949

The U.S. Department of Energy (DOE) in conjunction with Pacific Northwest Laboratory (PNL) offers students the unique opportunity to study a wide range of ecosystems, which include ocean, desert, forest, river, and stream, that span the State of Washington. Students should be interested in discovering how ecosystems function, interrelate, and change. This program emphasizes intensive field experiences, and participants need to be able physically to work in a variety of terrains. Combining field study with advanced satellite technology, students study biology, chemistry, computer science, and math. PNL scientists also present seminars on topics such as food irradiation, robotics, and molecular biology. Application deadline: contact program or State Department of Education for information.

❖ Natural Resources Career Workshop for High School Students

Host School:	Central Wisconsin Environmental Station
Type:	Summer study
Location:	Amherst Junction, WI
Duration:	One week
Dates:	Four sessions: June through August (One week is tailored especially for minority students.)
Qualifications:	Grades 11 and 12 and first year of college
	Students should be interested in exploring career opportunities in the field of natural resources.
Housing:	Students are housed at the Environmental Station, which has dining, sleeping, and meeting lodges along with trails and waterfront.
Costs:	$190 for room, board, and program costs. Scholarship funds are available from sponsors and local conservation groups for needy students.
Credits Given:	1 college credit is available for students who are at least entering 12th grade.
Contact:	Natural Resources Career Workshop for High School Students
	Central Wisconsin Environmental Station
	7290 County MM
	Amherst Junction, WI
	(715) 824-2428

These workshops are designed to give participants a look at careers in natural resources. The focus is on opportunities in resource management and environmental protection. The program is held at the Central Wisconsin Environmental Station, a rustic facility overlooking glacial Sunset Lake. Students take part in field trips to facilities such as a fish hatchery, a wildlife refuge, a water treatment plant, and a paper mill in order to examine potential work sites. Evening presentations by professionals give students a look at career paths and college preparation needed to work in the field of natural resources. Participants have many opportunities to explore the environment while learning about careers. A special session for minority students includes presentations by minority professionals. Applications are considered on a rolling basis until each session is full.

❖ High School Field Ecology and Field Natural History

Host School:	Teton Science School
Type:	Field experience
Location:	Various sites in Wyoming
Duration:	Four weeks to six weeks, depending upon program chosen
Dates:	Early July through early August
Qualifications:	Grades 10-12 (Exceptional students entering grade 9 will also be considered.)
	Students should be enthusiastic and self-motivated.

Housing:	Except for time spent in the back country, participants are housed in modern dormitory-style log cabins. Meals are provided at the dining hall.
Costs:	$1,650 for the four-week Field Natural History course; $1,975 for the six-week Field Ecology course. The program fee includes instruction, food, housing, and program transportation. Financial aid is available.
Credits Given:	1 or 2 semesters of elective high school credit
Contact:	High School Field Ecology and Field Natural History
	Teton Science School
	PO Box 68
	Kelly, WY 83011
	(307) 733-4765; FAX (307) 739-9388

These coed field courses offer firsthand experience in field biology, ecology, and/or natural history in the spectacular outdoor classrooms of the Greater Yellowstone Ecosystem. Participants investigate the natural world, study the key concepts of ecology, and design and carry out biological field research. The first week is spent exploring the surrounding plant communities through observation, field guides, and work in the Murie Museum. During the next weeks, participants camp off-site, learning land management skills, or live at the Robin Lange Field Research Station in the Bridger-Teton National Forest where they learn field research techniques and carry out a group research project. Additional time is spent investigating ecological or water systems as participants hike in the mountains and canoe on a lake. The course culminates with a week-long back-country trip exploring the natural beauty of the Teton Mountains of northwest Wyoming. Application deadline: contact program for information.

❖ Junior High Field Ecology

Host School:	Teton Science School
Type:	Field experience
Location:	Jackson Hole, WY
Duration:	Twelve days
Dates:	Late June through early July
Qualifications:	Grades 7-9
	Students should be enthusiastic and motivated.
Housing:	Except for time spent on the backpacking trip, participants stay in modern dormitory-style log cabins on the Teton Science School campus; meals are served in the dining room. Participants are supervised at all times.
Costs:	$770 includes instruction, housing, meals, and transportation during the program. Financial aid is available.
Credits Given:	None
Contact:	Junior High Field Ecology
	Teton Science School
	PO Box 68
	Kelly, WY 83011
	(307) 733-4765; FAX (307) 739-9388

Held in the beautiful natural setting of Jackson Hole, Wyoming, this field experience introduces young scientists to the Greater Yellowstone Ecosystem and to its natural history. Participants hike in many different terrains, canoe a glacial lake in Grand Teton National Park, learn fire ecology at a burn site, float the Snake River, climb Jackson Peak (learning alpine ecology in the process), and spend four days in the back country on a low-impact, backpacking trip. Throughout, a trained biologist/naturalist accompanies the group and aids students in understanding their surroundings. Students also participate in ongoing field research that is being conducted by one of the staff members. Applications deadline: rolling admissions after March 1.

❖ Young Scholars in Yellowstone National Park

Host School: Northwest College
Type: Field experience
Location: Powell, WY, and Yellowstone National Park
Duration: Four weeks
Dates: Early July through beginning of August
Qualifications: Grade 12

Students should be interested in a field research experience in environmental studies. The program is limited to 20 students.

Housing: While on campus, students are housed in supervised dormitories and eat in the college's cafeteria. In Yellowstone Park, the group camps at Bridge Bay campground, supervised by five instructors.

Costs: No cost to students. Room, board, and transportation costs of up to $150 are paid for the students by a grant from the National Science Foundation and Northwest College. In addition, each participant receives a stipend of $65 per week.

Credits Given: 3 college credits in chemistry from Northwest College.
Contact: David Barkan
Young Scholars in Yellowstone National Park
Northwest College
231 West 6th Street
Powell, WY 82435
(307) 754-6410

This is a unique, physically challenging program that combines field work with laboratory study in environmental science. Participants begin with three days on campus, preparing for their research project. The next two weeks are spent in the field at Yellowstone National Park, collecting research samples and accumulating data. Samples will include biological, geological, and environmental chemical specimens that will be used to answer research questions. Students may explore areas such as the effect of ultraviolet light on algae populations, genetic variability of plants pioneering in burn areas, and the bioaccumulation of metals in area rivers. The last two weeks of the program are spent back on campus, studying the collected samples and organizing data. Student participants will be expected to carry out a research project with the help of their science teacher during the following school year. Application deadline: May 21.

❖ Environmental Studies Program

Host School: The School for Field Studies

Type:	Field experience
Location:	Dependent on program chosen
Dates:	Various starting dates during the summer
Qualifications:	Grade 12 and college
	Students should have an interest in environmental studies and a desire to learn more about the world.
Housing:	Participants are housed in field accommodations that might include dormitories, platform tents, or other area housing. Local food is enjoyed at each site.
Costs:	Summer-program tuition ranges from $2,850 to $3,680. Students are also responsible for their transportation costs to and from program site and for personal gear. All food, scientific equipment, and housing are provided. Need-based financial aid is available.
Credits Given:	All courses carry college credit through Northeastern University.
Contact:	Environmental Studies Program
	The School for Field Studies
	16 Broadway
	Beverly, MA 01915-4499
	(508) 927-7777; FAX (508) 927-5127

The School for Field Studies provides a unique opportunity for firsthand study of the environmental problems that confront the world today. Students come away from this program with a heightened awareness of environmental issues and with the feeling that their efforts can make a difference in finding solutions. The summer programs involve teams of 24 to 32 students and three faculty members. Teams travel to sites all over the world, depending upon the program chosen. Recent courses have included Tropical Reforestation in Australia; Sea Lion and Dolphin Conservation in Baja, Mexico; a Wildlife Management course in Kenya; a Marine Parks Management course in the Caribbean; and a course in Tropical Forest Ecology in Costa Rica. Additional field experiences are also available. Application deadline: rolling admissions; apply early.

HEALTH SCIENCE

❖ Yale Summer Psychology Program (YSPP)

Host School:	Yale University
Type:	Summer study
Location:	New Haven, CT
Duration:	Four weeks
Dates:	Late June to late July
Qualifications:	Grades 10-12
	Students are selected for the program on the basis of a test taken locally, the Sternberg Triarchic Abilities Test (STAT). The test measures strengths in analytic, creative, and practical intelligence. High school record and recommendations are also considered.
Housing:	Students are housed in a residential college on the Yale University campus. Meals are provided in a university dining hall.
Costs:	$2,500 covers tuition, housing, meals, academic materials, and

social and recreational activities. Some need-based scholarships
are available.

Credits Given: Earned credits dependent on results of the Advanced Placement
exam in Psychology

Contact: Yale Summer Psychology Program (YSPP)
Yale University
Department of Psychology
Box 11A, Yale Station
New Haven, CT 06520
(203) 432-4656

Participants in the Yale Summer Psychology Program (YSPP) explore the field of
psychology through lectures and discussions, small group activities, and independent
projects. Topics covered in the program include the biological bases of behavior, personality, social development, intelligence, language, consciousness, motivation, and emo-
tion; abnormal psychology; and psychotherapy. The course can be used as preparation for
the Advanced Placement exam in Psychology. The students will also be participants in
a research program investigating intelligence. Additional activities for participants include speakers, museum visits, and social, recreational, and athletic events. Application
deadline: April 1.

❖ Summer Scholars Program in Medicine and Public Health

Host School: University of Miami

Type: Summer study

Location: Coral Gables, FL

Duration: Three weeks

Dates: Middle to end of July

Qualifications: Grades 11 and 12
Students should be interested in a career in health care.

Housing: Students live in the four-person, two-bedroom suites of the
university's residential college, supervised by resident advisors.
Meals (three per day on weekdays, two each day on weekends)
are provided in the dining halls. A full range of extracurricular
activities are available.

Costs: $3,300 includes tuition, room and board, field trips, and special
excursions. Limited scholarships are available; application
deadline for financial aid: March 1.

Credits Given: 6 college credits

Contact: Dr. Mary Lou King
Summer Scholars Program in Medicine and Public Health
University of Miami
PO Box 248005
Coral Gables, FL 33124-1610
(305) 284-2727; FAX (305) 284-4235

Taught by faculty from Miami's Medical School, this program focuses on current trends
in health care and preventive medicine. Visits to Jackson Memorial Hospital, Sylvester
Cancer Institute, Camillus Health Concern for the Homeless, and the Miami Project to
Cure Paralysis provide students with a firsthand look at current medical practices.

Students also take two 3-credit University of Miami courses. Genetics and Society explores today's knowledge of genes, studying topics such as cloning, gene regulation, gene therapy, and the molecular basis of cancer. Lab work provides hands-on insights into genetics. Health Behavior and Preventive Medicine examines the role of health-related behaviors—diet; tobacco, alcohol, and drug use; physical activity—in relation to patterns of disease and death in the United States in the 1990s. Application deadline: rolling admissions.

❖ Adventures in Veterinary Medicine

Host School: Tufts University School of Veterinary Medicine
Type: Summer study
Location: North Grafton, MA
Duration: Two weeks
Dates: Two sessions: mid-June through early July and mid-July through late July
Qualifications: First session: grade 12; second session: grades 10 and 11
    Students should be interested in a career in veterinary medicine.
Housing: Not available. This is a commuter program only.
Costs: $995 covers all costs including tuition, materials, field trips, lab fees, and 10 lunches. A limited number of partial scholarships are available for students with demonstrated financial need.
Credits Given: None
Contact: Ms. Hillary Lambert
    Adventures in Veterinary Medicine
    Tufts University School of Veterinary Medicine
    Administration Building
    200 Westboro Road
    North Grafton, MA 01536-1895
    (508) 839-5302 ext. 4743

This summer day program is designed to provide an intensive introduction to a career in veterinary medicine. Participants take short courses dealing with such subjects as wildlife medicine, anatomy, small- and large-animal medicine, and animal handling. They also "shadow" current veterinary students during their surgical and medical assignments in areas such as intensive care, surgery, anesthesia, and radiology. Each session features a day-long field trip, as well as tours of Tufts research, lab, and farm facilities. Student teams choose and research a topic for presentation at the end of the progam. A variety of speakers also address participants on topics currently important in veterinary medicine as well as presenting career opportunities. Application deadline: April 15.

❖ Medical Technology Summer Institute

Host School: Western Michigan University
Type: Summer study
Location: Kalamazoo, MI
Duration: One week
Dates: Late June
Qualifications: Grades 11 and 12

Students must currently be enrolled in a Michigan public or private school.

Housing: Students are housed in the dormitory at Western Michigan University. Students have access to the recreational facilities of the university.

Costs: $150 covers total costs to the student. (The balance of the costs of the program is supported by state funds.) Local and state need-based scholarships are available to help offset the registration fee.

Credits Given: None

Contact: Dr. Jack Humbert
Medical Technology
Western Michigan University
Kalamazoo, MI
(616) 387-3700

This program is for the student interested in pursuing a career in any health-related field. An intensive, week-long institute, it combines a study of medicine, related medical technologies, and marketing. Under the guidance of faculty and representatives from the medical community, students explore medical technology as it applies throughout the life cycle from neonatology to gerontology. Participants explore areas such as holistic medicine, high tech diagnostics, and rehabilitative services through hands-on learning, case studies, career shadowing, simulations, field trips, and discussion groups. A futuristic videotape marketing a health product in the year 2025 is produced. A wide range of recreational activities are available. Applications are submitted through the student's high school guidance office. Application deadline: March 2.

❖ Exploration in Biology and the Health Professions

Host School: Cornell University

Type: Summer study

Location: Ithaca, NY

Duration: Six weeks

Dates: Late June to early August

Qualifications: Grade 12 or first year of college
The program is open to students of superior academic ability as reflected in high school record and PSAT/SAT scores.

Housing: Summer College participants live in Cornell dormitories staffed by resident advisors and program assistants. Students have access to a variety of athletic facilities.

Costs: $3,800 includes tuition, room and board, fees, and health services. Books, supplies, and transportation are the student's responsibility. A limited number of need-based full and partial scholarships are available for gifted students. Several minority scholarships are also available.

Credits Given: 6 to 8 college credits

Contact: Exploration in Biology and the Health Professions
Cornell University
Cornell University Summer College
B 12 Ives Hall, Box 158

Ithaca, NY 14853-3901
(607) 255-6203; FAX (607) 255-8942

Students choose two courses from Cornell's Summer College list of classes. In addition they take the noncredit seminar Exploration in Biology and the Health Professions. The seminar helps students get a realistic picture of careers in the biological sciences. Lectures are presented by physicians who describe their subspecialties and by Cornell faculty members engaged in basic research in biological disciplines, including biotechnology, animal behavior, and applied ecology among many others. Weekly discussion groups encourage further career exploration. Workshops are also offered on college admissions, college study skills, time management, math study, and on personal-growth issues such as stress management. The Summer College also offers a full range of sports and cultural activities. Application deadline: April 17.

❖ Exploration in Psychology

Host School:	Cornell University
Type:	Summer study
Location:	Ithaca, NY
Duration:	Six weeks
Dates:	Late June through early August
Qualifications:	Grade 12 or first year of college
	The program is open to students of superior academic ability as reflected in high school record and PSAT/SAT scores.
Housing:	Participants live with other members of the Summer College program in Cornell dormitories supervised by resident advisors and program assistants. Students have a wide variety of athletic facilities available to them.
Costs:	$3,800 covers tuition, room and board, and fees. Transportation, books, and supplies are the student's responsibility. A limited number of need-based full and partial scholarships are available for gifted students. A number of minority scholarships are also available.
Credits Given:	6 to 8 college credits
Contact:	Exploration in Psychology
	Cornell University
	Cornell University Summer College
	B 12 Ives Hall, Box 158
	Ithaca, NY 14853-3901
	(607) 255-6203; FAX (607) 255-8942

A special seminar, developed as part of Cornell's Summer College, gives students contemplating a career in the field of mental health an opportunity to explore the theoretical, research, and applied aspects of psychology. Included are site visits to a number of social agencies, talks with practitioners in the field and with Cornell faculty members, and an opportunity to participate in research projects. Career options and appropriate course selection are discussed. Participants take a college-level course in human development or in psychology and choose another course from the offerings of the Summer College. In addition, students participate in workshops on college admission, study and math skills, and stress and time management and have available a full range of sports, cultural, and literary activities. Application deadline: April 17.

✦ Exploration in Veterinary Medicine

Host School:	Cornell University
Type:	Summer study
Location:	Ithaca, NY
Duration:	Six weeks
Dates:	Late June through early August
Qualifications:	Grade 12 and first year of college
	The program is open to students of superior academic ability as reflected in high school record and PSAT/SAT scores.
Housing:	Students live in Cornell dormitories with other members of the Summer College. The dorms are supervised by resident advisors and program assistants. Students also have access to a wide variety of athletic facilities.
Costs:	$3,800 covers tuition, room and board, and fees. Transportation, books, and supplies are the student's responsibility. A limited number of need-based full and partial scholarships are available for gifted students. A number of minority scholarships are also available.
Credits Given:	6 to 8 college credits
Contact:	Exploration in Veterinary Medicine
	Cornell University
	Cornell University Summer College
	B 12 Ives Hall, Box 158
	Ithaca, NY 14853-3901
	(607) 255-6203; FAX (607) 255-8942

A special program run as part of Cornell's Summer College for high school students, Exploration in Veterinary Medicine allows participants to gain insights into careers as veterinarians. Through lectures, lab work, visits, and demonstrations, students learn about the modern practice of veterinary medicine, including biotechnology, large-animal surgery, animal behavior, and the use of computers, as well as the other topics of current interest. In addition to the Exploration seminar, students choose two college-credit courses from the Summer College offerings and participate in workshops on college admission, study skills, and stress and time management: A full range of sports, cultural, and literary activities is available. Application deadline: April 17.

✦ Research Apprentice Program in Veterinary Medicine for Minority High School Students

Host School:	Cornell University School of Veterinary Medicine
Type:	Internship
Location:	Ithaca, NY
Duration:	Six weeks
Dates:	Late June through the beginning of August
Qualifications:	The program is open to current high school students who are interested in health-related research and limited to minority

students: those who identify themselves as Black, Hispanic, American Indian, Alaskan native, Pacific Islander, or Asian. Students should be U.S. citizens or have a permanent visa.

Housing: Participants live in the Cornell University dormitories and eat in the university dining halls.

Costs: None. Student interns receive minimum wage for their work. Room and board are subsidized by the College of Veterinary Medicine.

Credits Given: None

Contact: Ms. Shenetta Selden
Research Apprentice Program in Veterinary Medicine for Minority High School Students
Cornell University School of Veterinary Medicine
C-112 Schurman
Ithaca, NY 14853

This program offers students who are interested in health-related research the opportunity to work in veterinary research laboratories under the guidance of scientists committed to helping students understand the scientific information as well as develop the technical skills needed to pursue these studies. Interns become familiar with the many facets of the College of Veterinary Medicine, and learn about requirements for admission to veterinary school along with career opportunities in the field. Recreational and athletic facilities as well as cultural and social activities are available to participants. Application deadline: February 28.

❖ Pennsylvania Governor's School for the Health Care Professions

Host School: University of Pittsburgh
Type: Summer study
Location: Pittsburgh, PA
Duration: Five weeks
Dates: Early July through early August
Qualifications: Grade 12
The program is open to students interested in pursuing careers in health care and human service. Applicant's parents or guardians must be full-time residents of Pennsylvania. Former Governor's School participants are ineligible.

Housing: Students live in the dormitories at the University of Pittsburgh, supervised by college-student counselors. Meals are provided at the university dining facilities. The athletic, recreational, and cultural facilities of the university are available to the participants.

Costs: Full scholarships are provided to all participants covering instructional costs, supplies, room and board, and activities. Students are responsible for transportation to and from the university and for incidental expenses.

Credits Given: None
Contact: Pennsylvania Governor's School for the Health Care Professions
University of Pittsburgh
Pittsburgh, PA 15260
Information Hotline: (717) 524-5244

Funded and developed by the Hospital Association of Pennsylvania in cooperation with the Governor's Schools, the program provides participants with classes, observational experiences, independent research, and the opportunity to "shadow" health care professionals as they work. The program enrolls students interested in medicine, dentistry, nursing, physical therapy, pharmacy, and occupational therapy, among other health care professions. Students take a curriculum composed of a science core (anatomy, physiology, chemistry, and physics), a health-care-issues core (policy, prevention issues), and a communications core (ethics, computers, psychosocial behavior). Elective courses explore areas such as genetics and holistic interventions. Recreation and field trips are part of the program. Application deadline: March 6.

❖ Summer Research Program for High School Students

Host School:	University of Texas Medical Branch at Galveston
Type:	Internship
Location:	Galveston, TX
Duration:	Eight weeks minimum
Dates:	Early June through end of July
Qualifications:	Grades 11 and 12
	The program is open to high-ability students who are at least 16 years old and who have demonstrated an interest in and aptitude for science as evidenced by grades and standardized test scores, science hobbies or projects, recommendations, and a student essay. Special consideration is given to applicants who are disadvantaged economically, educationally, ethnically, or physically.
Housing:	Students can live in the university's dormitories, supervised by resident advisors.
Costs:	Students are responsible for all living expenses: room, meals, transportation, and incidentals. Students are paid minimum wage, earning about $1,360 for the eight weeks. Housing is available in the university's dorms for about $250. Limited housing and travel stipends are available for disadvantaged students.
Credits Given:	None
Contact:	Dr. Clifford Houston
	Summer Research Program for High School Students
	University of Texas Medical Branch
	Microbiology Department
	Galveston, TX 77555-1019
	(409) 772-0135

In this program, which is sponsored by the National Institutes of Health, the National Science Foundation, and others, each student is placed for at least eight weeks in an ongoing research team. A faculty preceptor teaches the student needed skills and presents an overview of the goals of the research. The student becomes familiar with the advanced technology used in this research, including such techniques as culturing cells, electrophoresis, chromatography, electrophysiology, data analysis by microcomputer, and biochemical assays. Participants also take part in a weekly research seminar and present their research to the group. Counseling about future career options in science and teaching careers is provided. Social activities, field trips, and weekly discussion groups covering topics such as philosophy and ethics complete the program. Application deadline: April 5.

❖ Veterinary Enrichment Program

Host School:	College of Veterinary Medicine, Texas A&M University
Type:	Summer study
Location:	College Station, TX
Duration:	Three days
Dates:	Three sessions: early June, mid-June, and late June
Qualifications:	Grades 11 and 12
	The program is limited to college-bound disadvantaged and/or Black or Hispanic students interested in careers in the field of veterinary medicine.
Housing:	Students live in the air-conditioned dormitories at Texas A&M University and have meals in the dining hall.
Costs:	$150 covers the cost of the program to students. Applicants may apply for full and partial scholarships by calling the office of Biomedical Science at (800) 874–9591 for an abbreviated Financial Aid Form (FAF).
Credits Given:	None
Contact:	Lyndon Kurtz
	Veterinary Enrichment Program
	Texas A&M University
	College of Veterinary Medicine
	College Station, TX 77843-4465
	(800) 874-9591

Participants in this program have an opportunity to explore possible careers in the field of veterinary medicine. Students attend special classes, observe clinical diagnoses and treatment of animal patients, and learn about the broad diversity of opportunities available to people who graduate with doctorates in veterinary medicine. Changes in the field of veterinary science as well as preparation needed to become qualified for veterinary school are discussed. Application deadline: April 15.

❖ Science Careers Opportunity Enhancement (SCOPE)

Host School:	Institute for Pre-College Enrichment, Prairie View A&M University
Type:	Summer study
Location:	Prairie View, TX
Duration:	Two weeks
Dates:	Two sessions: middle to late June and middle to late July
Qualifications:	Grades 10-12
	The program is open to serious students who rank in the upper third of their class, who are interested in a career in the health sciences, and who are U.S. citizens.
Housing:	Students live in the dormitories at Prairie View and take meals in the dining hall.
Costs:	Participants are responsible only for a $50 activity fee and

transportation to and from the university. Participants are awarded grants from the Science and Engineering Recruitment Fund of the Texas Education Agency that pay the cost of tuition, room and board, books, and supplies.

Credits Given: None
Contact: Hal Walker
Institute for Pre-College Enrichment
Prairie View A&M University
PO Box 66
Prairie View, TX 77446-0066
(409) 857-2055; (800) 622-9643

Workshops at the Institute are designed to stimulate students' interest in science and technical careers while they experience a taste of college life and get a look at the opportunities available to them at Prairie View A&M. Student participants in SCOPE learn about careers in the health sciences, including the fields of medicine, dentistry, and veterinary medicine. In addition, courses designed to strengthen basic skills needed by those pursuing health science careers are given. Participants have many chances to interact with professionals working in these fields and to learn about opportunities for future careers. Selection is competitive and on a rolling basis. Application deadline: April 1.

❖ Summer Scholars: Premedical Studies

Host School: Washington & Lee University
Type: Summer study
Location: Lexington, VA
Duration: Four weeks
Dates: Early to end of July
Qualifications: Grade 12
The program is open to academically oriented students who have a strong secondary school record and are interested in the health fields.
Housing: Students are housed in the residence halls at Washington & Lee, eat at the dining halls, and have access to recreational, sports, computer, and laboratory facilities and libraries.
Costs: $1,650 covers tuition, meals and housing, and program expenses. Textbooks and personal expenses are not included. Limited financial aid is available.
Credits Given: None
Contact: Summer Scholars: Premedical Studies
Washington & Lee University
Special Programs
Lexington, VA 24450-9904
(703) 463-8723

In this program, one of six summer curricula offered to Summer Scholars at Washington & Lee, participants take three daily one-hour classes within a chosen field. The premedical offerings include the basic sciences of biology and chemistry, as well as a course designed to improve writing skills. The science classes include experimental laboratories, lectures by professors and health-care professionals, and visits to nearby schools of medicine and veterinary medicine. Students gain a realistic view of the demands and expectations of professionals working in the field of health care. Physical education activities are planned for all participants each afternoon. Workshops on college selection, application, career planning, and study skills, along with other topics of interest to college-bound students, are offered. Application deadline: April 30.

❖ Dimensions in Nursing

Host School:	University of Wisconsin, Eau Claire: School of Nursing
Type:	Summer study
Location:	Eau Claire, WI
Duration:	One week
Dates:	Mid-July
Qualifications:	Grades 10 and 11
	The program is open to all students interested in exploring possible careers in the field of nursing. The program was designed primarily for minority students, but all students are welcome.
Housing:	Students are housed in double rooms in a university dormitory. Participants are supervised by a program assistant. Meals are provided.
Costs:	$250 covers the cost of tuition, room and board, and materials. Full scholarships are available through the support of the Wisconsin Department of Public Instruction Minority Scholarship Program. Application for the program and scholarship are on the same form.
Credits Given:	None
Contact:	Dr. Marjorie Bottoms
	Dimensions in Nursing
	University of Wisconsin, Eau Claire: School of Nursing
	Eau Claire, WI 54702-4004
	(715) 836-5287

Dimensions in Nursing is a career-exploration program designed to develop the health-assessment and -promotion skills of its participants while increasing their awareness of opportunities in the field of nursing. Students complete assessments of their own health risks and discuss ways of maintaining a healthful life-style. Risk factors, such as alcohol and drug abuse, stress management, and healthful nutrition and exercise are all topics that are explored during the week. Through field trips and interaction with professionals in the health field, participants get a look at the changing field of nursing as it is practiced today. Students also learn about college life and participate in seminars concerned with college admissions, financial aid, and college success. Application deadline: May 1.

MARINE SCIENCE

❖ Discovery Hall Program: High School Summer Program in Marine Science

Host School:	Marine Environmental Sciences Consortium/Dauphin Island Sea Lab
Type:	Summer study/Field experience
Location:	Dauphin Island, AL

Duration:	Four weeks
Dates:	Two sessions: early June through early July and mid-July through early August
Qualifications:	Grades 10-12 and first year of college
	This program is for students interested in a field-based course in marine science. A course in general biology is a prerequisite.
Housing:	Students live on campus in air-conditioned double-occupancy rooms. Meals are provided.
Costs:	$825 includes tuition, room, and board. A $20 application fee is an additional cost.
Credits Given:	High school credit is recommended by the Alabama State Department of Education
Contact:	Ms. Jenny Cook
	Discovery Hall Program: High School Summer Program in Marine Science
	Marine Environmental Sciences Consortium/Dauphin Island Sea Lab
	PO Box 369-370
	Dauphin Island, AL 36528
	(205) 861-2141 ext. 41

Sea Lab is the campus of the Marine Environmental Sciences Consortium, composed of 21 Alabama colleges and universities that have pooled their resources to form one marine campus. This intense, academic program introduces students to the marine environment through classroom lecture, laboratory, and field activities. Much of the time is spent in the field examining different marine communities. Field activities include the exploration of a salt marsh, beach profiling, shark tagging, and trawling aboard the Sea Lab's 65-foot research vessel. Students learn the mechanics of marine field research along with class instruction that investigates such topics as principles of oceanology, marine invertebrates and vertebrates, ecology, and human interactions with marine environments. Students participate in lab and field dissections, an individual research project, and panel discussions with professional researchers. Application deadline: March 12.

❖ Catalina Island Marine Institute: Sea Camp

Type:	Science camp
Camper Level:	Ages 12 to 17
Location:	Catalina Island, CA
Duration:	Three weeks
Dates:	Two sessions: early to late July and late July to mid-August
Housing:	Campers are housed on the 90-acre campus and take meals in the dining hall.
Costs:	$1,650 covers room and board, as well as all activities, lab fees, and boat transportation.
Contact:	Mr. Ross Turner
	Catalina Island Marine Institute: Sea Camp
	PO Box 1360
	Claremont, CA 91711
	(909) 625-6194

Along with traditional summer camp activities, Sea Campers have a unique marine science experience at this Toyon Bay, Catalina Island, facility. The marine science program finds campers exploring giant kelp beds, rocky intertidal zones, and the sandy ocean bottom while they learn about the organisms that inhabit each environment. Marine biologists instruct participants in courses like marine biology; oceanography; marine invertebrate behavior; and sharks, skates, and rays. Basic and intermediate sailing classes, advanced sailing and racing techniques, boardsailing, and basic seamanship are some of the classes available. Sea Camp diving courses ranging from skin diving to seven levels of scuba instruction provide campers with the skills needed for field marine exploration. Classes in underwater photography and video teach campers how to capture their discoveries on film. Sea Camp is accredited by the American Camping Association.

❖ Precollege Summer Scholars Program

Host School:	University of California, San Diego
Type:	Summer study
Location:	La Jolla, CA
Duration:	Five weeks
Dates:	End of June through the beginning of August
Qualifications:	Grade 12
	A 3.3 grade point average is required for students taking Marine Science; a 3.5 grade point average for students taking the Field Experience in Marine Biology program.
Housing:	Men and women students are housed separately in a campus dormitory, along with resident assistants. Meal cards are issued for 21 meals per week.
Costs:	$2,150 includes room, board, tuition, and all fees. A limited number of scholarships are awarded based on need and grade point average.
Credits Given:	4 college credits
Contact:	Precollege Summer Scholars Program
	University of California, San Diego
	9500 Gilman Drive
	La Jolla, CA 92093-0179
	(619) 534-7074; FAX (619) 534-8271

The Precollege Summer Scholars Program, offered through the collaboration of the University of California, San Diego, and the Scripps Institution of Oceanography, provides rising seniors with two courses in marine biology. Fifty students are enrolled in Introduction to Marine Science, a survey course, while students considering a career in marine biology may opt for the more intensive Field Experience in Marine Biology. All students are involved in lectures, labs, projects, and field trips, as well as sports and social activities, and receive instruction in the use of and have access to the Macintosh equipment in the campus computer lab. Optional scuba classes leading to open water certification as well as all campus recreational facilities are available to participants. Application deadline: May 1.

❖ Young Scholars Ocean Science Institute

Host School:	California State University, Long Beach

Type:	Summer study
Location:	Long Beach, CA
Duration:	Four weeks
Dates:	End of July to end of August
Qualifications:	Grades 9 and 10
	The program is open to high-ability students with a strong interest in science.
Housing:	Students are housed in Cal State dormitories supervised by mature counselors. Meals are provided in the university dining hall.
Costs:	About $850 covers student expenses, which include on-campus room and board and educational field trips. No tuition is charged to participants. Need-based scholarships are available for some participants.
Credits Given:	None
Contact:	William Ritz
	Young Scholars Ocean Science Institute
	California State University, Long Beach
	Science and Math Education Institute
	Long Beach, CA 90840-4501
	(301) 985-4801

The Ocean Science Institute, supported by a grant from the National Science Foundation, is conducted on the campus at Cal State, Long Beach, and at a number of ocean study sites. Participants receive hands-on experiences in the sciences through laboratories and field work, special presentations, lectures, and demonstrations. A special feature of this program is a "shadowing" program, matching each student with a professor working in an area of interest to the student. Each student completes a research project. Special activities are conducted aboard the university's research ship, the *R/V Yellowfin*. In addition, students participate in three days of ocean study at the Orange County Marine Institute and Catalina Island as well as other field trips and a full program of evening and recreational activities. Application deadline: May 15.

❖ Oceanology at Occidental College

Host School:	Occidental College
Type:	Summer study
Location:	Los Angeles, CA
Duration:	Five weeks
Dates:	Early July through early August
Qualifications:	Grade 12
	Participants should be fascinated by the ocean, highly motivated, and have had courses in biology, chemistry or physics, and mathematics.
Housing:	Students live in the Occidental dormitory under the guidance of a head resident and two resident advisors. Twenty meals per week are provided. Some day students who live in the Los Angeles area may also attend.
Costs:	About $1,700 for tuition and fees. Room and board is $950. Partial scholarships are available.

Credits Given: 4 college credits
Contact: Dr. Gary Martin
Oceanology at Occidental College
Occidental College
Department of Biology
1600 Campus Road
Los Angeles, CA 90041-3314
(213) 259-2890

Located near the Los Angeles harbor, and using the facilities of The Moore Laboratory of Zoology and the college Biology Department, as well as the college-owned 85–foot oceanographic research ship, Occidental offers a comprehensive oceanology program. The course work consists of lectures and labs Monday through Thursday. All of Friday is spent aboard the *R/V Vantuna.* The course of study includes topics such as chemical and physical oceanography, navigation, marine organisms, and marine ecology. Visiting scientists supplement the areas of expertise of the faculty of Occidental College. Social activities, including trips to Disneyland, concerts, and beaches, are organized by the resident advisors (Occidental students). The college admissions staff also presents seminars on college selection and essay writing. Application deadline: May 22.

❖ Summer Marine Biology Program

Host School: Santa Catalina School
Type: Summer study
Location: Monterey, CA
Duration: Four weeks
Dates: Late June through mid-July
Qualifications: Grades 10-12
Students should be interested in marine biology.
Housing: Boys and girls live in separate dormitories of the Santa Catalina
School and are supervised by resident faculty members.
Costs: $2,100 for resident students; $1,050 for day students
Credits Given: One year of high school credit for marine biology
Contact: Katie Aime
Summer Marine Biology Program
Santa Catalina School
Director of Summer Programs
1500 Mark Thomas Drive
Monterey, CA 93940
(408) 655-9386

This challenging program in marine biology uses the California coast as an outdoor laboratory, allowing the students to study the marine organisms found in tide pools, kelp beds, and sandy beaches. Along with lectures at the school, students use the lab facilities at Monterey Bay Aquarium and participate in field studies at other area marine labs and aboard research vessels. Classes meet for six hours a day, Monday through Friday, with an additional four hours on Saturday. A full recreational program is supervised by an Activities Director. The program is available to both resident students and day students. Application deadline: May 1.

❖ Seacamp San Diego

Type:	Science camp
Camper Level:	Grades 7–12
Location:	San Diego, CA
Duration:	One week
Dates:	Seven camps: July and August
Housing:	Campers live in the dormitories of the University of California, San Diego. Meals are provided.
Costs:	$675 includes tuition, room and board, and all costs except transportation to and from the program.
Contact:	Seacamp San Diego
	3669 Mt. Arlane Drive
	San Diego, CA 92111-3904
	(619) 571-0449

Seacamp combines traditional classroom learning and laboratory experiences with an intensive field experience in marine biology. At the University of California, San Diego, campers get an early taste of college life, while taking advantage of the Pacific location of the campus to discover the marine world. Daily hands-on classes provide background knowledge supplemented by trips and field work. Participants snorkel in a marine reserve, explore the tide pools of the Pacific shoreline, are introduced to scuba diving, and take a trip on a research vessel. Field trips take campers behind the scenes at Sea World and to the laboratories at the Scripps Institution of Oceanography. Recreational activities including volleyball, water sports, and a beach barbecue complete this fun- and learning-filled program.

❖ Circumnavigation

Camper Level:	High school and college
Type:	Science camp
Location:	New Haven, CT
Duration:	Five days
Dates:	End of June to beginning of July
Housing:	Campers are housed aboard ship.
Costs:	$425 for Schooner members; $475 for nonmembers
Contact:	Pamela Wuerth
	Circumnavigation
	Schooner, Inc.
	60 South Water Street
	New Haven, CT 06519
	(203) 865-1737

During this unusual program, participants live and work as both crew and marine biologists aboard the 91-foot gaff-rigged schooner *Quinnipiac*. The students stand watch; share deck, navigation, and galley duties; and collect and record scientific data as the schooner sails to various ports of call, including Mystic, CT, and Port Jefferson, NY. A day-camp program, entitled "Seafaring Scientists," is also available for students entering grades 5 through 8.

❖ Seacamp

Type:	Science camp
Camper Level:	Ages 12 to 17
Location:	Big Pine Key, FL
Duration:	Eighteen days
Dates:	Three sessions throughout the summer
Housing:	Campers are housed in dormitories on the Seacamp campus. Meals are taken in the dining hall.
Costs:	About $1,900 per session, with an additional fee of $315 for scuba courses.
Contact:	Ms. Grace Upshaw
	Seacamp
	Seacamp Association
	Route 3 Box 170
	Big Pine Key, FL 33043
	(305) 872-2331

The camp, situated in the Florida Keys, provides a unique physical environment for studying marine science in the waters of both the Atlantic Ocean and the Gulf of Mexico. Participants study marine communities, animal behavior, marine zoology, botany, marine geology, and the place of humans in the sea. Advanced studies are provided for students interested in scientific research. Campers use snorkel equipment to study live communities. Campers 13 and 14 years old can take a junior scuba course. Campers 15 and older are eligible for beginning through advanced scuba certification. Canoeing, lifesaving, and other traditional camp activities complete the summer program. The camp is accredited by the American Camping Association.

❖ Summer Scholar Program in Marine Science

Host School:	University of Miami
Type:	Summer study
Location:	Coral Gables, FL
Duration:	Three weeks
Dates:	Middle to end of July
Qualifications:	Grades 11 and 12
	Strong interest in marine science is necessary for this program. It is recommended that participants have completed the W.S.I. or senior lifesaving courses because swimming is required in the program.
Housing:	Students are housed in the four-person suites of the university's residential college. Three meals per day are served weekdays, with two meals per day on weekends. Students are supervised by resident assistants.
Costs:	$3,300 includes tuition, room and board, field trips, and planned excursions. Limited scholarships are available; financial aid deadline is March 1.
Credits Given:	6 college credits
Contact:	Dr. Linda Farmer
	Summer Scholar Program in Marine Science

University of Miami
PO Box 248005
Coral Gables, FL 33124-1610
(305) 284-2727; FAX (305) 284-4235

Participants in this exciting summer program examine the physical features of the oceans, discover the chemistry of seawater, and explore the structure of marine and estuarine ecosystems. Students utilize the unique South Florida location, traveling to the Florida Keys as well as Biscayne Bay. Field work takes place aboard research vessels and while snorkeling over the coral reefs. Throughout the program, students work on research projects. The program includes two intensive University of Miami courses, each carrying three credits: Survey of Oceanography provides an introduction to oceans and their importance to humankind; Marine Environments of South Florida emphasizes the interaction between living organisms and their physical environment. A full range of extracurricular activities is also included. Application deadline: rolling admissions.

❖ LUMCON/NSF Marine Science Young Scholars Program

Host School:	Louisiana Universities Marine Consortium
Type:	Summer study/Internship
Location:	Chauvin, LA
Duration:	Six weeks
Dates:	Late June through end of July
Qualifications:	Grade 12
	The program is limited to Louisiana students interested in careers in marine science.
Housing:	Students are housed at the Marine Center and take their meals at the site.
Costs:	None. The program's costs are covered by a grant from the National Science Foundation. Students are provided with room and board and also receive a stipend of $100 per week for the six-week program.
Credits Given:	None
Contact:	Dr. Michael Dagg
	LUMCON/NSF Marine Science Young Scholars Program
	Louisiana Universities Marine Consortium
	8124 Highway 56
	Chauvin, LA 70344
	(504) 851-2800

Outstanding students have a unique opportunity to explore careers in marine science while engaging in university-level scientific research. Participants begin the program with two weeks of lectures and laboratory experiences at the LUMCON (Louisiana Universities Marine Consortium) Marine Center. Students explore such subjects as biological oceanography, barrier-island beach ecology, processes of coastal and wetlands change, and fisheries oceanography. This is followed by a three-day research cruise aboard the research vessel R/V *Pelican*. The rest of the program time is spent engaged in independent research in the laboratory of one of LUMCON's research scientists. Most projects involve both laboratory and field work. Application deadline: April 16.

❖ Summer Sea Session

Host School:	Maine Maritime Academy
Type:	Field experience/Summer study
Location:	Castine, ME
Duration:	Five days
Dates:	Two sessions: late June and early July
Qualifications:	Grades 9-12
	This program is for students who are interested in careers involving working on the ocean or in marine science.
Housing:	Students are housed in the Maine Maritime Academy dormitory, supervised by dorm counselors. Meals are taken at the Academy.
Costs:	$325 includes tuition, room, and board.
Credits Given:	None
Contact:	Prof. John Barlow
	Summer Sea Session
	Maine Maritime Academy
	Castine, ME 04420
	(207) 326-4311 ext. 296 or 211

This intensive program finds participants spending up to 14 hours each day in maritime activities. The program includes classroom, laboratory, and field instruction in basic navigation, seamanship, ocean safety, and marine science. Students are introduced to the principles of physics, chemistry, biology, and geology from the point of view of their relationship to the marine environment. One field trip focuses on the hydrography and biology of the Penobscot Estuary, while the second focuses on sailing and seamanship aboard the historic gaff-rigged schooner *Bowdoin* while observing marine mammals. Students have access to the Academy's recreational facilities during free time. Application deadline: March 30.

❖ Invitation to Marine Discovery Camp

Type:	Science camp
Camper Level:	Grades 7–12, in the top 30 percent of school class
Location:	Hattiesburg, MS
Duration:	One week
Dates:	Late July
Housing:	Boys and girls are housed on separate floors of a university dormitory in four- to six-person suites, supervised by camp counselors.
Costs:	$325 covers all instruction, materials, field trips, housing, and meals. Day campers pay $275 for camp activities and lunch and dinner daily.
Contact:	Professor Lawrence Bellipanni
	Invitation to Marine Discovery Camp
	PO Box 8298
	Southern Station
	Hattiesburg, MS 39406
	(601) 266-4740

This Sunday-through-Friday program on the University of Southern Mississippi Gulf Park campus overlooking the Gulf of Mexico gives campers the opportunity to learn about the marine environment of southern Mississippi while having fun. Activities include trips to barrier islands, trawling expeditions, laboratory work, canoeing on a bayou, aquaculture studies, and tours of marine and oceanographic facilities along with other marine science adventures. Campers are taught by college professors, high school teachers, and practicing biologists. Recreational activities include swimming, tennis, fishing, volleyball, and baseball. Application deadline: July 3.

❖ Math & Marine Science Program

Host School:	University of New Hampshire
Type:	Summer study
Location:	Durham, NH
Duration:	Three weeks
Dates:	Late June through mid-July
Qualifications:	Grade 10
	The program is limited to students from New Hampshire and southern Maine. Applicants must have completed a year of high school algebra and science with at least a B average.
Housing:	Students are housed on campus during the three weeks of the program, but return home for the weekends. Meals are provided.
Costs:	The National Science Foundation covers all costs of the program except for a $100 registration fee.
Credits Given:	None
Contact:	B. Sharon Meeker
	Math & Marine Science Program
	University of New Hampshire
	Sea Grant Extension Program
	Kingman Farm/UNH
	Durham, NH 03824
	(603) 749-1565

Students explore the field of marine science by working on a project contrasting the environment at the Isles of Shoals with that of the Great Bay Estuary. They collect data using marine science equipment and then analyze the data through the use of computers. Participants have an opportunity to work closely with scientists, mathematicians, and computer experts to test hypotheses based on their field studies. An overnight field trip takes the students to the Shoals Marine Lab on Appledore Island for a close-up look at the island's environment. Each student also comes to the campus on four Saturdays during the school year, accompanied by a math or science teacher who acts as the student's mentor. Application deadline: April 29.

❖ Coast Trek: A Marine Science and Environmental Studies Program for the Academically Gifted

Host School:	University of North Carolina at Wilmington
Type:	Summer study
Location:	Wilmington, NC
Duration:	One week
Dates:	Eight sessions: June through August
Qualifications:	Ages 11 through 14

Students should be identified as academically gifted and interested in marine and environmental studies.

Housing: Students are housed in air-conditioned facilities of the university, in walking distance of all campus activities. The participants are fully supervised at all times. Meals are provided in the dining hall.

Costs: $425 includes housing, meals, instructional and lab fees, and transportation to and from all program activities.

Credits Given: None

Contact: Ms. Rosemary Talmage
Coast Trek: A Marine Science and Environmental Studies Program
University of North Carolina at Wilmington
Public Service and Extended Education
601 South College Road
Wilmington, NC 28403-3297
(919) 395-3195; FAX (919) 350-3990

Coast Trek offers bright young people the opportunity to study the unique marine life that inhabits the Atlantic coastal waters near the campus of the University of North Carolina at Wilmington. Participants assemble and stock individual salt water aquaria with organisms they collect during field trips to the surrounding inlets, marshes, and sounds. Laboratory studies research the behavior, life cycle, and environment of specimens collected by the students. Enrichment activities such as guest speakers, programs, and outings, and a full selection of recreational and social events round out the program. Students also have access to the university's athletic facilities. Application deadline: April 30.

❖ Summer Field Studies in Marine Biology

Host School: Roger Williams College

Type: Summer study

Location: Bristol, RI

Duration: One week

Dates: Two sessions: the last week in July; the first week in August.

Qualifications: Grades 9-12
The program is open to students who have completed an introductory course in biology and who are interested in exploring the field of marine biology.

Housing: Students live in double rooms in a waterfront residence hall at Roger Williams College. The dormitories are supervised by residence hall staff 24 hours a day. Meals are served in the cafeteria. A snack bar is also open daily.

Costs: $595 covers instruction, materials, lodging, and meals.

Credits Given: None

Contact: Dr. Thomas Doty
Summer Field Studies in Marine Biology
Roger Williams College
School of Science and Mathematics
Bristol, RI 02809-2921
(401) 254-3454

This program introduces students to typical New England coastal ecosystems. Through lectures, laboratories, and hands-on experimentation, participants learn about the interrelationships between organisms and their environment. Laboratories emphasize hands-on marine studies through dissections, collections, and microscopic examination of marine organisms. Field trips to a marsh in Nanaquaket, to the rocky coast of Newport, and to the pebble beach at Roger Williams College, along with trips to the New England Aquarium and a whale watch on the Atlantic Ocean, supplement the academic program. Application deadline: June 1.

❖ Marine Science for Junior Scholars

Host School:	Coastal Carolina College
Type:	Summer study
Location:	Conway, SC
Duration:	Two weeks
Dates:	Two sessions: middle to late June, and early to middle July
Qualifications:	Grade 9 or 10
	The program is open to motivated students interested in marine science. Students must be at least 14 years old.
Housing:	Students are housed in campus residence halls, supervised 24 hours per day by counselors and faculty members. Meals are provided.
Costs:	$850 includes tuition, room, and board. Students who wish to take PADI open-water scuba diving certification pay an additional $230. Financial aid is available to help defray tuition costs.
Credits Given:	None
Contact:	Dr. Robert Young
	Marine Science for Junior Scholars
	Coastal Carolina College
	Marine Science Department
	PO Box 1954
	Conway, SC 29578
	(803) 349-2277

Participants in this program have full use of the extensive marine studies facilities at Coastal Carolina College. Through the experiences provided in this program, students gain an appreciation and knowledge of the coastal marine environment and understand the concerns involving current marine issues. Classroom discussions focus on topics that include salt marsh ecology, aquaculture, marine chemistry, geological cycles, and waves and beaches. Students also do extensive field and laboratory work, including sediment coring of fossil-bearing deposits, specimen collections, survey of estuarine environments, and bird identification, and participate in directed research projects. Scuba instruction and recreational activities, including racquetball, tennis, swimming, and basketball, complete the program. Application deadline: April 30.

❖ Sea Camp

Type:	Science camp
Camper Level:	Three levels: ages 10 to 12, 13 to 16, and 14 to 16 (advanced camper)
Location:	Galveston, TX

Duration:	Five days
Dates:	Numerous sessions from early June through end of July
Housing:	Campers live in supervised dormitories on the Texas A&M University, Galveston (TAMUG), campus on Pelican Island. Staff is present 24 hours a day. All meals are provided.
Costs:	$525 for Sea Camp; $575 for advanced Sea Camp
Contact:	Mr. Sammy Ray
	Sea Camp
	TAMUG Sea Camp Director
	PO Box 1675
	Galveston, TX 77553-1675
	(409) 740-4525

Sea Camp is a project of Texas A&M University and the Texas Sea Grant College. Campers explore the wonders of the Galveston Island area through the use of research vessels, oceanographic equipment, and laboratories facilities, all combined with the guidance and knowledge of a professional staff that helps campers experience the water environment firsthand. Activities include exploring an oyster reef, touring a sea turtle hatchery, and trawling from the 42-foot R/V *Roamin' Empire*. A recreational program complements the marine studies. The advanced camp for 14 to 16 year olds emphasizes vertebrates and invertebrates and provides longer hours in the field and laboratory.

❖ Marine Science Pre-College Summer Program

Host School:	Marine Science Consortium
Type:	Summer study
Location:	Wallops Island, VA
Duration:	One week
Dates:	End of June through early August
Qualifications:	Grade 8 through first year of college
	Students must be at least 13 years old and have an interest in learning about marine science.
Housing:	Students are housed in Spartan dormitories containing bunk beds and bathrooms. Resident counselors live in the dormitories and supervise students during nonclass periods. Marine science instructors supervise students during field trips and activities.
Costs:	$325 per week covers room and board, instructional costs, equipment, supplies, and research cruises. The scuba course has an additional fee of $85.
Credits Given:	None
Contact:	Mr. Jerry Greene
	Marine Science Pre-College Summer Program
	Marine Science Consortium
	Box 16
	Enterprise Street
	Wallops Island, VA 23337
	(804) 824-5636; FAX (804) 5638

The Marine Science Consortium is administered by its member universities. It is located on the Eastern Shore of Virginia between the Atlantic Ocean and Chesapeake Bay, providing it with biologically diverse natural laboratories. The Consortium offers a number of different precollege summer programs, including Marine Biology, Oceanography, Experimental Ecology & Behavior, Wetland Ecology & Aquatic Botany, Advanced Marine Science, Shark or Dolphin Behavior, and an Open Water Scuba Course (minimum age 16). Participants may register for one or more sessions. All classes are field and laboratory intensive. The Consortium facilities include three research vessels, oceanographic field equipment, and 10 laboratory classrooms equipped with microscopes and saltwater aquaria. A variety of other educational programs are offered to school groups during the academic year. Application deadline: Contact program for information.

❖ Marine Science Camps at Island Institute

Type:	Science camp
Camper Level:	Children ages 6 and over, adults, families, teachers (advanced camp also available)
Location:	Spieden Island in the San Juan Islands, WA
Duration:	One week (scuba program: two weeks)
Dates:	Mid-June through late August
Housing:	Safari-style tents and cots provide housing; a swimming pool and jacuzzi add to relaxation.
Costs:	$695 for one-week program; teacher and family rates are also available.
Contact:	Ms. Jane Howard
	Marine Science Camps
	Island Institute
	4004 58th Place, SW
	Seattle, WA 98116
	(206) 938-0345; FAX (206) 932-2341

Island Institute provides total immersion in marine science while participants experience a unique camping vacation. Campers explore the underwater marine world, observe and track marine mammals including resident killer whales, and experience a variety of habitats on this private, rustic island in the San Juan Islands of Washington State. Marine scientists give formal and informal presentations during the week, while tours of the island, hiking, sea kayaking, and explorations of tide pools and shoreline, along with trips on the Institute's 43-foot boat all combine to broaden participants' appreciation for and understanding of marine resources. Other academic and recreational programs are also offered during the summer and the academic year.

❖ Summer Program in Marine Science

Host School:	Marine Science Consortium–West ▓▓▓▓ University
Type:	Summer study
Location:	Wallops Island, ▓▓
Duration:	Four weeks
Dates:	Late June through late July
Qualifications:	Grades 9-12
	The program is limited to highly motivated hearing-impaired students interested in hands-on study of marine science.
Housing:	Faculty, counselors, and students are housed together in the

dormitory on the campus of the Marine Science Consortium. Meals are served in the cafeteria.

Costs: Student stipends cover all program costs. Travel expenses and personal recreational allowances are the responsibility of the participants.

Credits Given: None

Contact: Dr. Joseph Marshall
Summer Program in Marine Science
Marine Science Consortium-West Virginia University
Department of Biology
PO Box 6057
Morgantown, WV 26506-6057
(304) 293-5201; FAX (304) 293-6363

This innovative program is held on the campus of the Marine Science Consortium at Wallops Island, ███████ Through lectures, laboratory work, and field trips, students explore the world of marine science. Topics covered include coastal, beach, and marsh ecology; shipboard and oceanographic techniques; animal behavior; marine biology; and other related areas. Field trips to the National Aquarium in Baltimore, MD, to NASA rocket operations, to the National Oceanic and Atmospheric Administration's weather station, and to the Assateague National Wildlife Refuge give students a view of real-life science and career opportunities in the marine sciences. In addition to group experiences, each student completes a research project under the supervision of a faculty member. Recreational activities and evening hours are supervised by resident recreational counselors. Application deadline: June 10.

PHYSICAL SCIENCE

❖ Student Science Training Program (SSTP) in Calculus–Physics

Host School: University of Hawaii at Hilo

Type: Summer study

Location: Hilo, HI

Duration: Seven weeks

Dates: Mid-June through the end of July

Qualifications: Grades 11 and 12
Participants should be highly motivated students who have demonstrated ability in mathematics and science and have completed two years of high school science courses and have had Algebra II, Plane Geometry, and Trigonometry.

Housing: Students are housed with counselor/tutors in the Hale Aloha Dormitory. Men and women are housed on separate floors. Meals are served at the Campus Center Cafeteria. Facilities of the university are open to the participants.

Costs: Approximately $1,400 for room and board, books, and fees. Tuition for Hawaii residents is paid by the state. Nonresident students have an additional cost of $600 for tuition. Financial aid is available for qualified students in need of assistance.

Credits Given: None

Contact:	Professor Suk Hwang
	Student Science Training Program (SSTP) in Calculus-Physics
	University of Hawaii at Hilo
	523 West Lanikaula Street
	Hilo, HI 96720-4091
	(808) 933-3319; FAX (808) 933-3693

Rudiments of Calculus–Physics is an intensive summer program. Students attend three hours of lecture four days a week and break into recitation-discussion groups two afternoons each week. An hour a day is devoted to a computer class; each student also conducts two three-hour physics experiments per week. On Wednesdays, participants take field trips to scientific laboratories and installations on the island including trips to the Hawaii Volcano Observatory, the Mauna Kea Astronomical Observatory, the Mauna Loa Geophysical and Solar Corona Observatories, and the Ocean Thermal Energy Conservation Laboratory. During the later part of the program, students may be invited to participate in individual research projects under the supervision of university faculty. Application deadline: March 8.

❖ DOE High School Honors Research Program in Particle Physics

Host School:	Fermi National Accelerator Laboratory
Type:	Internship
Location:	Chicago, IL
Duration:	Two weeks
Dates:	Middle to late June
Qualifications:	Grade 12 or first year of college
	Students must show superior academic achievement and recognition in science and/or mathematics. They should have completed at least one year each of physics and calculus and have some knowledge of computers. Students selected by State Departments of Education.
Housing:	Students are housed in approved facilities arranged by the Laboratory. Meals are provided.
Costs:	None. All expenses are paid by the sponsoring agencies, including transportation for the student to and from the facility.
Credits Given:	None
Contact:	Mr. Richard Stephens
	DOE High School Honors Research Program in Particle Physics
	Fermi National Accelerator Laboratory
	ER-80
	U.S. Department of Energy
	Washington, DC 20585
	(202) 586-8949

Sponsored by the U.S. Department of Energy (DOE) and the Fermi Accelerator Laboratory, this program gives 58 high school seniors the opportunity to interact with physicists and graduate students at a state-of-the-art scientific research center. The facility is a proton accelerator that provides the ability to carry out research in high-energy particle physics. Student participants join groups of researchers from the United States and around the world doing frontier research on the properties of elementary particles, using the world's highest energy particle accelerator. Application deadline: contact program or State Department of Education for information.

❖ DOE High School Honors Program in Materials Science

Host School:	Argonne National Laboratory
Type:	Internship
Location:	Argonne, IL
Duration:	Two weeks
Dates:	Middle to late June
Qualifications:	Grade 12 or first year of college
	Students should show superior academic achievement and recognition in science. Completion of courses in biology, chemistry, and physics preferable. One student from each state will be selected for this program. Contact individual State Department of Education for information.
Housing:	Students will be housed at a nearby college. Meals are provided.
Costs:	None. All expenses are paid for by the sponsoring agencies, including transportation for the student to and from the Laboratory.
Credits Given:	None
Contact:	Mr. Richard Stephens
	DOE High School Honors Program in Materials Science
	Argonne National Laboratory
	ER-80
	U.S. Department of Energy
	Washington, DC 20585
	(202) 586-8949

Sponsored by the U.S. Department of Energy (DOE) and Argonne National Laboratory, the program provides high school seniors with hands-on experience in ceramics and superconductivity. Activities are designed to develop curiosity, expose students to a research atmosphere, and provide interaction with scientists and peers. Lectures and demonstrations focus on current and potential applications of superconducting ceramics in basic science, engineering, electronics, and medical research. Students have access to the libraries of the Laboratory. Each student participant is expected to prepare a short paper on possible uses of superconductivity, give an oral presentation, and demonstrate an understanding of the principles of superconductivity. Application deadline: Contact program or State Department of Education for information.

❖ Young Scholars Program: An Introduction to Analog and Digital Electronics

Host School:	Ball State University
Type:	Summer study
Location:	Muncie, IN
Duration:	Four weeks
Dates:	Late June through mid-July
Qualifications:	Grades 11 and 12
	The program is open to academically able students with minimum

	math and science grades of 3.6 and an overall GPA of at least 3.4. Algebra, geometry, and at least one laboratory science course are prerequisites.
Housing:	Resident students are housed in one wing of a university residence hall, supervised by regular residence hall staff. All student participants eat the noon meal together.
Costs:	$190 for housing for resident students, and about $400 for meals. Commuter students pay a meal cost of $110. All instructional fees are provided by the National Science Foundation. NSF also has limited stipends available to help needy students with housing and travel costs.
Credits Given:	6 college credits
Contact:	Dr. David Ober An Introduction to Analog and Digital Electronics Ball State University Department of Physics and Astronomy Muncie, IN 47306 (317) 285-8860; FAX (317) 285-1624

Sponsored by the National Science Foundation (NSF), this Young Scholars Program is designed to excite students about science and technology and to encourage them to consider careers in these fields. No previous experience in electronics is assumed. Students begin by learning about AC and DC circuits using prototype boards, signal generators, and oscilloscopes. They move on to a study of amplification, filtering, and oscillators, followed by a study of digital electronics and computer interfacing. Evening activities, including instruction on computer usage as well as discussions on careers and current issues in science, are planned. Follow-up activities performed after the participants return home involve the use of computer interfaces that students will build and use for experiments. Application deadline: April 21.

❖ Physical Sciences Institute

Host School:	Jackson State University
Type:	Summer study
Location:	Jackson, MS
Duration:	Four weeks
Dates:	July
Qualifications:	All high school students are eligible; preference is given to students entering grade 12. Students must have a minimum score of 20 on the ACT. Women and minority students are especially encouraged to apply.
Housing:	Students are housed in the dormitories on the Jackson State campus. Meals are provided.
Costs:	Program costs are covered by the Mississippi Science Partnership, and students receive a $100 grant upon successful completion of the Institute. Participants are responsible for their own transportation to and from the campus.
Credits Given:	None
Contact:	Physical Sciences Institute Jackson State University

Mississippi Science Partnership
PO Box 17450
Jackson, MS 39217-0350
(601) 968-2969; FAX (601) 968-8623

The Physical Sciences Institute was created to increase the number of students interested in pursuing careers in science and technology. Activities are provided to enrich the students' background knowledge and to improve basic skill areas. Lectures in physics, astronomy, and mathematics as well as a survey of selected research fields are provided. Students are introduced to scientific research through seminars and laboratories. Special attention is given to improvement of communication skills, test-taking abilities, analytical thinking, and laboratory skills. Students are encouraged to use these skills to solve real-life problems. Field trips to places like the Davis Planetarium, the Hughes Aircraft Company, and Stennis Space Center and recreational activities complete the program. Application deadline: May 21.

❖ Young Scholars Program: Investigations in Trajectories

Host School: Mississippi State University
Type: Summer study
Location: Mississippi State, MS
Duration: Five weeks
Dates:: End of June through end of July
Qualifications: The program is open to students interested in exploring the field of aerospace engineering.
Housing: Students are housed in the dormitories at Mississippi State University and take meals in the dining hall.
Costs: None. The program is fully funded by the National Science Foundation. A $300 stipend is also provided to cover students' transportation costs and incidental expenses.
Credits Given: None
Contact: Keith Koenig
Young Scholars Program: Investigations in Trajectories
Mississippi State University
Aerospace Engineering
PO Drawer A
Mississippi State, MS 39762
(601) 325-3623; FAX (601) 325-7730

Students who elect to participate in Investigations in Trajectories have the opportunity to explore the growing field of aerospace engineering. The program is interdisciplinary in nature. Students learn about the motion of objects through the atmosphere by both classroom study and laboratory experimentation. Areas of study include physics, engineering, mathematics, and computer science. Application deadline: March 15.

❖ Advanced Chemistry Education Seminar (ACES)

Host School: Missouri Western State College
Type: Summer study
Location: St. Joseph, MO
Duration: Four weeks

Dates:	End of June through late July
Qualifications:	Grades 11 and 12 and first year of college
	Academically exceptional students interested in science-related careers are eligible for the program.
Housing:	Students are housed in the university dormitories. They may elect to stay on campus or return home on weekends. Meals are provided. The campus recreational and athletic facilities are available for student use.
Costs:	$665 covers tuition, room, and board for resident students. Commuting students pay a seminar fee of $425. Social and personal expenses are additional. Scholarships are available if financial aid is needed.
Credits Given:	5 college credits
Contact:	Dr. Gerald Zweerink
	Advanced Chemistry Education Seminar (ACES)
	Missouri Western State College
	4525 Downs Drive
	St. Joseph, MO 64507-2294
	(816) 271-4371

The Advanced Chemistry Education Seminar (ACES) was designed to provide high-ability high school students with practical training in chemistry. Unlike first-year college chemistry courses, this seminar includes laboratory and lecture sessions in analytical, organic, inorganic, and biochemistry, all presented emphasizing the practical applications of each discipline. The organic chemistry, for example, is related to synthetics used in everyday life, while the analytical chemistry is applied to maintaining a safe, clean environment. Friday field trips take the participants to nearby chemical industries. Social events are planned throughout the program, and a canoe trip in southern Missouri highlights each ACES program. Application deadline: May 11.

❖ Technology, Education, Kids: TEK Camp

Type:	Science camp
Camper Level:	Grades 5–9
Location:	Blair, NE
Duration:	One week
Dates:	Late June through early July
Housing:	Campers live in air-conditioned Holling Hall. Students are supervised by dorm counselors. Meals are served in the Campus Center.
Costs:	$170 covers the cost of room and board, recreational activities, and materials. Staff and instructional costs are provided by Eisenhower, Title II, funds. Some additional funds may be available to underserved populations.
Contact:	Dr. Kay Ferguson
	Technology, Education, Kids: TEK Camp
	Associate Professor of Education and Psychology
	Dana College
	Blair, NE 68008
	(402) 426-7279

This is a program for kids who are fascinated by high-tech science applications, telecommunications, and environmental issues. Campers build their own robot, use telecommunications to communicate with students across the country, use Hypercard, build thermistors, conduct experiments, and travel to the DeSoto Wildlife Refuge. The instructors are master teachers. TEK Camp is held at Dana College in Blair, Nebraska, where the campers have access to the excellent recreational and sports facilities of the college.

❖ Young Scholars Research Program in Chemistry

Host School:	State University of New York at Binghamton
Type:	Internship
Location:	Binghamton, NY
Duration:	Six weeks
Dates:	End of June through the first week of August
Qualifications:	Grade 12
	Applicants must be science-oriented students with a strong background in mathematics and must have a high school average of at least 90 or rank in the top 15 percent of their class.
Housing:	Students live in a reserved section of the residence hall under the supervision of resident counselors. Meals are served in the dining hall. Students have access to the libraries, computing center, and sports facilities of the university.
Costs:	None. The program is completely funded by the National Science Foundation and SUNY Binghamton and includes the cost of room, board, tuition, fees, and minimal participant travel.
Credits Given:	4 college credits
Contact:	Young Scholars Research Program in Chemistry
	State University of New York at Binghamton
	Department of Chemistry
	PO Box 6000
	Binghamton, NY 13902-6000
	(607) 777-2208

Participants in the Young Scholars Research Program become active members of a research team engaged in some aspect of current chemistry research. Students may choose to take part in study in one of the traditional areas such as inorganic, organic, analytical, or physical chemistry or to participate in ongoing research in neurochemistry, biochemistry, chemical physics, or geochemistry. Students also have an opportunity to study one of the most rapidly expanding fields of chemistry—materials chemistry. In addition to the research participation, students take part in seminars and discussions and trips to IBM, Corning Glass, and environmental research facilities. Weekend activities include both educational and recreational field trips. Application deadline: April 1.

❖ DOE High School Honors Research Program at the National Synchrotron Light Source (NSLS)

Host School:	Brookhaven National Laboratory
Type:	Internship
Location:	Upton, NY

Duration:	Two weeks
Dates:	Late July through early August
Qualifications:	Grade 12
	Students must demonstrate superior academic achievement and recognition in science and/or math. Advanced placement classes in physics, chemistry, and/or biology are desirable. One student from each state is selected; contact State Department of Education for information.
Housing:	Students are housed in approved facilities arranged by the Laboratory. Meals are provided.
Costs:	None. All expenses are paid by the sponsoring agencies, including transportation to and from the facility.
Credits Given:	None
Contact:	Mr. Richard Stephens
	DOE High School Honors Research Program at the National Synchrotron Light
	Brookhaven National Laboratory
	ER-80
	U.S. Department of Energy
	Washington, DC 20585
	(202) 586-8949

Sponsored by the U.S. Department of Energy (DOE) and the Brookhaven National Laboratory, this unique program gives high school seniors an opportunity to work at a state-of-the-art research facility. The major theme of this program is the study of basic and applied research in physical and life sciences. Current research at NSLS includes investigations in biology (protein structure), technology (photo etching), chemistry (photoemission spectroscopy), and physics (surface structures), as well as in other disciplines. Students attend lectures, visit laboratories, and interact with lab scientists and engineers. They also perform several experiments on NSLS beam lines, the world's brightest source of X and vacuum ultraviolet radiation. Written lab reports and oral presentations are required. Application deadline: contact program or State Department of Education for information.

❖ Nuclear Science and Technology

Host School:	North Carolina State University
Type:	Summer study/Internship
Location:	Raleigh, NC
Duration:	Four weeks
Dates:	Late June through mid-July
Qualifications:	Grade 12
	Students should have a demonstrated aptitude and interest in science or engineering.
Housing:	Students are housed in the University Towers residence hall, supervised by resident counselors. Meals are provided at the dormitory.
Costs:	$400 towards room and board. Tuition and the rest of the room and board costs are provided by the sponsors. Scholarships are available and awarded based on need.

Credits Given: None
Contact: Professor Thomas Elleman
Nuclear Science and Technology
North Carolina State University
Department of Nuclear Engineering
Box 7909
Raleigh, NC 27695-7909
(919) 515-3620

This program, supported by the National Science Foundation, introduces students to nuclear science and its applications through lectures, laboratory experiences, field trips, and participation in research. The program aims to increase awareness of high school students of the role of nuclear energy and nuclear techniques in solving problems that affect modern society. The first two weeks are devoted to a study of nuclear science through lectures and laboratories. In the last two weeks, the students take part in research projects, guided by faculty members and graduate students who serve as mentors. Evening programs involve discussions on scientific ethics, the Manhattan Project, and military applications of nuclear energy. Students have use of NCSU athletic and recreational facilities. Application deadline: May 1.

❖ Young Scholars Program in Physics

Host School: Francis Marion University
Type: Summer study
Location: Florence, SC
Duration: Three weeks
Dates: Mid-June through early July
Qualifications: Grade 12 (Exceptional 11th graders with strong academic
backgrouns may be accepted.)
Students should have a strong interest in exploring opportunities in
science and mathematics. Applicants should have completed
algebra I and II and geometry. High school physics is not a
prerequisite.
Housing: Students are housed in air-conditioned dormitories on the Francis
Marion campus and have meals in the dining hall.
Costs: None. All costs, except transportation and social-activity expenses,
are covered by a grant from the National Science Foundation.
Limited financial aid is available to defray transportation costs
and provide stipends on a need basis.
Credits Given: None
Contact: Dr. R. Seth Smith
Young Scholars Program in Physics
Francis Marion University
Department of Chemistry and Physics
Florence, SC 29501
(803) 661-1453

This program focuses on modern physics. Topics covered include atomic and nuclear structure, elementary particles, quantum mechanics, laser spectroscopy, relativity, and superconductivity. Students perform experiments, analyze data, and have an opportunity to be involved in a research project with a faculty scientist. Through the research experience, participants are introduced to modern research techniques, and function as researchers themselves. Research areas include nuclear and laser physics, spectroscopy, x-ray diffraction, and magnetic resonance imaging among other areas of study. Field trips expose students to technical advances through visits to the GE Superconducting Magnet Facility, the McLeod Regional Medical Facility, and Oak Ridge National Laboratory. Application deadline: April 16.

❖ Advanced Chemistry Applications Program

Host School:	Tarleton State University
Type:	Summer study/Internship
Location:	Stephenville, TX
Duration:	Five to ten weeks
Dates:	Session I: June through the first week in July; session II: early July through mid-August
Qualifications:	Grade 12
	Students should be at least 16 years old by May 31 and be interested in chemistry or a related field. Applicants should have SAT scores of at least 1000 or an ACT score of at least 24.
Housing:	Housing and meals are available in the university residence halls.
Costs:	Students receive partial scholarships towards college course fees. Students also receive a parttime salary for their research work.
Credits Given:	College credits are awarded. Number of credits depends upon classes selected.
Contact:	Advanced Chemistry Applications Program
	Tarleton State University
	Department of Physical Sciences
	Box T-69, Tarleton Station
	Stephenville, TX 76402
	(817) 968-9143

Each student in this program takes at least one class in chemistry or a related discipline while being actively involved in research with a university faculty member. Students may choose from several possible areas of research, including studies in the free radical reactions of organic compounds, the synthesis and reactions of substituted aromatic compounds, and a study of alkali metal tellurides in liquid ammonia solutions. Students may choose to participate in the program for either one or both sessions and will receive a partial scholarship as well as a parttime salary. Application deadline: April 5.

GENERAL SCIENCE

❖ Summer Minority Student Science Training Program

Host School:	Alabama A&M University
Type:	Summer study/Internship
Location:	Normal, AL
Duration:	Five to six weeks, depending upon program chosen
Dates:	Mid-June through end of July
Qualifications:	Grades 4 through first year of college (Students entering grades 11,

12, and the first year of college may apply for internship program.)

Housing: Housing is provided on campus; meals are taken in the university cafeteria.

Costs: There are no program costs. Housing and meals are free for resident students. Students will receive stipends of $375 to $450 for precollege program and stipends of $1,350 for first-year college program.

Credits Given: None

Contact: Dr. Jerry Shipman
Summer Minority Student Science Training Program
Alabama A&M University
PO Box 326
Normal, AL 35762
(205) 851-5316

Alabama A&M sponsors a variety of student science programs, both residential and commuter, supported by the National Science Foundation and directed to students entering grades four through first year of college. The elementary and middle school program (students grades 5–9) are for commuter students only; the high school programs serve both commuter and residential students. Students in the Research Participation (internship) Program are involved in research experiences intended to provide information about modern trends in science, mathematics, and engineering disciplines as well as career opportunities. The goal of the Science Training Program is to provide science research and/or enrichment experiences and to motivate minority students to consider careers in science and engineering. Application deadline: April 15.

❖ Horizons Unlimited: The Science Program

Host School: University of Arizona

Type: Summer study

Location: Tucson, AZ

Duration: One week

Dates: Mid-June

Qualifications: Grades 11 and 12
Students should be enthusiastic about learning and have at least a 3.0 GPA. Applicants should rank in the top 25 percent of their class.

Housing: Students live in a university dormitory, supervised by residence hall counselors. Meals are taken in the dining hall.

Costs: Approximately $191 for tuition, room, program fee, and application fee. Meals are not included but average $50 per week. Need-based financial aid is available. Scholarship deadline: May 7.

Credits Given: 1 college credit

Contact: Horizons Unlimited: The Science Program
University of Arizona
Office of Academic Programs
College of Agriculture, Forbes 211
Tucson, AZ 85721
(602) 621-1374

Students can explore science courses, experience college life, gain self-confidence, and acquire college credit in this program offered at the University of Arizona. Participants choose from a variety of offerings; selections include classes in genetic engineering, computer applications in the natural sciences, chemical ecology, health and biology of animals, issues in environmental protection, fitness, nutrition and food technology, solar energy applications, and landscape architecture, along with several other science classes. Classes include field work, laboratory experiments, lectures, and discussions. In addition to the academic component, students participate in social events and campus happenings and have the opportunity to assess their academic preparation for college. The university also sponsors a variety of internship programs for minority students entering grades 11 and 12. Application deadline: May 21.

❖ **Lawrence Hall of Science: Summer Science Camps—Outdoor Skills and Backpacking Camp, Wildlife Research Camp, and Forestry Research Camp**

Type:	Science camp
Camper Level:	Ages 10 to 13 and ages 14 to 18
Location:	Berkeley, CA, and sites in the Sierra Nevada Mountains
Duration:	Five days
Dates:	July through August
Housing:	Campers' accommodations range from dormitories to wilderness camping.
Costs:	About $340 to $540, depending upon camp chosen. Fees include meals, lodging, transportation to and from UC Berkeley, and instruction. A limited number of need-based scholarships are available.
Contact:	Lawrence Hall of Science: Summer Science Camps University of California, Berkeley Berkeley, CA 94720 (510) 642-5134

The first few days of the Lawrence Hall of Science's Backpacking Summer Camp for younger students are spent at Camp Lodestar in the Sierra Foothills concentrating on outdoor skills, including shelter building, map reading, and stargazing along with participation in a full recreational sports program. Then, participants leave for a four-day backpacking adventure in the Sierra Nevada Mountains, with separate routes chosen for novice and experienced backpackers. Campers explore lakes and streams, observe and identify wildlife, and may possibly get a chance to play in a snowfield in July. Older students may choose the Forestry Research Camp, working with ecologists, entomologists, and wildlife experts at the research station near Georgetown in the Sierra Nevadas. Wildlife Campers spend time at the research facility at Sagehen Creek in the high Sierras. There, they work with scientists on a variety of wildlife research projects, learning field techniques along the way.

❖ **YMCA Camp Oakes: Basic Wilderness Camp**

Type:	Science camp
Camper Level:	Ages 12 to 16
Location:	San Bernadino Mountains, CA

Duration:	Two weeks
Dates:	Two sessions: Middle to end of July, middle to end of August
Housing:	Accommodations range from cabins to wilderness camping.
Costs:	$620
Contact:	Mr. Frank McRae
	YMCA Camp Oakes
	PO Box 90995
	Long Beach, CA 92314
	(310) 496-2756; (800) 642-2014; FAX (310) 425-1169

The Basic Wilderness Camp is designed to promote the enjoyment of wilderness areas while teaching campers how to have minimal impact on the environment. In this co-ed program, campers gain experience in all areas of outdoor living skills, including activities such as orienteering, trailmarking, outdoor cooking, firebuilding, and backpacking. Only two hours from Los Angeles, Camp Oakes is located high in the San Bernadino Mountains, close to Big Bear Lake and the San Gorgonio Wilderness area. In this smog-free environment, campers participate in a program that progresses from basic camping skills and trail hiking to a three-day backpacking trip in the surrounding national forest. Camp Oakes is accredited by the American Camping Association.

❖ Committee for Advanced Science Training (CAST) Research Program

Host School:	California Museum of Science and Industry
Type:	Internship
Location:	California sites dependent on project
Duration:	Ten weeks
Dates:	Summer
Qualifications:	Grades 11 and 12
	Students who are interested in research and who are residents of Los Angeles, Orange, and Riverside, California, counties are eligible. All applicants must take an exam in biological and physical sciences; the top one-third are interviewed by science specialists for selection for one of 15 assignments.
Housing:	None provided; all participants are commuters.
Costs:	None. A stipend of $500 is paid to each student researcher.
Contact:	Ms. Yoshi Yamasaki
	Committee for Advanced Science Training (CAST) Research Program
	California Museum of Science and Industry
	Educational Symposia Programs Coordinator
	700 State Drive
	Los Angeles, CA 90037
	(213) 744-7444

The program seeks to bring promising secondary students in direct contact with outstanding research scientists. Each of 15 students is assigned to work on an ongoing laboratory research project at a research facility near home. Students are guided by the supervising scientist. All student researchers participate at the Committee for Advanced Science Training (CAST) Scientific Meeting in October by means of a poster presentation describing their research projects. Application deadline: February 22. Written exam is scheduled for the middle of March.

❖ DOE High School Supercomputer Honors Program

Host School:	Lawrence Livermore National Laboratory
Type:	Internship
Location:	Livermore, CA
Duration:	Two weeks
Dates:	Middle to end of June
Qualifications:	Grade 12 or first year of college
	Students must demonstrate superior academic achievement and recognition in science and/or mathematics, be computer literate, and be U.S. citizens. One student from each state is selected for this program; contact individual State Department of Education for information.
Housing:	Students are housed in approved facilities arranged by the Laboratory. Meals are provided.
Costs:	None. All expenses are paid by the sponsoring agencies, including transportation for the student to and from the facility.
Credits Given:	None
Contact:	Mr. Richard Stephens
	DOE High School Supercomputer Honors Program
	Lawrence Livermore National Laboratory
	ER-80
	U.S. Department of Energy
	Washington, DC 20585
	(202) 586-8949

Sponsored by the U.S. Department of Energy (DOE) and a host laboratory, this program gives high school students firsthand experience working in a state-of-the-art research facility and interacting with research scientists. High school students selected for this program get hands-on experience using the world's fastest and most sophisticated computers at the Lawrence Livermore Laboratory's National Magnetic Fusion Energy Center. The program seeks to encourage students to regard supercomputers as research tools and to motivate them to study computer science. Students solve problems in mathematics, physics, and computer graphics. Each student is also expected to complete a programming project that demonstrates the capacities of supercomputers. Application deadline: contact program or State Department of Education for information.

❖ Caltech Young Engineering and Science Scholars (YESS)

Host School:	California Institute of Technology
Type:	Summer study
Location:	Pasadena, CA
Duration:	Four weeks
Dates:	Early to late July
Qualifications:	Grade 12
	The program is open to outstanding students interested in the sciences and/or engineering. Students from backgrounds

	traditionally underrepresented in science and engineering are especially encouraged to apply.
Housing:	Students live in supervised Caltech dormitories and are provided with meals. Participants have access to the university's research, including libraries and athletic facilities.
Costs:	No program costs to the participants. Tuition, room and board, and all books are covered. Students are responsible only for transportation to and from the university and for personal expenses. Limited need-based financial aid is available for transportation costs.
Credits Given:	None
Contact:	Caltech Young Engineering and Science Scholars (YESS) California Institute of Technology 2-98 Caltech Pasadena, CA 91125 (818) 356-6207

YESS (Young Engineering and Science Scholars) exposes high school seniors to the process of actually doing science. Participants take laboratory-based classes in biology, physics, and earth and planetary science. The biology class introduces students to modern molecular biology. The earth and planetary science course includes applications of chemistry and physics to explain phenomena such as earthquakes and volcanoes. Other classes include mathematics (calculus or precalculus), art, and art history. Field trips to the Jet Propulsion Laboratory and to the Getty Museum of Art allow students to utilize the resources of the greater Los Angeles area. High school activities are not duplicated; students are exposed to the joys of intensive scientific research. Application deadline: April 23.

❖ Young Scholars Summer Session (YSSS)

Host School:	University of Colorado at Boulder
Type:	Summer study
Location:	Boulder, CO
Duration:	Five weeks
Dates:	Late June through late July
Qualifications:	Grade 12 The program is open to academically motivated students whose grades place them in the top 10 to 15 percent of their high school class.
Housing:	YSSS participants are housed together in one of the central campus dormitories. Resident advisors live in the halls and serve as mentors and recreational program leaders. Meals are served at the residence halls each day except Sunday.
Costs:	About $2,000 for tuition, room, and board for in-state students and about $2,800 for out-of-state students. Books cost about $60 and about $50 per week is needed for incidentals. A limited number of scholarships are available. Scholarship application deadline: May 1.
Credits Given:	3 college credits
Contact:	Dr. Donna Vocate

Young Scholars Summer Session (YSSS)
University of Colorado at Boulder
Director
Campus Box 73
Boulder, CO 80309-0073
(303) 492-5421

YSSS (Young Scholars Summer Session) participants choose among special sections of regular University of Colorado at Boulder courses, including anthropology, astronomy, and general biology. Students attend small classes (between 10 and 20 students) that are offered exclusively for program participants and that meet for at least three hours each day. In addition to rigorous academics, an auxiliary program of YSSS offers opportunities for hiking in the mountains, swimming at Boulder Reservoir, exploring Denver, attending the Shakespeare festival, and a long weekend camping trip. Additionally, a College Prep Workshop offers information on colleges and universities throughout the United States. Application deadline: May 15.

❖ America's Adventure Camping Program Inc.

Type:	Science camp
Camper Level:	Grades 9–12 (grouped by age)
Location:	Golden, CO
Duration:	Four weeks
Dates:	July or August depending upon program selected.
Housing:	Most of the programs' accommodations involve tent camping; campers plan meals and shop for and prepare food.
Costs:	About $2,500 for the 28–day programs. All food, lodging, tuition, equipment, and laundry costs are included.
Contact:	Mr. Abbot Wallis
	America's Adventure Camping Program Inc.
	23418 Fescue Drive
	Golden, CO 80401
	(303) 526-0806; (800) 222-3595

America's Adventure is a private camping program that provides wilderness camping experiences to small groups of teenagers. The programs center on three- to five-day learning experiences and may include skills instruction and experiences in backpacking and mountaineering, technical rock climbing, white water rafting, sailing, wind surfing, mountain biking, and horseback riding, depending upon the program selected. All staff members are over 21. America's Adventure is a member of the American Camping Association.

❖ Summer Scientific Seminar

Host School:	United States Air Force Academy
Type:	Summer study
Location:	Colorado Springs, CO
Duration:	One week
Dates:	Two sessions: mid-June and Late June
Qualifications:	Grade 12
	The program is open to students interested in becoming Air Force

Academy cadets. Applicants must be ranked in the top third of their class and have scores of at least 50 Verbal, 55 Math on the PSAT (500 V and 550 M on SAT), or composite of 24 on the ACT.

Housing:	Students live in a cadet dormitory and eat in the dining hall.
Costs:	$100 plus transportation costs to and from the Air Force Academy. Limited financial aid is available.
Credits Given:	None
Contact:	Summer Scientific Seminar
	United States Air Force Academy
	HQ USAFA/RRMX
	2304 Cadet Drive, Suite 211
	USAF Academy, CO 80840-5025
	(719) 472-2236

This program offers participants a unique opportunity to get a firsthand look at academic and student life at the U.S. Air Force Academy. Students choose from a wide variety of scientific seminars focusing on topics such as metaphysics, astronomy, geopolitics, computer-aided drawing, electronics, field biology, airmanship, and technical writing, along with many other selections. Tours of the laboratories and flight line are also available to the participants. Evening programs include informational sessions and athletic and recreational activities. Current cadets host and escort students and provide guidance as well as information about life as a cadet. Students gain an understanding of the opportunities available to scientists and engineers in the Air Force. Application deadline: early February.

❖ Science Transition Program

Host School:	Central Connecticut State University
Type:	Summer study
Location:	New Britain, CT
Duration:	Three weeks
Dates:	End of June through mid-July
Qualifications:	Grades 9 and 10
	The program is for students who exhibit a high potential for science studies but who are not currently achieving at their ability level.
Housing:	Students live in the campus residence halls. Meals are provided in the dining hall.
Costs:	No cost to the participants. Fees for tuition, housing, meals, and supplies are all provided by the program's sponsors.
Contact:	Dr. George Clarke
	Science Transition Program
	Central Connecticut State University
	Dean, School of Arts and Sciences
	1615 Stanley Street
	New Britain, CT 06050
	(203) 827-7279

Supported by the National Science Foundation along with several corporate sponsors,

Science Transition seeks those students who show a high potential for science studies but who are not the top scholars in their classes at this time. It is believed that these are students who may, with the right environment and encouragement, grow to meet their potential. The program consists of an interdisciplinary exploration of the worlds of ecology, space, marine science, and human life seen from the perspectives of biology, chemistry, earth science, and physics. Other features of the program include a mentoring program matching individual participants with role models and a support program for parents to help them encourage their children in their studies. Women and minority students are especially encouraged to apply. Application deadline: April 10.

❖ University of Connecticut—NSF Young Scholars Program

Type:	Internship
Location:	Storrs, CT
Duration:	Six weeks
Dates:	Early July through mid-August
Qualifications:	Grades 11 and 12
	The program is designed for outstanding students from Connecticut, Massachusetts, and Rhode Island who are interested in science and mathematics. Underrepresented minority students and women are especially encouraged to apply for this program. Admission is competitive.
Housing:	Students are housed in the university residence hall and have their meals provided.
Costs:	No cost to the student participants. The program provides a $500 stipend to each participant. All program costs are covered by grants from the National Science Foundation and from the University of Connecticut.
Contact:	John Tanaka
	University of Connecticut—NSF Young Scholars Program
	University of Connecticut, Storrs
	Honors Program, Box U-147, Room 113
	241 Glenbrook Road
	Storrs, CT 06269-2147
	(203) 486-4223

Sponsored by the University of Connecticut, Storrs, and the National Science Foundation (NSF), this intensive six-week research experience targets outstanding students interested in pursuing careers in science and engineering. Interns work on individual research projects with professor mentors; participate in research-progress meetings; attend seminars on scientific ethics, problem-solving techniques, and philosophy of science; and interact with other Young Scholars. Students present their research findings at a symposium at the end of the six weeks. In addition to the research experience, students participate in organized recreational, athletic, and social events. Field trips are planned for each weekend. Application deadline: March 26.

❖ Smithsonian Institution's Intern '94

Type:	Internship
Location:	Washington, DC

Duration:	About six weeks
Dates:	Late June through early August.
Qualifications:	Grade 12
	Acceptance is based on a demonstrated interest in a particular subject area or career. Minority students and students with disabilities are especially encouraged to apply.
Housing:	Housing in a university residence hall is provided.
Costs:	None. Each intern earns an allowance of $700 to cover meals and living expenses. Round-trip travel tickets are provided for students living outside of the Washington, DC, area.
Contact:	Intern '94
	Smithsonian Institution
	Office of Elementary and Secondary Education
	A & I, Room 1163, MRC 402
	Washington, DC 20560
	(202) 357-3049

Thirty high school seniors are invited to participate in the Smithsonian Internship program each summer; students have a unique opportunity to explore possible career options at the same time they are exploring the Smithsonian and Washington, DC. Each intern spends about 35 hours per week working in a particular office with a Smithsonian professional. Students apply for one of the specific openings that are listed on the application booklet. Science-related internships include positions at the National Air and Space Museum, at the National Museum of Natural History, at the National Zoological Park, at the Office of the Assistant Secretary for Science, and at the Office of Plant Services. Interns may build exhibits, care for primates, mount birds, maintain collections, label specimens, or perform a variety of other tasks. The entire group of interns tour sites that many visitors to Washington never see. Application deadline: March 12.

❖ The Technology Connection

Host School:	Florida Atlantic University
Type:	Summer study
Location:	Boca Raton, FL
Duration:	One week
Dates:	Two sessions: Early July for grades 7–9; mid-July for grades 10–12
Qualifications:	Grades 7 through 12
	The program is open to students interested in exploring technology and its applications. Women and minority students are especially encouraged to apply.
Housing:	Students live in the dormitories and have meals in the dining hall.
Costs:	$295 includes all program costs, room, and board. A limited number of full and partial need-based scholarships are available.
Credits Given:	None
Contact:	Dr. Roger Messenger
	The Technology Connection
	Florida Atlantic University
	College of Engineering
	Boca Raton, FL 33431
	(407) 367-3400

The Technology Connection provides participants with laboratory experiences designed to transform math and science principles into reality. Students participate in a variety of hands-on engineering laboratory activities including work in digital electronics, microprocessors, analog electronics, robotics, data acquisition, and communications. Lectures by the engineering faculty, a tour of an industrial manufacturing facility, and participation in a design contest all combine to give students a realistic look at the applications of technology. Participants experience life on a college campus and attend workshops on college admissions, financial aid, and career opportunities. Evening programs complete the program. Application deadline: April 15.

❖ Florida Accelerated Initiatives Seminar (FAIS)

Host School:	University of Florida at Gainesville
Type:	Summer study
Location:	Gainesville, FL
Duration:	Four weeks
Dates:	Early July to early August
Qualifications:	Grades 9 and 10
	Students must be highly qualified academically. The program is especially interested in minority and women students traditionally underrepresented in science and engineering.
Housing:	Participants and residential staff live in the Beaty Towers Residence Hall on the University of Florida campus. Participants are supervised 24 hours a day. The FAIS Meal Plan provides all meals.
Costs:	$1,900 covers all costs for students other than personal spending money and transportation to and from Gainesville. Full and partial scholarships may cover most or all of these expenses for a large number of Florida-resident participants.
Credits Given:	None
Contact:	Dr. Elizabeth Abbot
	Florida Accelerated Initiatives Seminar (FAIS)
	University of Florida at Gainesville
	Florida Foundation for Future Scientists
	111 Norman Hall
	Gainesville, FL
	(904) 392-2344

The Florida Accelerated Initiatives Seminar (FAIS) provides multidisciplinary academic activities and one-on-one interchange with professional role models to add to students' knowledge and to help them make informed decisions about career goals. Students enroll in one of three modules—Biotechnology, Marine Sciences, or Earth and Space Sciences Technology—which include lecture and hands-on laboratory work, as well as site visits. Workshops in time management, research methodology, career development, and ethical issues as well as classes in computer applications complete the program. The program also sponsors recreational activities. Application deadline: March 1.

❖ Student Science Training Program (SSTP)

Host School:	University of Florida at Gainesville

Type:	Internship/Summer study
Location:	Gainesville, FL
Duration:	Eight weeks
Dates:	Mid-June through early August
Qualifications:	Grade 12 (Some highly qualified 11th-grade students accepted.) The program is open to high-ability students interested in careers in science and engineering.
Housing:	Participants and residential staff live in the Beaty Towers Residence Hall on the University of Florida campus. Students live in suites consisting of two double-occupancy bedrooms, kitchen, bath, and living room. Participants do their own shopping and prepare their own meals.
Costs:	$2,100 covers all costs with the exception of personal spending money and transportation to and from Gainesville. All or much of these costs can be met through scholarship grants to a large number of Florida-resident students.
Credits Given:	Dual high school and college credit is available.
Contact:	Dr. Elizabeth Abbot Student Science Training Program (SSTP) University of Florida at Gainesville 111 Norman Hall Gainesville, FL 32611 (904) 392-2310

This is an intensive research-participation program in which students perform research in laboratories in close association with individual faculty mentors. The emphasis is on research participation in the fields of science, mathematics, computers, and engineering. In addition to working in a laboratory, participants attend lectures on current topics and attend classes in computer programming and statistics. Students also participate in seminars and workshops covering topics such as ethics, oral presentations, study strategies, computer applications, research and technical writing, and career exploration. Planned weekend activities include sports and social activities as well as scientific field trips. Students may also take a college-level class if they desire. Application deadline: March 1.

❖ Young Scholars Program

Host School:	Florida State University
Type:	Summer study
Location:	Tallahassee, FL
Duration:	Six weeks
Dates:	Mid-June through late July
Qualifications:	Grade 12 (A few exceptionally qualified 11th graders have been accepted.) Students must have completed 11th grade in a Florida public or private high school, have at least a B average (unweighted), and score at the 90th percentile or better in science or mathematics on a national standardized test.
Housing:	Students are housed in separate men's and women's wings of Osceola Hall, a private residence hall on the edge of the FSU

campus near the science center. Fulltime counselors live with the students. Meals are provided at Osceola Hall's dining room.

Costs: All program costs including tuition, housing, meals, and weekend excursions (approximately $2,500) are met through scholarships provided by the National Science Foundation, the Florida Department of Education, and FSU. Participants pay for textbooks, transportation to and from Tallahassee, and incidental living expenses.

Credits Given: None

Contact: Dr. D. Ellen Granger
Young Scholars Program
Florida State University
Department of Biological Science
237 Conradi Building, B-142
Tallahassee, FL 32306-2043
(904) 644-6747

This Young Scholars Program for Florida high school students provides formal course work in math, computer science, and science ethics for all participants. Elective courses in molecular biology, modern physics, or science communication are chosen by the student. The emphasis in all courses and their associated laboratories is on problem solving on integrating theory with applications, and on the ethical issues involved in science and technology. Students choose research projects from computer-based, laboratory, or field research projects. Students have full university privileges, including access to recreational facilities and social and cultural events. On weekends, students take trips to Wakulla Springs, St. Marks Wildlife Refuge, the Florida State University (FSU) Marine Lab, and Gulf beaches at Panama City, FL. Application deadline: March 15.

❖ Math and Science Spectacles

Host School: Wesleyan College

Type: Summer study/Science camp

Location: Macon, GA

Duration: Two weeks

Dates: Three sessions: Middle to late June, middle to late July, and the first two weeks in August

Qualifications: Grades 6-9

The program is limited to middle school girls interested in mathematics and science. Session I is for girls entering grades 6 and 7; session II, entering 7 and 8; session III (Spectacles Squared), for gifted girls entering grade 9.

Housing: Students live in the college's residence hall with resident assistants (one per eight students) and the camp coordinator. Meals are in the dining hall.

Costs: $750 covers the cost of tuition, housing, meals, and field trips for sessions I and II; $850 for session III. A limited number of partial scholarships are available.

Credits Given: None

Contact: Math and Science Spectacles
Wesleyan College

4760 Forsyth Road
Macon, GA 31297-4299
(912) 477-1110 ext. 359; FAX (912) 477-7572

The Spectacles program was begun to provide middle school girls with the opportunity to change the way they see their world at a time when young women make decisions about their interest and abilities in science and math. The program works in cooperation with the U.S. Department of Energy and Oak Ridge National Laboratory to provide exciting activities, field trips, and science experiences. Besides numerous exploratory activities, students participate in field trips to Atlanta to visit SciTrek and the Fernbank Science Center and a three-day trip to Oak Ridge National Laboratory and the Chattanooga Aquarium. Spectacles Squared is a more intensive program and provides more time at Oak Ridge Labs. Students have the opportunity to use the college's science laboratories, computer facilities, and sports complex. Application deadline: May 15.

❖ Idaho Science Camp

Host School:	University of Idaho
Type:	Summer study
Location:	Moscow, ID
Duration:	Two weeks
Dates:	Middle to late June
Qualifications:	Grades 9-11.
	This program is for students interested in exploring career opportunities in science and engineering.
Housing:	Students live on campus in the university dormitory under the supervision of counselors. Meals are provided in the dining hall.
Costs:	$350. Full and partial need-based scholarships are available.
Credits Given:	None
Contact:	Margrit von Braun
	Idaho Science Camp
	University of Idaho
	College of Engineering
	JEB 142
	Moscow, ID 83843
	(208) 885-6438

This career exploration program held on the campus of the University of Idaho involves students in career exploration through hands-on activities, including experiments in water chemistry, bridge construction, and computer programming. Students take classes in mathematics, physical science, and environmental science, including investigations of current importance such as the problems regarding hazardous wastes. The program includes field trips relating to the subjects under study, as well as work on science and engineering projects. A full program of recreational activities is also provided. Campus tours and informal talks with counselors and instructors allow participants to engage in some early planning for college. Application deadline: May 3.

❖ Summer "AD"Ventures in Mathematics, Science, and Technology I & II

Host School:	Illinois Mathematics and Science Academy (IMSA)

Type:	Summer study
Location:	Dependent on program
Duration:	Ten days to two weeks
Dates:	Early June
Qualifications:	The program is limited to Illinois students who have scored at or above the 90th percentile on local norms during most recent standardized testing program. Applicants should have demonstrated interest in science and mathematics.
Housing:	Participants are housed on the campuses of the participating institutions. Meals are provided.
Costs:	"AD"Venture I: $250; "AD"Venture II: $400. Financial aid is available on a need basis. For information about financial aid, please call (708) 801-6989.
Credits Given:	None
Contact:	Summer "AD"Ventures in Mathematics, Science, and Technology I & II
	Illinois Mathematics and Science Academy (IMSA)
	1500 West Sullivan Road
	Aurora, IL 60506
	(708) 801-6989

The summer "AD"Ventures program takes students beyond the usual limits of junior and senior high school work in the fields of science, mathematics, and computer science. Innovative instructors are encouraged to develop and field test curriculum aligned with the newest developments in educational research; participants benefit from exposure to these new teaching methods and materials. The cirruculum focuses on enrichment activities designed to promote scientific curiosity and to develop problem-solving skills. Each summer the activities are arranged around a central theme; a recent summer program explored the impact of mathematics, science, and technology on society. The programs are held at different sites including Eastern Illinois University in Charleston and the Illinois Mathematics and Science Academy (IMSA) in Aurora. Application deadline: January 1.

✦ Women in Science and Engineering Program (WISE)

Host School:	Illinois Institute of Technology
Type:	Summer study
Location:	Chicago, IL
Duration:	Two weeks
Dates:	Middle through end of July
Qualifications:	Grades 10-12
	This program is for girls who enjoy science and mathematics and have an interest in exploring career options in these areas.
Housing:	Day students may live at home, but all students are strongly encouraged to live on campus in the ITT Residence Hall.
Costs:	$350 for room and board for the two weeks. There is no charge for tuition or fees.
Credits Given:	None
Contact:	Women in Science and Engineering Program (WISE)
	Illinois Institute of Technology

Office of Admission
10 West 33rd Street
Chicago, IL 60616-3793
(312) 567-5250; (800) 448-2329

The Women in Science and Engineering (WISE) Program seeks to encourage young women to explore career opportunities in science and engineering. The program includes a number of interesting laboratory investigations, hands-on projects developed and taught by women undergraduate students, and tours of Chicago-area engineering companies, as well as career and personal-development components. WISE's network of over 250 women working in science and engineering in the Chicago area volunteer to talk with participants and serve as role models and mentors. Small group discussions between WISE participants and undergraduate women as well as Interest Inventories and personality testing help the participants to make informed decisions about their future career path. Application deadline: June 25.

❖ National High School Institute—Engineering and Science

Host School:	Northwestern University
Type:	Summer study
Location:	Evanston, IL
Duration:	Five weeks
Dates:	End of June through end of July
Qualifications:	Grade 12
	Competitive selection based on student interest and achievements. Applicants should rank in the top 20 percent of their high school class.
Housing:	Students live in university residence halls supervised by trained counselors. Meals are provided in the university dining hall. Students have access to University facilities including the libraries, athletic facilities, Lake Michigan, and the University Center.
Costs:	$2,320 covers tuition, room, board, fees, social activities, and field trips. Personal incidental expenses and transportation costs are not included. Financial aid is available on an as-needed basis.
Credits Given:	None
Contact:	Ms. Lynn Goodnight
	National High School Institute—Engineering and Science
	Northwestern University
	2299 North Campus Drive
	Evanston, IL 60208
	(708) 491-3026; (800) 662-NHSI

Northwestern's National High School Institute is the oldest and largest university-based program for high school students. Participants are introduced to college-level study, gain practical experience, and interact closely with college faculty. Challenging experiences in mathematics, science, engineering, and biomedical engineering are provided. Each student chooses five minicourses along with an independent or small-group research project. Lecture-demonstrations, computer programming instruction, and field trips complete the academic program. Students also interact with other exceptional high school students while participating in the cultural and social activities that are part of the Institute program. Application deadline: April 30. Early admissions: April 1.

❖ Career Awareness Experiences in Science and Mathematics (CAESM)

Host School:	Western Illinois University
Type:	Summer study/Internship
Location:	Macomb, IL
Duration:	Three weeks with two follow-up sessions during the school year.
Dates:	Early through late June
Qualifications:	Grade 8
	The program is open to high-ability students with a demonstrated interest in science and mathematics. Most participants are from rural, downstate Illinois and return home on weekends.
Housing:	Students are housed in the Olson Conference Center on campus and supervised by adults at all times. Students leave campus late on Friday afternoons and return Sunday evenings.
Costs:	No fees for room, board, or tuition. Parents will be reimbursed $50 for travel expenses at the end of the summer session.
Credits Given:	None
Contact:	Dr. John Beaver
	Career Awareness Experiences in Science and Mathematics
	Western Illinois University
	Horrabin Hall-47
	Macomb, IL 61455
	(309) 298-2065; (309) 298-1777

This program, supported by the National Science Foundation, consists of instructional and experiential activities on campus during the summer as well as a one-week internship with a practicing scientist, engineer, or mathematician, plus two days of follow-up colloquia and once-a-month, interactive-television program sessions during the school year. On campus, participants perform hands-on lab experiments in biology, chemistry, physics, math, and geology; participate in discussions of ethical issues relevant to science and technology; and receive career information. Field trips to area research facilities are a part of the program. Application deadline: April 17.

❖ Futures in Science and Technology

Host School:	University of Illinois, Urbana-Champaign
Type:	Summer study
Location:	Urbana, IL
Duration:	Four weeks
Dates:	July
Qualifications:	Grades 11 and 12
	Students should have proven ability in math and science and interest in science or engineering as a career option.
Housing:	Students live in residence halls on campus with counselors. All meals are provided in the residence hall cafeteria. Students may use the university's sports facilities including swimming, tennis, and golf.

Costs:	$2,000 includes tuition, room and board, supplies, field trips, and class notes. A limited amount of need-based financial aid is available.
Credits Given:	None
Contact:	David Powell
	Futures in Science and Technology
	University of Illinois, Urbana-Champaign
	1304 West Green Street, Room 207
	Urbana, IL 61801-2982
	(800) 843-5410

This is a challenging exploration of science and technology. Everyone takes an interdisciplinary course, Materials for Engineering, that bridges the gap between pure and applied science. Each student chooses four of six courses designed as an overview of major topics in science and technology. These courses include Microelectronics and Biotechnology, Current Topics in Science and Technology, Computer Design, and Engineering Math and Problem Solving. Labs provide extensive hands-on experiences, and some students have the opportunity to work with a professor on a research project. On Fridays, participants tour major research facilities and labs. Seminars about choosing a college and academic planning as well as career guidance are held. A full range of sports and social activities are also planned. Application deadline: April 15.

❖ Young Scholars Program: Exploration of Careers in Science

Host School:	Indiana University
Type:	Summer study/Internship
Location:	Bloomington, IN
Duration:	Eight weeks
Dates:	Mid-June through mid-August
Qualifications:	Grades 11 and 12
	The program is limited to Indiana high school students who have an interest in science or mathematics.
Housing:	Participants live in a university dormitory comprised of five-room suites (three bedrooms, kitchen, and bath), supervised by a staff of high school science teachers. Meals are served in the dining facilities. Students have access to Indiana University's athletic facilities and cultural events.
Costs:	No cost to participants. Grants from National Science Foundation, the Howard Hughes Foundation, and the University pay all expenses. All participants earn a $600 stipend plus $100 travel costs. Needy students may apply for larger stipends.
Credits Given:	None
Contact:	Young Scholars Program: Exploration of Careers in Science
	Indiana University
	College of Arts and Sciences
	Kirkwood Hall #104
	Bloomington, IN 47405
	(812) 855-5397

This program provides an exploration of science careers by combining two weeks of study with a six-week research-participation experience. Participants learn about research methodology, explore current topics in science, and consider ethical issues through lectures, demonstrations, field trips and tours, and laboratory experiments. After two weeks exploring fields such as astronomy, anthropology, geology, math, optometry, physics, and psychology, participants are assigned to research teams in the student's area of interest and conduct research under the guidance of a mentor-scientist. Presentation of research results concludes this section of the program. Students also have the opportunity to participate in an anthropological dig and enjoy recreational and social programs. Application deadline: April 1.

❖ Student Science Training (SST) Programs in Stellar Astronomy and Nuclear Radiation Applications

Host School:	Ball State University
Location:	Muncie, IN
Type:	Summer study/Internship
Duration:	Four weeks
Dates:	Late June through mid-July
Qualifications:	Grade 12
	The program is open to academically able students interested in an intensive research experience.
Housing:	Students are housed in a supervised university residence hall. Meals are provided.
Costs:	Approximately $1,140 for resident students. Commuting students pay about $660, which includes lunch. A limited amount of scholarship aid is available.
Credits Given:	College credits may be available
Contact:	Dr. David Ober
	Student Science Training (SST) Programs
	Ball State University
	Department of Physics and Astronomy
	Muncie, IN 47306
	(317) 285-8860; FAX (317) 285-1624

Students in the Student Science Training Program participate in classroom and laboratory instruction during the first week of this program, gaining background knowledge and laboratory skills needed for the research experience. During the remaining three weeks, each student conducts individual scientific research in a chosen area under the supervision and guidance of a faculty sponsor. Students choose from two general research areas. Investigations in Stellar Astronomy centers on the use of small telescopes and astrophotography. Students use the university observatory and planetarium in their studies. Nuclear Radiation Applications—Radon studies environmental radiation. Students utilize gamma-ray detectors, neutron-activation analysis, and computers in their research. Application deadline: April 21.

❖ GERI Summer Residential Programs

Host School:	Purdue University
Type:	Summer study
Location:	West Lafayette, IN
Duration:	COMET, one week; STAR and PULSAR, two weeks; NOVA, three weeks

Dates:	Late June through late July, depending on program
Qualifications:	Grades 5-12
	Students must be nominated by their schools and have an A-/B+ average. Applicants for COMET need to have a minimum IQ of 125; qualifying SAT scores are needed for the more advanced programs.
Housing:	Students are housed two to a room in Meredith Hall, a Purdue dormitory. Students are supervised for program counselors. Meals are provided in the dining hall.
Costs:	Program fees depend upon program chosen, depend upon program duration and if college credits are awarded. Fees range from $495 to $1965. Covered are room and board, tuition, and books. Financial aid is available. Financial aid application deadline: May 3.
Credits Given:	3 to 5 college credits for the NOVA program
Contact:	GERI Summer Residential Programs
	Purdue University
	1446 South Campus Courts, Building G
	West Lafayette, IN 47907-1446
	(317) 494-7243

The Gifted Education Resource Institute (GERI) provides intensive, challenging summer programs for academically gifted students. The youngest children attend COMET, a one-week program that exposes students to courses that include spatial math, molecular chemistry, fantasy literature, and creative writing. The two-week programs, STAR and PULSAR, offer classes that include physics, archaeology, calculus, computer science, critical thinking, abstract algebra, leadership, Shakespeare, and comparative anatomy. High school students may choose the three-week NOVA, which offers college-credit courses in plane analytic geometry and calculus, social problems, or economics. Sports, recreational events, and cultural trips are part of the program. Qualified applicants are accepted as applications are received. Application deadline: June 2.

❖ Challenges for Youth—Talented and Gifted (CY–TAG)

Host School:	Iowa State University
Type:	Summer study
Location:	Ames, IA
Duration:	Three weeks per session (Students may attend both sessions if desired.)
Dates:	Two sessions: Mid-June through early July; mid-July through early August
Qualifications:	Grades 8-10
	Gifted students qualify on the basis of high scores on the Scholastic Aptitude Test (SAT) or the ACT; qualifying scores vary by course of study chosen.
Housing:	Participants are housed in an air-conditioned dormitory, supervised by residence advisors responsible for groups of 12 students. Meals are taken in a buffet-style cafeteria; vegetarian meals are available.
Costs:	$1,025 covers most program costs, room board, and tuition.

Students may attend both sessions or two siblings may attend one session each for one fee of $1,950. A limited amount of need-based financial aid is available.

Credits Given:	High school credit may be awarded by the student's home school.
Contact:	Amy Napolski
	Challenges for Youth—Talented and Gifted (CY-TAG)
	Iowa State University
	W172 Lagomarcino Hall
	Ames, IA 50011-3180
	(515) 294-1772; (800) 262-3810 ext. 1772

The Challenges for Youth—Talented and Gifted (CY-TAG) program seeks to challenge, motivate, and intellectually stimulate gifted students by providing a fast-paced, intensive program of study complemented by exciting social, recreational, and cultural activities. Students choose from a number of course offerings each session; each session provides a total of 99 hours of instructional time. Offerings include courses in chemistry, computer science (C-Language), agricultural science, engineering mechanics, mathematics, philosophy, physics, and psychology. Laboratory experiments and group and individual projects involve students in hands-on learning. Students entering grades 9 and 10 may also choose mentorship opportunities, working directly with professors and graduate students in an area of mutual interest. Application deadline: April 16.

❖ Explorations!

Host School:	Iowa State University
Type:	Summer study
Location:	Ames, IA
Duration:	One or two weeks, depending on session (Students may attend any number of sessions.)
Dates:	Late June through the end of July
Qualifications:	Grades 8–10
	The program is open to gifted students who score at or above the 97th percentile on standardized tests such as the Iowa Test of Basic Skills.
Housing:	Students are housed in an air-conditioned dormitory supervised by residential advisors who live with each group of 10 to 12 students. Meals are provided in the Dining Center; vegetarian meals are available.
Costs:	$395 per one-week session and $725 per two-week session covers tuition, room, board, and activities fees. Financial aid is not available.
Credits Given:	None
Contact:	Amy Napolski
	Explorations!
	Iowa State University
	W172 Lagomarcino Hall
	Ames, IA 50011-3180
	(515) 294-1772; (800) 262-3810 ext. 1772

Explorations! is designed to give gifted young people the opportunity to investigate academic interests in a relaxed atmosphere. Students are challenged through hands-on experimentation, personal involvement, and participation in individual and small-group projects. Students choose one course each session from the available offerings. Choices in the scientific area include classes like Cosmic Movements—The Science of Astronomy, Robotics in Motion, Probability Theory, Attention! It's Your Environment, and Motion, Time, and Energy. A full program of recreational and social activities is planned by the residence hall staff along with sporting events and career-exploration activities. Application deadline: April 16.

❖ Secondary Student Training Program (SSTP); Research Participation Program

Host School:	University of Iowa
Type:	Internship
Location:	Iowa City, IA
Duration:	Eight weeks or six weeks, depending on program
Dates:	Middle of June or end of June through early August
Qualifications:	Grades 11 and 12 and first year of college
	High-ability students or students who are especially motivated in science and/or math are eligible. Acceptance is competitive; early application is recommended.
Housing:	Participants live in university residence halls, supervised by counselors. Meals are provided except on Sunday evening.
Costs:	$1,550 for the eight-week program; $1,150 for the six-week program. Includes tuition, fees, room, and board. The National Institutes of Health offers financial aid for minority students. Iowa residents may get aid from the local American Cancer Society. Other limited financial aid is available.
Credits Given:	4 or 3 college credits available, depending upon program chosen
Contact:	Ms. Kathy Foss
	Secondary Student Training Program (SSTP): Research Participation Program
	University of Iowa
	450 Van Allen Hall
	Iowa City, IA 52242
	(319) 335-1173

This program is for the student who wonders what scientific research is and what a career as a scientist would be like. Participants spend about 40 hours each week doing hands-on research and study on a laboratory project that is of interest to the student. Projects are available in numerous areas, including biochemistry, biology, computer science, dentistry, exercise science, pediatrics, physiology, psychology, and surgery. Most projects involve the use of computers in library research, word processing, and data analysis. Students present their results at a formal symposium at the end of the program. Seminars are held discussing ethical issues, public policy, scientific practice, and career planning. There are a variety of social and recreational activities also planned. Application deadline: rolling admissions, generally closed by April 15.

❖ High School SUMMIT (Superior and Unique Methods of Motivation for the Intellectually Talented)

Host School:	Pittsburg State University
Type:	Summer study
Location:	Pittsburg, KS
Duration:	Two weeks
Dates:	Mid-June
Qualifications:	Grades 9-12
	Gifted and talented students, as documented by testing, accelerated placement in classes, and school personnel recommendations, are eligible for the program.
Housing:	Participants live in a supervised residence hall and eat their meals on campus. Pittsburg State University facilities are open to SUMMIT participants.
Costs:	$550 for resident students; $445 for commuter students. Fees include all educational materials, lab supplies, instructional and recreational expenses, housing and three meals a day for resident students, lunch and dinner for commuter participants. Limited financial aid is available.
Credits Given:	None
Contact:	Ms. Peggy Czupryn
	High School SUMMIT
	Pittsburg State University
	SUMMIT Coordinator
	215 Russ Hall—Division of Continuing Studies
	Pittsburg, KS 66762
	(316) 235-4179

The SUMMIT (Superior and Unique Methods of Motivation for the Intellectually Talented) program provides participants with experiences not commonly found in their home schools. High school students take a science and technology program that consists of classroom lectures with a heavy emphasis on hands-on laboratory experiences and research methods. Recreational activities, study, and social events are planned for evenings and weekends. Applications are reviewed beginning March 1.

❖ Precollege Academic Experience in Mathematics and Science (PAEMS)

Host School:	Georgetown College
Type:	Summer study
Location:	Georgetown, KY
Duration:	Two weeks
Dates:	Late June to early July
Qualifications:	Students interested in and with an aptitude for mathematics, natural science, and computer science are eligible for the program.
Housing:	Students live in the college residence hall and eat in the college cafeteria. Dormitories are supervised by adult head residents and student assistants. All participants have access to the cultural and recreational facilities of the college.

Costs:	$350 covers all costs to the student. The program is partially supported by a grant from Johnson & Johnson. A few need-based scholarships are available.
Credits Given:	None
Contact:	Dr. Charles Boehms
	Precollege Academic Experience in Mathematics and science (PAEMS)
	Georgetown College
	Biology Department
	400 East College Street
	Georgetown, KY 40324-9989
	(502) 863-8087

Participants are divided into subgroups of 10 students working with a professor and laboratory assistant. Mornings are devoted to studying math and computer science including programming, word processing, and interactive activities along with experiences in problem solving, probability, and statistics. Biology, with an exploration of the basic concepts in modern genetics, and chemistry, including chemical analysis, are studied in the afternoons. Extensive laboratory experiments are performed and data collected and analyzed. Global science issues are explored through special presentations, computer games, field trips, and visits to laboratories. A team approach is used to solve global problems. Recreational and cultural activities are planned to add fun to the learning experience. Application deadline: April 1.

❖ Science and Technology Camp

Host School:	Transylvania University
Type:	Summer study
Location:	Lexington, KY
Duration:	Six days or five days, depending on program
Dates:	Two sessions: late June and end of June through early July
Qualifications:	Grades 11 and 12: Science and Technology camp.
	Grades 8-12: Academic camp.
	The program is open to students interested in science and having at least a B average.
Housing:	Students live in Transylvania's residence halls and eat three meals daily in the cafeteria. University recreational and sports facilities are available to participants.
Costs:	$300 covers cost of room, board, tuition, and supplies for the one-week program. A limited number of partial, need-based scholarships are available. The fee for the five-day program is $250.
Credits Given:	None
Contact:	Dr. James Miller
	Science and Technology Camp
	Transylvania University
	Division Chair, Natural Sciences and Math
	300 North Broadway
	Lexington, KY 40508
	(606) 233-8155 or (606) 233-8228

Not truly a "camp," the Science and Technology program offers students an opportunity to experience life as college students while enhancing the participants' awareness of current research in the sciences and its applications and stimulating interest in possible careers as scientists. During the camp's six days, six different scientific areas are explored through lectures, discussions, and sessions dealing with practical applications. Hands-on activities complement the program. Students also visit local laboratories to view current science research in action. Students have access to Transylvania's IBM 4361 computing system as well as library and laboratory facilities. Recreational and sports activities are available. A five-day long Academic Camp that emphasizes computers is also available for students entering grades 8–10 and grades 10–12. Participants in this program have computer skills that range from beginner to advanced. Application deadline: May 1.

❖ D-Arrow: A Wilderness Trip Camp

Type:	Science camp
Camper Level:	Ages 11 to 17 (Trips limited to specific age groups.)
Location:	Freeport, ME
Duration:	Various trips available ranging from one to eight weeks in length
Dates:	Throughout summer
Housing:	Wilderness camping.
Costs:	$575 to $3,400, depending upon length and program chosen.
Contact:	Mr. John Houghton
	D-Arrow: A Wilderness Trip Camp
	RFD 3 Box 231B
	Freeport, ME 04032
	(207) 725-4748

D-Arrow offers young people a chance to experience wilderness camping, canoeing, fishing, and swimming in a spectacular natural setting. Participants may shoot white water, descend a wilderness river, observe wildlife, and hone their camping skills. Programs for younger participants explore many of Maine's most beautiful waters. Older campers may choose the challenging 300-mile canoe trip that explores the rivers of northern Quebec. Here, they will see the unmatched scenery of this northern region with its sheer cliffs and raging waterfalls and experience superb fishing, as well as insects and, sometimes, near-freezing nights. D-Arrow is accredited by the American Camping Association.

❖ Chewonki Co-ed Wilderness Expeditions

Type:	Science camp
Camper Level:	Ages 13 to 18
Location:	Wiscasset, ME
Duration:	Three to seven weeks, depending upon trip chosen
Dates:	Various dates, late June through mid-August
Housing:	Wilderness camping.
Costs:	$2,100 to $4,050, depending upon trip chosen and its length. The only additional costs are for transportation to and from camp and required T-shirts. Scholarships may be available for campers

with demonstrated need. Application deadline for scholarships: March 1.

Contact: Mr. Dick Thomas
Chewonki Co-ed Wilderness Expeditions
The Chewonki Foundation
RR 2, Box 1200 D
Wiscasset, ME 04578
(207) 882-7323; FAX (207) 882-4074

Chewonki Wilderness trips range along the coastal regions, the mountains, and the rivers of Maine and into eastern Canada. These trips are meant for teens who are interested in challenging wilderness experiences and nature and ecology. The focus of the trip depends upon the program chosen. The Thoreau Wilderness Trip explores waterways and mountain regions, traveling both by canoe and on foot. Other trips involve sea kayaking, boatbuilding, canoeing, hiking, and a Mariner Trip for sailing and rowing. All participants (ten campers and two leaders per trip) help to gather firewood, cook meals, and clean up. Campers gain an appreciation for nature in all its forms and learn to distinguish between what is meaningful and what is superfluous in their own lives. Campers and counselors come from all over the country and the world and represent a variety of interests and backgrounds; respect for others' beliefs and ideas is one of the goals of the summer. Chewonki is accredited by the American Camping Association.

❖ Summer Student Grants at the National Institutes of Health

Host School: The Foundation for Advanced Education in the Sciences, Inc.
Type: Internship
Location: Bethesda, MD
Duration: At least eight weeks
Dates: Summer
Qualifications: Open to all full-time high school, college, graduate school, and medical/dental school students who are at least 16 years of age.
Housing: Interns are responsible for their own living arrangements.
Costs: Students receive a monthly stipend, depending upon educational level. Current high school students receive $600 per month; newly graduated students receive $675. College students receive $750–900 per month, college graduates are paid $1,050 per month. A limited number of $500 supplementary housing allowance grants may be available.
Contact: Summer Student Grants at the National Institutes of Health
The Foundation for Advanced Education in the Sciences, Inc.
One Cloister Court, Box 101
Bethesda, MD 20814-1460
(301) 496-7976; FAX (301) 402-0174

The Foundation for Advanced Education in the Sciences (FAES) Summer Student Grants provide stipends for students working in a National Institutes of Health laboratory. Each student must be involved in a supervised original research project that exposes the student to the principles of biomedical research. The student must conduct his or her scientific research for a period of at least eight weeks during the time from June through September. Each student applying for a grant must identify an NIH sponsor/laboratory. Students submit an application to FAES that includes a description of the proposed research project and a statement by the proposed supervisor. A transcript of the student's academic grades for the previous four years is also part of the application. Grades and academic preparation are used to distinguish among otherwise equally qualified applicants. Application deadline: March 31.

❖ Northeast Science Enrichment Program

Host School:	University of Massachusetts at Amherst
Type:	Summer study
Location:	Amherst, MA
Duration:	Five weeks
Dates:	Mid-July through mid-August
Qualifications:	Grade 10
	The program is open to motivated minority (African American, Hispanic American, Native American) and underserved (poor, rural, disadvantaged) students from Connecticut, New Hampshire, Maine, Massachusetts, upper New York, Rhode Island, and Vermont.
Housing:	Students live in supervised dormitories on the University of Massachusetts campus. Meals are provided in the university dining facilities.
Costs:	No cost to the student. All expenses of the program are paid by the sponsoring organizations. Parents are reimbursed for travel expenses. Each student also receives a $20 weekly stipend during the five weeks of the program and a concluding stipend of $150.
Credits Given:	None
Contact:	Northeast Science Enrichment Program University of Massachusetts at Amherst Department of Mathematics and Statistics Lederle Graduate Research Center Amherst, MA 01003 (413) 545-1909; FAX (413) 545-1801

The Northeast Science Enrichment Program, sponsored by the National Cancer Institute, seeks to encourage underrepresented and underserved students to consider careers in science and mathematics by exposing them to these fields at an early age. Hands-on courses in biology, physics, math, chemistry, computer science, and language arts are combined with a variety of other educational experiences. Field trips to the Boston Museum of Science, data collection on the research vessel *Envirolab*, and seminars by scientists broaden the participant's background. Daily recreational activities and a variety of cultural events complete the program. Application deadline: March 31.

❖ Math and Science for Minority Students (MS²)

Host School:	Phillips Academy
Type:	Summer study
Location:	Andover, MA

Duration:	Six weeks per summer for three summers
Dates:	Beginning of July through mid-August
Qualifications:	Grade 10 (for initial program)
	The program is limited to math- and science-oriented African American and Hispanic students from Atlanta, Baltimore, Boston, Chicago, Cleveland, Dayton, Ft. Worth, Louisville, Memphis, New York, and Washington, DC, and to any Native Americans.
Housing:	Students live in the dormitories at Phillips Academy supervised by resident advisors. Meals are taken in the dining halls. Recreational programs take place four afternoons each week; participants choose from a wide range of activities.
Costs:	No program costs to the participants. The $9,000 cost is covered by grants from donors. The only expenditure for students is for transportation and incidental expenses. Financial aid to meet these expenses is available.
Credits Given:	None
Contact:	Mr. Walter Sherrill
	Math and Science for Minority Students (MS^2)
	Phillips Academy
	Director, Math and Science for Minority Students
	Andover, MA 01810
	(508) 749-4402

This unique program allows selected minority students to begin an intense study of math and science for three consecutive summers. Located on the campus of Phillips Academy, Andover, the oldest incorporated boarding school in the nation, the program offers students challenges to better prepare them for possible careers in science and related fields. Nine hours of science and math classes and four hours of English classes (incorporating writing, library skills, and computer literacy) or college counseling sessions occur weekly. Over three summers, participants take biology, chemistry with lab, a physics course, and math courses. MS^2 students also take part in a full range of athletic and recreational activities, and field trips. Senior students visit area colleges each Wednesday. Application deadline: January 8.

❖ Program in Mathematics for Young Scientists—PROMYS

Host School:	Boston University
Type:	Summer study
Location:	Boston, MA
Duration:	Six weeks
Dates:	Late June through early August
Qualifications:	Grades 10-12
	Ambitious high school students interested in exploring the creative world of mathematics are eligible for the program.
Housing:	Students are housed in the Boston University Dormitories supervised by a staff of college-aged counselors. Meals are provided.
Costs:	$1,300 for room and board. Books may cost an additional $100.

Other costs (including travel) should not exceed $500. Need-based financial aid is available.

Credits Given:	None
Contact:	Professor Glenn Stevens
	Program in Mathematics for Young Scientists—PROMYS
	Boston University
	Department of Mathematics
	111 Cummington Street
	Boston, MA 02215
	(617) 353-2560; FAX (617) 353-8100

Participants in this unique program are challenged with solving a large assortment of mathematical problems in number theory and become familiar with the art of mathematical discovery. Daily lectures are combined with problem sets under the guidance of research mathematicians. Each student belongs to a problem-solving group that meets three times each week with a professional mathematician. Participants are involved in numerical exploration and the formulation and critique of conjectures, and learn the techniques of proof and generalization. More advanced students may also study combinatorics and modern geometry. Lectures by guest speakers provide a broad view of mathematics and an understanding of its role in the sciences. Application deadline: June 1.

✤ Science and Engineering Honors Program

Host School:	Boston University
Type:	Internship
Location:	Boston, MA
Duration:	Six weeks
Dates:	Late June through early August
Qualifications:	The program is open to academically able and motivated students interested in science research. Students should have at least a B+ average and minimum combined SAT scores of 1100 or PSAT scores of 110. Participants must be at least 16 years of age.
Housing:	Students live in single-sex dormitories on the campus of Boston University. Meals are provided. Resident assistants are available, as is 24-hour security.
Costs:	Approximately $1,500 for fees and room and board. Tuition is covered by a grant from the National Science Foundation's Young Scientist Program. Need-based financial aid is available to help defray some of the additional expenses.
Contact:	Dr. George Zimmerman
	Science and Engineering Honors Program
	Boston University
	Physics Department
	590 Commonwealth Avenue
	Boston, MA 02215
	(617) 353-2189; (617) 353-6000

Thirty high school students participate in ongoing research under the direction of a Preceptor (an experienced faculty member). Areas of study include physics, engineering, biology, astronomy, and chemistry. Graduate students also act as additional resources for the high school intern. Each student joins a research team and works in an assigned laboratory 30 to 40 hours each week. This experiential program gives students the opportunity to experience a research environment and to learn directly about career options in scientific research. The program is supplemented by seminars and field trips and recreational activities. Application deadline: May 1.

❖ Research Science Institute

Host School:	The Center for Excellence in Education in Collaboration with the Massachusetts Institute of Technology (MIT)
Type:	Summer study/Internship
Location:	Cambridge, MA
Duration:	Six weeks
Dates:	Late June through early August
Qualifications:	Grade 12
	Academically excellent students who have demonstrated superior achievement in mathematics, the sciences, and verbal skills are eligible for the program. Math PSAT scores should be at least 70, and combined math and verbal PSAT scores should be at least 135.
Housing:	Housing and meals are provided at MIT. A full range of field trips including whale watching and a camping weekend in New Hampshire's White Mountains, along with trips to research facilities, are included.
Costs:	No cost to the students for tuition, room, and board. Students are responsible only for transportation to and from the program.
Credits Given:	None
Contact:	Ms. Maite Ballestero
	Research Science Institute
	The Center for Excellence in Education
	7710 Old Springhouse Road, Suite 1000
	McLean, VA 22102
	(703) 448-9062; FAX (703) 442-9513

The Research Science Institute offers its participants six of the most intellectually stimulating weeks of their lives. During the first week, on-campus morning classes focus on the newest developments in mathematics, physical and biological science, and the humanities; afternoons are spent learning the technical skills needed for scientific research, including computer skills, quantitative research methods, and design. The next four weeks are spent in off-campus internships under the guidance of mentors. Projects focus on math, biology, engineering, or physical science at research sites at the Massachusetts Institute of Technology (MIT), Harvard, and other facilities in the Boston area. Students make oral and written presentations during the last week of the program. Many participants enter the Westinghouse Talent Search. Application deadline: February 1.

❖ MIT MITES—Minority Introduction to Engineering & Science

Host School:	Massachusetts Institute of Technology (MIT)
Type:	Summer study

Location:	Cambridge, MA
Duration:	Six weeks
Dates:	Late June through the end of July
Qualifications:	Grade 12
	The program is open to minority students (American Indian, Black American, Mexican American, and Puerto Rican) who have demonstrated above-average ability and have an interest in the study of science and mathematics. Applicants should have completed precalculus or trigonometry.
Housing:	Students are housed in supervised dormitories at MIT and are provided with three meals a day. Participants have access to campus resources, including libraries and athletic facilities.
Costs:	No cost for room, board, and tuition. Students are required to provide their own transportation to and from MIT. A limited amount of financial aid is available to help needy students with transportation costs.
Credits Given:	None
Contact:	MIT MITES—Minority Introduction to Engineering & Science
	Massachusetts Institute of Technology
	Room 1-211
	77 Massachusetts Avenue
	Cambridge, MA 02139
	(617) 253-3298

This rigorous program introduces minority high school students to careers in science and engineering. Classroom work centers on math, physics, biology and chemistry, humanities, writing and design; daily assignments are given. One-on-one and mass tutoring sessions are held most evenings. Highlighting the program are design contests aimed at developing student solutions to specified problems. Career exploration is provided through presentations by faculty and practicing engineers and scientists. Also included are field trips to area installations and industries. On weekends and holidays, social events such as a harbor cruise and dance and a trip to a major league baseball game are held. Application deadline: February 26.

❖ Radcliffe Summer Program in Science

Host School:	Radcliffe College of Harvard University
Type:	Summer study
Location:	Cambridge, MA
Duration:	Eight weeks
Dates:	End of June through late August
Qualifications:	Grade 12 (must be at least 16 years old) or first year of college.
	Young women with special interest in science and mathematics are eligible for the program.
Housing:	Students living on campus are housed with other high school students in Harvard dormitories where they are supervised by Radcliffe/Harvard undergraduates who serve as resident proctors.
Costs:	$4,700 is the total cost. This includes $2,500 for tuition, $2,000 for

room and board, $200 program and lab fees, and $25 application fee. Need-based full and partial scholarships are available.

Credits Given: 8 college credits
Contact: Radcliffe Summer Program in Science
Radcliffe College of Harvard University
106 Fay House
10 Garden Street
Cambridge, MA 02138
(617) 495-8626

This intensive program allows young women to expand their understanding of several disciplines of science and to explore possible future careers. The program's unique eight-credit core course, Frontiers of Science, includes lectures on major topics in physics, chemistry, and biochemistry; hands-on laboratory modules in the natural sciences and computers and math; discussion groups led by graduate teaching fellows; and weekly presentations by prominent women scientists. Participants also attend weekly Career Conversations with women scientists and engineers and go on numerous field trips to scientific laboratories, industries, and installations in the Boston area. Application deadline: rolling admissions.

❖ Smith Summer Science Program

Host School: Smith College
Type: Summer study/Internship
Location: Northampton, MA
Duration: Four weeks
Dates: Early through end of July
Qualifications: Grades 9-12
Young women with an interest in exploring the field of science are eligible for the program.
Housing: The 50 participants live in a college house along with nine Smith students who serve as supervisors and advisors. Meals are provided in the house dining room.
Costs: $2,695 covers the cost of all program activities. Financial aid is available for a limited number of participants.
Credits Given: None
Contact: Dr. Gail Scordilis
Smith Summer Science Program
Smith College
Sabin Reed #435
Clark Science Center
Northampton, MA 01063
(413) 585-3879; FAX (413) 585-3786

The emphasis of Smith's program is to give 50 young women of all levels of interest in science a chance to explore and to gain hands-on experience in the doing of science. Students participate in two research projects with Smith faculty, choosing from such offerings as The Chemistry of Everyday Life, The Innocent Eye—to develop the art of seeing, Electronics and Laser Optics, and Mysteries of the Mind. Students usually spend four hours a day in the lab and field, while free time is filled with organized sport and recreational activities. A series of college planning workshops are also a part of the program. Application deadline: May 1; early admissions: March 1.

❖ Brandeis Summer Odyssey

Host School:	Brandeis University
Type:	Summer study
Location:	Waltham, MA
Duration:	Four weeks
Dates:	Early July through beginning of August
Qualifications:	Grades 10-12
	Competitive admissions; applicants must have at least a B average.
Housing:	Students are housed in supervised Brandeis University residence halls along with resident advisors. Meals are provided in the dining hall.
Costs:	$2,600 covers all costs, including instruction, texts, food, housing, field trips, and recreational activities. Financial aid is available through the National Science Foundation's Young Scholars Program for students choosing science cores and electives. Financial aid deadline: April 15.
Credits Given:	None
Contact:	Ms. Jane Schoenfeld
	Brandeis Summer Odyssey
	Brandeis University
	PO Box 9110
	Waltham, MA 02254-9110
	(617) 736-2111; FAX (617) 736-3420

Participants in the Academic Study Program of the Summer Odyssey choose a core course in science, which covers material almost never seen in high school courses, along with an elective course. Core courses meet three hours a day, four days a week, and have focused on such areas as forensic medicine, biotechnology, the psychology and biology of stress, diseases and medicine, architecture, marine biology, scuba diving, marine ecology and physiology. These courses are project oriented and include field trips linking classroom study with the real world. Elective classes meet three days a week and are chosen from a variety of courses in the sciences and humanities. Weekly recreational field trips, lectures, and social and sports activities are planned. Application deadline: May 15.

❖ Brandeis Summer Odyssey Science Research Internships

Host School:	Brandeis University
Type:	Internship
Location:	Waltham, MA
Duration:	Eight weeks
Dates:	Mid-June through mid-August
Qualifications:	Grades 11 and 12
	Students are selected based upon extremely high achievement in a rigorous high school program, recommendations, and a demonstrated interest in scientific research.
Housing:	Students are housed in supervised Brandeis University residence halls. Meals are provided in the dining hall.

Costs:	$3,450 covers all costs, including food, housing, access to Brandeis facilities, and one recreational field trip per week. Financial aid is available for some interns through the National Institutes of Health's Minority High School Student Research Apprentice Program.
Contact:	Ms. Jane Schoenfeld Brandeis Summer Odyssey Science Research Internships Brandeis University PO Box 9110 Waltham, MA 02254-9110 (617) 736-2111; FAX (617) 736-3420

Interns spend their eight-hour days investigating an important research topic and assisting their faculty mentor's ongoing studies. Participants choose their topic for study from such areas as chemistry, computer science, physics, psychology, biology, and biochemistry. By the end of the program, it is expected that the students will have completed their projects and written papers detailing their laboratory experiences. Work by past interns has been cited in major journals, and some interns have qualified as Westinghouse Talent Search semifinalists. Recreational and social events are also planned. Application deadline: April 15.

❖ STRIVE for College and Careers in Science, Mathematics, and Engineering

Host School:	Worcester Polytechnic Institute
Type:	Summer study/Internship
Location:	Worcester, MA
Duration:	Four weeks
Dates:	Mid-July through early August
Qualifications:	Grade 12 The program is limited to Black, Hispanic, and Native American students.
Housing:	Participants are housed in supervised dormitories and are provided with meals. Students have access to WPI's facilities, including recreational and athletic facilities, libraries, and the college computer center.
Costs:	$950 covers tuition, food and housing, books, field trips, and recreational activities. Partial and full scholarships are available through a grant from United Technologies Corporation.
Credits Given:	None
Contact:	Mr. Ronald Macon STRIVE for College and Careers in Science, Mathematics, and Engineering Worcester Polytechnic Institute Office of Multicultural Affairs 100 Institute Road Worcester, MA 01609-2280 (508) 831-5819; FAX (508) 831-5485

This enrichment program is designed to expand each participant's knowledge and interest in science, mathematics, and engineering. During the first two weeks of the STRIVE program, students participate in Worcester Polytechnic Institute's (WPI) Frontiers Program, introducing students to the newest advances in science. Students select one area for study from choices that include biology, chemistry, civil engineering, mathematics, and physics. Students also study communication arts to improve communication skills. The last two weeks of the STRIVE program finds students working in a WPI laboratory or other approved site. Teams of two to three students are assigned research responsibilities in areas ranging from chemical engineering to biotechnology. Social activities, seminars, guest speakers, and field trips supplement the program. Application deadline: April 30.

❖ Michigan Arts and Sciences Summer Program

Type:	Summer study
Location:	Michigan, city dependent on program
Duration:	Two weeks
Dates:	Dependent on program
Qualifications:	Grades 9-12
	These programs are limited to Michigan private and public school students.
Housing:	Participants are housed in campus dormitories and are provided with meals.
Costs:	$150 is the total cost to the students; the balance is met through the state grant.
Credits given:	None
Contact:	Call the phone number given for information on the desired program(s).

The state of Michigan provides funds for two-week, residential, summer programs. Each participating college offers study in a particular scientific discipline. The focus of each program is listed below. Contact program of choice for more information.

Biomedical sciences: Alma College, Alma, MI 48801; (517) 463-7131

Chemistry, biomedical technology, and electronics: Western Michigan University, Kalamazoo, MI 49008; (616) 387-4951

Chemistry, physics, and engineering design: Michigan Technological University, Houghton, MI 49931; (906) 487-2920

Computers and robotics: Eastern Michigan University, Ypsilanti, MI 48197; (313) 487-1161

Environmental sciences: Adrian College, Adrian, MI 49221; (517) 265-5161

Medical technology: Western Michigan University, Kalamazoo, MI 49008; (616) 387-3700

❖ Upward Bound

Host School:	Cranbrook Science and Math Center
Type:	Summer study
Location:	Bloomfield Hills, MI
Duration:	Six weeks
Dates:	Late June through end of July

Qualifications:	Grades 10 and 11
	Applicants should be interested in science and math, have a grade point average of about 3.0, and have completed at least one high school math and one science class. Program is limited to students who will be the first in their family to attend college.
Housing:	Students live on the campus, a beautiful 315-acre site that is home to the Cranbrook Institute of Science, Cranbrook Schools, and the Academy of Art and Museum. Meals are provided.
Costs:	None. The program is free for qualified students, supported by a grant from the U.S. Department of Education. Transportation costs are also covered and will be arranged by the Cranbrook Science and Math Center.
Credits Given:	None
Contact:	Upward Bound
	Cranbrook Science and Math Center
	500 Lone Pine Road
	PO Box 801
	Bloomfield Hills, MI 48303-9862
	(313) 645-3676 or 645-3256

This program gives students from families who have not historically sent their children to college an opportunity to explore the possibilities of a career in science. While a part of the Cranbrook Educational Community, students work in scientific teams conducting research on topics such as the physics of motion, river and lake ecosystems, forest communities, and star study. Participants take accelerated classes in science and math studying biology/ecology, research methods, and methods of generating and displaying scientific data. Field trips to area laboratories and universities allow for career exploration. Students gain confidence as they improve their oral and written communication skills as well as study and research skills. Free time is for cultural and sports activities including horseback riding, canoeing, and camping. Application deadline: April 15.

❖ High School Honors Science Program: Research Internship

Host School:	Michigan State University
Type	Internship
Location:	East Lansing, MI
Duration:	Seven weeks
Dates:	Late June through early August
Qualifications:	Grades 11 and 12
	The program is open to students who are in the top 10 percent of their class and who have a keen interest in science.
Housing:	Students live in a supervised residence hall and have planned recreational programs available. Meals are provided in the dining hall.
Costs:	About $1,300 for room, board, and some instructional costs. The program is partially supported by the National Science Foundation. Participants must provide transportation to and from Michigan State, Sunday dinners, and personal expenses. Limited financial aid is available.
Contact:	Dr. Gail Richmond

High School Honors Science Program: Research Internship
Michigan State University
Division of Science Education
115 North Kedzie Laboratory
East Lansing, MI 48824
(517) 353-2958; (800) MSU-9191

Students spend seven weeks working on a research project in a well-equipped laboratory under the mentorship of a professional scientist and doctoral students. The intern chooses an area of study and a research topic from a list of possible choices. General areas include animal science, biochemistry, chemistry, entomology, genetics, microbiology, physiology, plant biology, pharmacology/toxicology, and physics. Participants present a talk about their project and the summer experience at their home school and are encouraged to enter their projects in science fairs. Many former participants have been recognized in the Westinghouse Talent Search. Field trips and seminars about current topics in science, ethical issues, and college admissions and scholarships round out the program.

❖ Academically Interested Minorities (AIM)

Host School:	GMI Engineering and Management Institute
Type:	Summer study
Location:	Flint, MI
Duration:	Six weeks
Dates:	Mid-July through late August
Qualifications:	Grade 12
	Limited to minority students, applicants must have at least a 3.0 grade point average in high school math, chemistry, and English classes, and have taken the equivalent of algebra I and II and geometry, chemistry (with lab), and two years of English.
Housing:	Students are housed in the dormitories of GMI Engineering and Management Institute. Meals are provided.
Costs:	No program costs to students. Tuition, room and board, and supplies and books are covered by grants from GMI and other donors. Participants need to provide their own personal spending money.
Credits given:	None
Contact:	Mr. Ron Knox
	Academically Interested Minorities (AIM)
	GMI Engineering and Management Institute
	1700 West Third Avenue
	Flint, MI 48504-4898
	(313) 762-9825; (800) 955-4464 ext. 9825

The Academically Interested Minorities (AIM) program is designed to help minority students make a smooth transition from high school to college. The program targets students interested in careers in science, engineering, or management. Students enroll in college-level classes in math, computer science, communications, humanities, and chemistry, arranged in a pattern similar to that found at many colleges. Tutoring periods are included in the schedule to provide students with the tools they may need to be successful in college. Fridays are reserved for career institutes in which students work with professional engineers or administrators to learn about career options and how to set and achieve professional goals. Tours are also arranged as part of the career-awareness activities. Evening social events complement the academic program. Application deadline: March 31.

❖ Summer Science Camps: Molecular Biology Camp, Chemistry and Physics Camp

Host School:	Hillsdale College
Type:	Summer study
Location:	Hillsdale, MI
Duration:	One week
Dates:	Mid-June
Qualifications:	Grades 9-10
	This program is for students interested in learning more about modern science. Twenty students for each camp are selected primarily from the local Michigan and surrounding tri-state area.
Housing:	Students live on campus, supervised by house mothers. Meals are provided. Students have access to the sports complex and other college facilities.
Costs:	$25 registration fee. A grant from the Donald L. Murdock Foundation provides tuition, books, room, and board. College credit may be obtained by passing an examination and paying a $50 administrative fee.
Credits Given:	College credit is available.
Contact:	Dr. Francis Steiner
	Summer Science Camps
	Hillsdale College
	Biology Department
	Hillsdale, MI 49242
	(517) 437-7341 ext. 2399

Hillsdale College provides two science camps designed to help students gain an appreciation of what science is all about. The program is dedicated to the idea that studying science can be both challenging and fun and that science is exciting and practical. Students who choose the Molecular Biology Camp explore the field of genetic engineering. Through lectures and laboratories, discussions and experiments, participants learn about topics that include gene cloning, recombinant DNA, bacterial transformation, and manipulation of DNA. The Chemistry and Physics Camp participants learn about areas that include chromatography, spectroscopy, holography, thermodynamics, and superconductivity. Registration is limited to the first 20 applicants for each camp. Application deadline: May 3.

❖ Summer Youth Program

Host School:	Michigan Technological University
Type:	Summer study
Location:	Houghton, MI
Duration:	One week to four weeks

Dates:	July (Four, consecutive, one-week sessions are held; students may attend as many as they wish.)
Qualifications:	Ages 12 through 18 (Many of the programs are for specific age groups.)
	This program is for students who wish to explore careers and academic areas not available at their home schools and who wish an early taste of college life.
Housing:	Resident students live in one of the university residence halls, supervised by residence counselors who also direct recreational activities. Meals are provided. Outdoor campsites provide accommodations on some of the field-based programs. Commuter students are provided with lunch and invited to all recreational activities.
Costs:	$350 per week for resident students includes room and board, tuition, books, and supplies. (Several of the field experiences have additional charges.) Commuting students pay $200 per week, including tuition, books, supplies, and lunches. Some need-based aid is available for Michigan residents.
Credits Given:	None
Contact:	Ms. Shalini Rudak
	Summer Youth Program
	Michigan Technological University
	Youth Programs Director—Educational Opportunity
	1400 Townsend Drive
	Houghton, MI 49931-1295
	(906) 487-2219

Michigan Tech offers more than 65 one-week Explorations designed to introduce students to different careers and to give participants a chance to develop new skills through laboratory, classroom, and field experiences. The Explorations cover a very wide range of studies and activities including field-based programs in mountaineering and orienteering, backpacking ecology, biking, biology and geology, wilderness backpacking, limnology (study of bodies of water), mineralogy and field geology, field ornithology, and forestry. Laboratory- and classroom-based studies are found in areas such as electronics, environmental issues, genetic engineering, computer-aided design, engineering, chemistry, computers, physics, and a number of allied medical fields. Social and cultural events are planned. Application deadline: Rolling admissions.

❖ YMCA Camp Menogyn: Wilderness Adventures

Type:	Science camp
Camper Level:	Ages 12 to 18, grouped by age and sex; (no co-ed trips)
Location:	Northeastern Minnesota and sites dependent on trip
Duration:	Seven to twenty days
Dates:	Late June through late August (Many sessions are available.)
Housing:	At the base camp, campers are housed in rustic cabins.
Costs:	From $305 for 7-day adventures to $1,025 for 20-day mountain hiking trips. Meals are provided. Participants camp out while on trips. Partial need-based camperships are available from the YMCA for Minneapolis residents.

Contact: Mr. David Palmer
          YMCA Camp Menogyn: Wilderness Adventures
          4 West Rustic Lodge Avenue
          Minneapolis, MN 55409
          (612) 823-5282

Menogyn specializes in canoeing and backpacking trips in wilderness areas. All trips are professionally led and emphasize fun and adventure. All sessions include the practice of skills necessary for wilderness travel including outdoor cooking and trip planning. Trips begin at Menogyn's base camp located on the edge of the Boundary Waters Canoe Area Wilderness in northeastern Minnesota. From here, backpacking and canoe trips travel to selected areas in the waters and woods of central Ontario, Isle Royale, and the Rocky Mountains. The program is accredited by the American Camping Association.

❖ Project SEE (Summer Education Experience)

Host School: University of Minnesota, Morris
Type: Summer study
Location: Morris, MN
Duration: Seven weeks
Dates: Mid-June through end of July
Qualifications: Grade 12
          The program is open to students academically talented in the
          sciences as evidenced by successful completion of at least two
          years of science and math courses. Underrepresented minority
          students, women students, and physically or economically
          disadvantaged students are especially encouraged to apply.
Housing: Students are housed in a modern residence hall under the
          supervision of a university student counselor, who also serves as
          a tutor for the program. Meals are taken in the campus dining
          hall. The university library, athletic, and recreational facilities
          are available to the participants.
Costs: No costs for tuition or housing, for which scholarships are awarded
          to all participants. A cash stipend to cover all food and some
          personal expenses is also awarded. Transportation to and from
          the university is not provided.
Credits Given: None
Contact: Thomas McRoberts
          Project SEE (Summer Education Experience)
          University of Minnesota, Morris
          231 Community Services Building
          Morris, MN 56267
          (612) 589-6450

Project SEE is designed to introduce students to scientific research and college-level classwork through the study of the various scientific disciplines, including biology, chemistry, geology, physical science, and computer science. Lectures are supplemented by independent research opportunities, discussions on scientific ethics, laboratory experimentation, and career exploration. Emphasis is on individual attention; the program has a faculty/student ratio of 1:4. Social, athletic, and recreational activities are available to the participants on the University of Minnesota, Morris, campus. Application deadline: April 30.

❖ Scientific Discovery Program—Young Scholar's/PREP Program

Host School:	St. Cloud State University (SCSU)
Type:	Summer study
Location:	St. Cloud, MN
Duration:	Five weeks
Dates:	Mid-July through mid-August
Qualifications:	Grades 10 and 11
	High-ability, high-potential students with a strong interest in science and/or mathematics are eligible for the program. Minority and women students are especially encouraged to apply.
Housing:	Participants are housed on the SCSU campus, supervised by mature counselors. Meals are provided in the university dining hall.
Costs:	No program costs. All expenses related to tuition, fees, books, room, and board are provided by grants from the National Science Foundation and the Department of Energy. Participants cover only incidental expenses and transportation. Limited financial aid for needy students is available.
Credits Given:	None
Contact:	Dr. Robert Johnson
	Scientific Discovery Program—Young Scholar's/PREP Program
	St. Cloud State University
	EB B 120A
	720 Fourth Avenue, South
	St. Cloud, MN 56301-4498
	(612) 255-4928

This unusual program allows participants to experience the chemical, biological, mathematical, statistical, and computer science disciplines through laboratories, demonstrations, lectures, and field trips—all as related to the field of water quality and solid waste management. As students acquire knowledge and skills, they apply their learning to group research projects that have both environmental and social significance in their home communities. After the institute concludes, the students continue their work at home with the help of SCSU faculty and local teachers. Other features of the program include the opportunity to shadow a working scientist or university professor and special evening presentations. Recreational activities, including a day-long canoe trip on the Mississippi River, are also featured. Application deadline: April 16.

❖ High School Summer Science Research Program

Host School:	University of Minnesota, Twin Cities
Type:	Internship
Location:	St. Paul, MN
Duration:	Eight weeks
Dates:	Mid-June through early August
Qualifications:	Grade 12

High-ability, high-achieving students with a demonstrated interest in the biological sciences are eligible for the program.

Housing: Residential students are housed at the university. Meals are provided. Commuter students are expected to return to their homes each night.

Costs: Each participant receives a stipend of $1,200 for the summer's work. Part of the funding for this program is targeted for support of minority students.

Credits Given: None

Contact: Dr. Bill Ganzlin
High School Summer Science Research Program
University of Minnesota, Twin Cities
College of Biological Sciences
223 Snyder Hall, 1475 Gortner Avenue
St. Paul, MN 55108
(612) 624-9717

The Summer Science Research Program is funded by grants from the Howard Hughes Medical Institute and the National Science Foundation. Each participant selects a faculty member with whom to work and spends the majority of the program time pursuing a research topic in the mentor's laboratory. Each student is expected to work in the lab for about 40 hours each week. In addition to the research component, all students attend seminars on the philosophy of science, scientific methodology, ethical issues, and science careers. The program has both residential and commuter components. Application deadline: March 12.

❖ Introduction to Engineering and Science Summer Institute

Host School: University of Missouri, Rolla
Type: Summer study
Location: Rolla, MO
Duration: Six weeks
Dates: Mid-June through late July
Qualifications: Grade 12
The program is open to minority students (African-American, Native American, Puerto Rican American, and Mexican American) interested in science and engineering. Admission is competitive.

Housing: Students live in the Thomas Jefferson Residence Hall and eat in its cafeteria. The residence hall is air-conditioned and includes a computer room, weight room, game room, pool, and deck area as part of its facilities.

Costs: $40 registration fee is the only cost to students. Tuition, supplies, room, and board fees are borne by the university along with the National Science Foundation and sponsoring companies.

Credits Given: None

Contact: Mr. Floyd Harris
Introduction to Engineering and Science Summer Institute
University of Missouri, Rolla

Director, Minority Engineering Program
107 Norwood Hall
Rolla, MO 65401-0249
(314) 341-4212

Participants in this program explore the various disciplines of science and engineering through laboratory and field exercises, study advanced mathematics and science, learn about real-world engineering and science from practicing professionals who serve as role models, and become acquainted with college life while interacting with peers from across the nation. The Summer Institute seeks to provide participants with a clear picture of science- and math-based careers and to stimulate interest in those careers through the use of role models and career guidance. Students also learn about the academic requirements needed to be successful in engineering and science. Recreational activities are planned. Application deadline: March 31.

❖ Jackling Mineral Industries Summer Careers Institute

Host School:	University of Missouri, Rolla
Type:	Summer study
Location:	Rolla, MO
Duration:	One week
Dates:	Three sessions: early, middle, and late June
Qualifications:	Grade 12
	Good students interested in the environmental, energy, materials, or minerals disciplines are eligible for the program.
Housing:	Food and housing are provided on campus by the Jackling Fund.
Costs:	About $85 for books, supplies, and fees. Students chosen for the research apprentice program will receive a stipend of $300. All other fees are met by the sponsors.
Credits Given:	None
Contact:	Dr. Ronald Kohser
	Jackling Mineral Industries Summer Careers Institute
	University of Missouri, Rolla
	School of Mines and Metallurgy
	305 McNutt Hall
	Rolla, MO 65401
	(314) 341-4734

Conducted by the School of Mines and Metallurgy, the Jackling Institute is designed to introduce high school students to career opportunities in ceramic, mining, geological, metallurgical, nuclear, and petroleum engineering and in geology and geophysics. Students participate in hands-on lab experiments from each of the seven departments and attend demonstrations and discussions with faculty and students. Students also gain an understanding of the academic and social life found on college campuses. Twenty student participants from the Institute are invited to participate in August in a three-week National Science Foundation internship during which they work with a University of Missouri, Rolla, faculty member on a research project. Application deadline: April 9.

❖ WISE: Women Investigating Sciences and Environments

Host School:	University of Nebraska, Lincoln
Type:	Summer study
Location:	Lincoln, NE
Duration:	Three weeks
Dates:	Early to late July
Qualifications:	Grade 8 at the time of the first Institute attended
	The program is limited to Nebraska rural and/or minority highly motivated girls who demonstrate a strong interest in mathematics, science, and technology.
Housing:	Students live in the dormitories of the university, supervised by resident assistants. Meals and recreational activities are provided.
Costs:	No institute costs. Tuition, room, and board, as well as use of computer and modem during the academic year, are covered by a grant from the National Science Foundation. Participants are responsible only for transportation and personal expenses.
Credits Given:	None
Contact:	Jan Wright
	WISE: Women Investigating Sciences and Environments
	University of Nebraska, Lincoln
	Department of Geology
	214 Bessey Hall
	Lincoln, NE 68588-0306
	(402) 472-4632

WISE: Women Investigating Sciences and Environments seeks to motivate young women to consider careers in science and technology just when studies show a drop-off of interest in the sciences among this group. To expand the career options open to young women, WISE provides summer institutes coupled with academic year follow-up. Each student selected is expected to attend at least two summer institutes focusing on scientific questions and the attempt to find answers. Through the use of college libraries, laboratories, and computers, the participants explore the world around them. One recent summer institute focused on physics and the physical aspects of environmental science; topics such as energy, radioactivity, climate changes, hydrology, and aircraft design were explored. Each girl takes home a computer and modem for follow-up contact during the year. Application deadline: April 1.

❖ Exploring Career Options in Engineering and Science (ECOES)

Host School:	Stevens Institute of Technology
Type:	Internship
Location:	Hoboken, NJ
Duration:	Two weeks
Dates:	Three sessions: late June to early July; middle to late July; late July to early August
Qualifications:	Grades 11 and 12
	The program is open to young women interested in career

	possibilities in science and engineering. Students should have demonstrated ability in science and mathematics.
Housing:	Participants live in Technology Hall, an air-conditioned dormitory with other ECOES students and are provided with three meals a day weekdays and with brunch and dinner on weekends. Recreational and learning facilities at Stevens are available to participants.
Costs:	$550 covers tuition, room, and board. A limited number of need-based scholarships are available.
Credits Given:	None
Contact:	Ms. Kathleen Bott
	Exploring Career Options in Engineering and Science
	Stevens Institute of Technology
	Office of Women's Programs
	Castle Point on the Hudson
	Hoboken, NJ 07030
	(201) 216-5245

Exploring Career Options in Engineering and Science (ECOES) offers women students the opportunity to explore the fields of science and engineering by choosing a research project, explore other engineering and science disciplines through hands-on laboratory experiments, interact with undergraduate students and professional engineers and scientists, and visit local industries. The highlight of the program is the independent research project chosen by the student and supervised by Stevens faculty and doctoral students in areas such as chemical, environmental, mechanical, or electrical engineering or in physics, materials science, biomedical science, or chemistry. A variety of social activities are also planned. Application deadline: May 10.

❖ Discovery

Host School:	Rutgers University, Cook College
Type:	Summer study/Internship
Location:	New Brunswick, NJ
Duration:	Five weeks
Dates:	Mid-July to mid-August
Qualifications:	Grades 11 and 12
	Minority students who are interested in the life and physical sciences and who are New Jersey residents are eligible for the program. Students should rank in the top third of their high school class or have demonstrated academic potential.
Housing:	Students are housed in the university residence halls and are provided with meals.
Costs:	No program costs to the students. Funds are provided by the sponsoring organizations.
Credits Given:	3 college credits
Contact:	Ms. Daulat Husain
	Discovery
	Rutgers University, Cook College
	Office of Resident Instruction, PO Box 231

New Brunswick, NJ 08903-0231
(908) 932-9650; FAX (908) 932-8880

Discovery is an enrichment and apprenticeship program designed to introduce participants to career opportunities in science and technology. The program consists of an
intensive summer session with academic year follow-up. The academic component
includes classroom instruction in mathematics and English, with extensive use of computers, and instruction in scientific research methodology. In the apprenticeship, students
get hands-on experience in the laboratory and field, learning lab techniques under the
guidance of a faculty sponsor and gaining firsthand knowledge about what a scientist
does. Fields include animal science, entomology, environmental science, meteorology,
and food science, among others. Workshops on career exploration and time management
complete the program. Application deadline: March 5.

❖ Douglass Science Institute for High School Women in Math, Science, and Engineering

Host School:	Douglass College of Rutgers University
Type:	Summer study
Location:	New Brunswick, NJ
Duration:	Three weeks
Dates:	Early through late July
Qualifications:	Grade 11
	The program is limited to women students who are interested in science, math, or engineering and who attend New Jersey high schools.
Housing:	Students are housed in a Douglass College residence hall supervised by resident advisors who are part of the Douglass Project for Women.
Costs:	$25 registration fee
Credits Given:	None
Contact:	Dr. Ellen Mappen
	Douglass Science Institute for High School Women in Math, Science, and Engineering
	Douglass College of Rutgers University
	Director, Douglass Project for Rutgers Women in Math and Science
	PO Box 270
	New Brunswick, NJ 08903-0270
	(908) 932-9197

The Douglass Science Institute encourages young women to consider careers in science,
math, and/or engineering by actively involving them in scientific learning and by providing appropriate role models. The program includes hands-on laboratories studying topics
such as lightwave communications and molecular approaches to the study of gene
activity. Students participate in workshops and activities concerned with environmental
science, engineering, mathematics, computer science, career options, and women's issues, as well as field trips to corporate and natural scientific sites. A math and science fair
is part of the program as is an opportunity to work on an individual research project.

Ninety percent of the student participants in the 1989 summer program went on to major in science, math, or engineering in college. Application deadline: April 15.

❖ Summer Academy in Technology and Science

Host School:	New Jersey Institute of Technology (NJIT)
Type:	Summer study
Location:	Newark, NJ
Duration:	Five weeks
Dates:	Early July through early August
Qualifications:	Grades 11 and 12
	Academically talented high school students who want to begin earning college credits are eligible for the program.
Housing:	Residential students are housed during the week in air-conditioned residence halls with specially trained dormitory counselors. Students arrive on campus on Sunday night of each week and leave during the day on Friday. Meals are provided.
Costs:	$141 per credit tuition. Additional fees are approximately $100. Room and board for residential students is $750. A small number of partial scholarships may be available.
Credits Given:	Up to 8 college credits
Contact:	Ms. Diana Muldrow
	Summer Academy in Technology and Science
	New Jersey Institute of Technology (NJIT)
	Center for Pre-College Programs
	University Heights
	Newark, NJ 07102
	(201) 596-3679

High school students can earn up to eight college credits at New Jersey Institute of Technology's (NJIT) Summer Academy. Courses available include choices of chemistry I and II, physics I, architecture, computer science, calculus I and II, management, and an interdisciplinary course titled Literature, Nature, and the American Mind. Summer Academy students may commute to the campus or live there. A midday break between classes provides time for students to enjoy athletic and recreational activities, career exploration, or library and laboratory research. NJIT has the largest computer science program in New Jersey and the eighth largest School of Architecture in the nation. Application deadline: March 15.

❖ The Summer Institute for the Gifted at Bryn Mawr College
(Similar programs are held on different dates at the George School, Newton, PA; Vassar College, Poughkeepsie, NY; and at Blair Academy, Blairstown, NJ)

Type:	Summer study
Location:	Verona, NJ
Duration:	Three weeks
Dates:	Late June through mid-July (Dates vary at each site—programs run throughout the summer.)
Qualifications:	Grades 5-7, grades 7-9, and grades 10-12

The program is open to students identified as gifted by meeting one of the eligibility criteria such as participation in Talent Searches, rank at 95th percentile on standardized tests, identified as gifted and participating in a gifted program, or identified through PSAT/SAT.

Housing: Students live in the college dormitories, supervised by a housemaster and group counselor. Three meals are provided daily. Weekend field trips and evening programs are also part of the summer experience.

Costs: $1,950 includes all program costs, room and board, tuition, and lab and computer fees, as well as special weekend-trip fees. Transportation, books, and personal expenses are not included.

Credits Given: Credit available for college-level courses.

Contact: Dr. Philip Zipse
The Summer Institute for the Gifted at Bryn Mawr College
Bryn Mawr College: College Gifted Programs
544 Bloomfield Avenue
Verona, NJ 07044-1817
(201) 857-2521

One of four summer institutes held by College Gifted Programs in cooperation with Thomas Edison State College of New Jersey, this program offers gifted students in three age groups a variety of classes. The youngest group could choose such courses as Foundations of Mathematics, Problem Solving, Computer Clinic, Experimental Chemistry, Cell Biology, or Death of the Dinosaurs. Middle-school students choose from selections include PSAT/SAT Math Prep, Principles of Biology, Chemistry, Robotics and Microelectronics, Introduction to Veterinary Medicine, and Spaceship Earth. The oldest students may take Trigonometry, Pascal, College Chemistry, Astronomy, or a number of other choices. College-credit courses are also available. A full recreational program is provided. Application deadline: April 30.

❖ New York State Summer Institute for Science and Mathematics

Host School: State University of New York at Buffalo

Type: Summer study/Internship

Location: Buffalo, NY

Duration: Three weeks

Dates: Late July to mid-August

Qualifications: Grades 11 and 12
The program is limited to New York State residents who are outstanding science and mathematics students.

Housing: Students are housed in the dormitories at the university and eat in the dining facilities.

Costs: $900 for tuition. Other costs are provided through state funding. Need-based tuition assistance is available.

Credits Given: None

Contact: New York State Summer Institute for Science and Mathematics
State University of New York at Buffalo
Room 685 EBA
State Education Department

Albany, NY 12234
(518) 474-8773

Sponsored by the New York State Education Department in association with the State University at Buffalo, this program is designed to enrich the scientific experiences of New York State students. Introduction to Investigations in Science involves the participants in several ongoing lab- and field-research investigations during the first week of the program. Activities in the biological, physical, and earth sciences are provided. The students perform field work at sites that include an active archaeological dig, a fossil-rich shoreline, and a nearby bog. Students form research teams and pursue independent research during the remaining two weeks. Students gain experience with scientific methodology and present their results. Social and recreational activities are planned for weekends and evenings. Application deadline: April 1.

❖ New York State Summer Institute for Science and Mathematics

Host School:	Syracuse University
Type:	Summer study
Location:	Syracuse, NY
Duration:	Three weeks
Dates:	Early to late July
Qualifications:	Grades 11 and 12
	The program is limited to New York State residents who are outstanding science and mathematics students.
Housing:	Students are housed in the dormitories and take meals in the dining facilities.
Costs:	$900 for tuition. Other costs are provided for through state funding. Need-based tuition assistance is available.
Credits Given:	None
Contact:	New York State Summer Institute for Science and Mathematics
	Syracuse University
	Room 685 EBA
	State Education Department
	Albany, NY 12234
	(518) 474-8773

Sponsored by Syracuse University in association with the New York State Education Department, Frontiers of Science acquaints the participants with the latest advances in science and mathematics. Each week of the program focuses on a different scientific discipline. The first week provides laboratory experiences in molecular biology and genetic engineering. During week two students explore physical science topics including superconductivity, artificial intelligence, and computer interfacing and robotics. The third week emphasizes field experiences in ecology and geology. Mathematics is studied as part of the science experience. Tours of area facilities and social and recreational activities are included. Application deadline: April 1.

❖ New York State Summer Institute for Science and Mathematics— Student Research Program in Science

Host School:	Syracuse University and SUNY, Buffalo
Type:	Internship

Location:	Buffalo, NY, or Syracuse, NY
Duration:	Seven weeks
Dates:	July through mid-August
Qualifications:	Grades 11 and 12
	This program is limited to outstanding science and math students who are New York State residents. Applicants must have completed three years of Regents sciences and three years of Regents math classes.
Housing:	Students live in the dormitories at Syracuse or SUNY Buffalo and have meals provided.
Costs:	$1,500 for tuition. Other program costs are paid by funds from the New York State Education Department. Some need-based tuition assistance is available.
Credits Given:	None
Contact:	Student Research Program in Science
	New York State Summer Institute for Science and Mathematics
	Room 685 EBA
	State Education Department
	Albany, NY 12234
	(518) 474-8773

Designed to provide a firsthand experience in scientific research, this program also allows students to realistically evaluate the potential of a future career in science and mathematics. Students elect an area of interest and are assigned to ongoing research teams. Some students are placed with scientists at Syracuse University in the departments of biology, chemistry, geology, or physics, while others work with researchers at the State University of New York (SUNY) at Buffalo, College of Environmental Science and Forestry, the Health Science Center, the Institute for Sensory Research, or the School of Engineering. Students in the Buffalo program may also be placed with teams at the Superconductivity Institute or Roswell Park Cancer Institute. A research-methods course and special lectures on topics such as AIDS, cancer research, and engineering are presented. Social, recreational, and athletic activities complete the program. Application deadline: April 1.

❖ The International Summer Institute

Host School:	Adelphi University
Type:	Summer study
Location:	New York, NY
Duration:	Three weeks
Dates:	Early through late July

Qualifications:	Grades 7–12
	This program is open to high-ability, achievement-oriented students.
Housing:	Resident students are housed in double rooms in air-conditioned dormitory suites supervised by undergraduate and graduate student counselors. Dorms are within easy walking distance to all campus facilities. Faculty and staff live on campus providing easy access to students. Meals are provided; Glatt kosher meals are available on request.

Costs:	$1,995 includes tuition, housing, all meals, and activities.
Credits Given:	None
Contact:	Mr. Jack Scheckner
	The International Summer Institute
	Adelphi University
	PO Box 843, Bowling Green Station
	New York, NY 10274
	(800) 292-4452

Founded by parents and faculty of New York City's specialized high schools for the academically gifted, the Institute provides a variety of academic programming along with sports coaching sessions, special faculty lectures, and visits to sites such as Brookhaven National Laboratory and Cold Spring Harbor Genetics Laboratory. Students take four classes a day, some lasting all session and others lasting only three to five days. Offerings include such subjects as aerospace and astronomy, biology and biotechnology, chemistry, computer science and research, environmental science and ecology, genetics and molecular biology, and math and physics problem solving. Recreation, sports, and social activities round out the program. Application deadline: May 15.

❖ Summer Research Training Program

Host School:	Pace University
Type:	Summer study/Internship
Location:	New York, NY
Duration:	Six weeks
Dates:	Early July through mid-August
Qualifications:	Grades 11 and 12
	The program is open to students who have a strong interest in the biological and biochemical sciences. Students who belong to groups underrepresented in the sciences are especially welcome.
Hou~ing:	This is mainly a commuter program, although dormitory housing can be arranged for students needing these accommodations.
Costs:	No program fees or costs to students. They are responsible for lunch and travel expenses.
Credits Given:	None
Contact:	Dr. Dudley Cox
	Summer Research Training Program
	Pace University
	Department of Biological Sciences
	1 Pace Plaza
	New York, NY 10038
	(212) 346-1895

Students interested in a research experience have the opportunity to work with Pace University upperclassmen who have participated in their undergraduate research program. Students are taught basic microbial techniques and perform experiments involving a variety of microorganisms. Students who have had previous exposure to microbiology are assigned to an advanced group. These students experiment with cutting DNA with restriction endonucleases, heredity unit transfer, and incorporation of plasmids. Students who continue with their studies after the six-week program have the opportunity to develop their own research studies. These studies often are appropriate for participation in science fairs and the Westinghouse Talent Search competition. Application deadline: Contact program for information.

❖ AISES Science Camp

Host School:	Clarkson University
Type:	Summer study
Location:	Potsdam, NY
Duration:	Two weeks
Dates:	Late July through early August
Qualifications:	Grades 8-10
	This program is limited to American Indian students interested in science and mathematics who are in the top half of their class.
Housing:	Students live in a Clarkson University dormitory, supervised by college student resident advisors who live with the participants. Meals are provided in the university dining hall.
Costs:	No program costs to participants. All expenses are covered by AISES and Clarkson University through the support of the Eastman Kodak Company.
Credits Given:	None
Contact:	AISES Science Camp
	Clarkson University
	Center for Continuing Education
	Potsdam, NY 13699-5570
	(315) 268-6647

Sponsored by AISES, the American Indian Science and Engineering Society, Science Camp at Clarkson University seeks to develop the participant's interest in science through a creative, hands-on approach; to strengthen their problem-solving skills; to increase awareness of opportunities in science and engineering; and to improve performance skills. Instruction in science, mathematics, and computer science is combined with workshops focusing on careers, personal development, and leadership training. Students interact with American Indian role models involved in scientific professions and participate in field trips during the program. Recreational activities are planned for each day of the program. Applications may be requested from AISES, 1085 14th St., Suite 1506, Boulder, CO 80302; phone: (303) 492-8658. Application deadline: Contact program for information.

❖ SCOPES

Host School:	Clarkson University
Type:	Summer study
Location:	Potsdam, NY
Duration:	One week
Dates:	July
Qualifications:	Grades 10-12
	Students interested in exploring career opportunities and possibilities for college majors are eligible for the program.
Housing:	Participants are housed in double occupancy rooms in a supervised

residence hall. Meals are provided at a university dining hall. Recreational and athletic facilities are available to the students.

Costs: $425 covers instruction, room, and board. Scholarships are available.

Credits Given: None

Contact: Mr. Richard Watkins
SCOPES
Clarkson University
Center for Continuing Education
Potsdam, NY 13699-5570
(315) 268-4425 or 268-6647

SCOPES gives participants a chance to sample college life; to explore career opportunities in engineering, science, and management; and to decide what college majors best suit their personal goals. Through testing instruments and classroom and group activities, students emerge better prepared to make decisions about future college and career choices. Lectures, laboratories, and discussions focus on areas such as accounting, applied psychology, biology, chemical engineering, finance, engineering management, physics, and technical communications, among other academic and career disciplines. A workshop titled "What College Life Is Really Like" helps participants gain a true understanding of the college experience. University professors and staff and industry representatives all interact with the students. Application deadline: June 19.

✦ Summer Research and Apprenticeship Program in Science and Mathematics

Host School: Clarkson University
Type: Internship
Location: Potsdam, NY
Duration: Five weeks
Dates: Early July through early August
Qualifications: Grades 11 and 12
The program is open to students with an interest in involvement in ongoing research projects in chemistry, biology, physics, psychology, mathematics, or computer science.

Housing: Students are housed in a university dormitory, supervised by project and residence hall staff. Meals are served in a campus dining hall. Students have access to the field house, pool, and other recreational facilities during free evening and weekend hours.

Costs: $550 to help defray food and housing costs. Students must provide transportation to and from the university. Other program costs are paid from the partial funding by Clarkson University and the National Science Foundation. Full scholarships may be available.

Credits Given: None

Contact: Dr. Christine Jungklaus
Summer Research and Apprenticeship Program in Science and Mathematics
Clarkson University

Biology Department
Potsdam, NY 13699-5630
(315) 268-3837

Participants have an opportunity to engage in daily laboratory interaction with faculty and postgraduate researchers at Clarkson University. Students are trained in usage of the most up-to-date laboratory equipment as they actively participate in their choice of ongoing research projects. Some examples of projects include studies on genetic engineering and chromatin analysis, measurement of radon exposure, experiments with a multigrid model for hurricane-track prediction, astrophotography, and physiological studies of pain perception and pain control. Application deadline: April 2.

❖ The Simons Summer Research Fellowship Program

Host School: State University of New York at Stony Brook
Type: Internship
Location: Stony Brook, NY
Duration: Six weeks
Dates: Early July through mid-August
Qualifications: Grade 12
Academically talented high school students who have completed their junior year with a record of outstanding achievement are eligible for the program.
Housing: Housing is available for students who wish to live on campus. Meals are provided for residential students.
Costs: No program costs. Commuting students receive a stipend of $750. Residential students receive a $600 fellowship in addition to room and board.
Contact: Ms. Donna DiDonato
The Simons Summer Research Fellowship Program
State University of New York at Stony Brook
Office of Undergraduate Studies
Stony Brook, NY 11794-3351
(516) 632-7080

The Simons Fellowship program was developed to foster student interest and skills in experimental research. Each student selected for the program engages in scientific research in an area of the student's interest. Research opportunities are available in the biomedical, life, physical, applied, and behavioral sciences. Simons Fellows are matched with faculty sponsors who serve as mentors and guides during the program. Up to three students from each school may be nominated for the program. Selected nominees complete the application and essay to apply for the program. Application deadline: April 1.

❖ Summer Science Program

Host School: Appalachian State University
Type: Summer study
Location: Boone, NC
Duration: Two weeks
Dates: Two sessions: middle to late June; late June to mid-July
Qualifications: Grades 7-12

	Gifted or talented students nominated by their school are eligible for the program.
Housing:	Students are housed in double rooms in a residence hall on the Appalachian State campus. Students will be supervised at all times by qualified specialists and counselors. Meals are provided in the dining hall.
Costs:	$610 includes tuition, room and board, lab fees, recreation, and health services. Applications received by April 1 receive a $20 reduction. A white-water rafting trip and cave exploration and hiking trips may be offered at additional cost.
Credits Given:	None
Contact:	Summer Science Program Appalachian State University Office of Conferences and Institutes University Hall Boone, NC 28608 (704) 262-3045

This enrichment program seeks to challenge gifted students through an in-depth classroom study of selected science concepts, small group laboratory investigations, field experiences, and individual research projects. Participants select two academic classes from such courses as Chemical Research, Experimental Computer Technology, The Web of Life, and Applied Psychological Concepts. Athletic activities and evening activities, including social events, workshops, and night hikes, round out the program. Application deadline: May 25.

❖ The Summer Enrichment Program for Gifted and Talented Youth at Camp Broadstone

Type:	Science camp
Camper Level:	Grades 4–9
Location:	Boone, NC
Duration:	Two weeks
Dates:	Three consecutive sessions: middle of June through end of July
Housing:	Campers live in rustic cabins and eat in the family-style lodge dining room.
Costs:	$500 per session includes tuition, room and board, and health and recreational services.
Contact:	The Summer Enrichment Program for Gifted and Talented Youth Appalachian State University Office of Conferences and Institutes, University Hall Boone, NC 28608 (704) 262-3045

An enrichment program of Appalachian State University, this program provides gifted and talented youth an opportunity to engage in creative investigations in science and the arts through the use of hands-on activities. Topics include Native Americans, environmental science, animal behavior, computers, chemistry, and physics, along with music and graphic and creative arts. Camp Broadstone is a 53-acre site located in a valley in the Blue Ridge Mountains. Extracurricular activities include rock climbing, canoeing, white-water rafting, a ropes course, and swimming, among other traditional camp activities. Application deadline: April 1.

❖ The Green River Preserve

Type: Science camp
Camper Level: Grades 4–8 (academically gifted students only)
Location: Cedar Mountain, NC
Duration: One, two, or three weeks
Dates: Late June through mid-August
Housing: Campers live in cabins nestled in the woods. Meals are taken in the lodge dining hall.
Costs: $390 for one-week session; $725 for two-week session; $1,030 for three-week session. Partial scholarships are available for campers needing financial assistance.
Contact: Mr. Sandy Schenk
The Green River Preserve
Box 1000
Cedar Mountain, NC 28718
(704) 885-2250 summer; (704) 324-5832 winter

The natural science camp at the Green River Preserve, a beautiful 3,400-acre private wildlife preserve in the Blue Ridge Mountains near Brevard, NC, uses its wilderness environment to promote learning through direct observation and discovery. Mentors (teaching staff) lead field trips and assist with independent learning projects, while counselors live with the campers and supervise all recreational and camping activities. Instructional activities are designed to avoid academic pressure and competition; environmental concepts and processes are explored. Subjects studied include forestry, ornithology, and time travel. A full program of recreational and enrichment activities complements this unique camping experience where it is OK to be smart and motivated.

❖ Summer Ventures in Science and Math (SVSM)

Type: Summer study
Location: Six campuses of the University of North Carolina system including UNC at Charlotte, UNC at Wilmington, Appalachian State University, East Carolina University, North Carolina Central University and Western Carolina University
Duration: Four weeks
Dates: Two sessions: mid-June through mid-July; early July through end of July
Qualifications: Grades 11 and 12
North Carolina residents only are selected based on academic ability, science and mathematics motivation, and emotional maturity.
Housing: Students live in university dormitories supervised by residential advisors who are also responsible for planning social, athletic, cultural, and co-curricular activities. Meals are provided in campus dining halls.
Costs: No costs for room, board, and tuition. Students' families are

responsible for transportation to and from assigned campus and personal expenses. Limited funds are available to help with these expenses for students with severe financial need.

Credits Given: None

Contact: Dr. William Youngblood
Summer Ventures in Science and Math (SVSM)
University of North Carolina
PO Box 2976
Durham, NC 27715
(919) 286-3366 ext. 523

A statewide program of the University of North Carolina system, Summer Ventures in Science and Math (SVSM) is administered by the North Carolina School of Science and Mathematics. Six campuses host the SVSM Institutes, each with a different program emphasis. The academic program is designed to provide students with experience in scientific inquiry and mathematical problem solving. Students develop laboratory skills and learn experimental design, instrumentation, mathematical modeling and problem solving, and data analysis while engaged in a research topic of individual interest. Computer applications, career guidance, and discussions about social issues are also part of the summer program. Application deadline: January 31.

❖ Intensive Summer Science Program (ISSP)

Host School: Bennett College and North Carolina A&T State University

Type: Summer study

Location: Greensboro, NC

Duration: Four weeks

Dates: Late June to mid-July

Qualifications: Grades 9-12
The program is limited to college-bound minority students who want to improve their mathematics and science skills and knowledge.

Housing: Participants are housed in dormitories on the Bennett College campus. Three meals a day are provided in the college dining hall. Students have access to the libraries of both Bennett College and North Carolina A&T State University.

Costs: $600 room and board for the four-week program. Program costs are paid by the sponsoring organizations and Bennett College and North Carolina A&T State University.

Credits Given: None

Contact: Dr. Nellouise Watkins
Intensive Summer Science Program (ISSP)
Bennett College
900 E. Washington Street
Greensboro, NC 27401-3239
(919) 273-4431; (800) 338-BENN

The program is designed to increase the mathematical skills of minority students while improving their knowledge of science. Biology, chemistry, and physics are taught from an interdisciplinary approach. Problem solving, computation, and analytical skills are strengthened in the mathematics portion of the program, while science process and concepts, along with laboratory experiences, provide the scientific focus. Computer science, including programming and computer-assisted instruction, helps students understand the role of computers in an information-based society. The students' communication skills are strengthened with classes that focus on reading, writing, and oral communication. Organized recreational activities, including sports, dances, movies, and forums, complete the program. Application deadline: April 23.

❖ Physical and Mathematical Sciences Academic Camps

Host School:	North Carolina State University
Type:	Summer study
Location:	Raleigh, NC
Duration:	Two weeks
Dates:	Middle through late June
Qualifications:	Grades 10-12
	The program is for highly motivated students interested in chemistry, mathematics and statistics, physics, or marine, earth, and atmospheric sciences.
Housing:	Students live in double rooms at University Towers residence hall. Resident counselors are available 24 hours a day. Three meals a day weekdays and brunch and dinner on weekends are provided.
Costs:	$700 for resident students, which includes tuition, room and board, weekend activities, and field trips; $350 for day students, which includes tuition, lunch, and field trips. Financial aid is not available.
Credits Given:	None
Contact:	Mr. Robert Savage
	Physical and Mathematical Sciences Academic Camps
	North Carolina State University
	College of Physical and Mathematical Sciences
	Box 8201
	Raleigh, NC 27695-8201
	(919) 515-6117

Three concurrent sessions offer students the opportunity to explore topics in a physical science of their choice. The chemistry program is designed to give students an understanding of chemical reactions through reading, labs, demonstrations, and firsthand exposure to chemical research activities. Field trips to regional labs are included. The mathematics and statistics program emphasizes the use of matrix algebra in problem solving and the use of computers in statistics. Hands-on activities and field trips complement this program. The session on physics, earth and atmospheric science emphasizes a hands-on approach to investigating physical processes in nature through field excursions, reading, labs, and demonstrations. Weekend activities are planned for resident campers. Application deadline: May 1.

❖ Women in Science and Mathematics Workshop

Host School:	College of Mount St. Joseph
Type:	Summer study

Location:	Cincinnati, OH
Duration:	Five days
Dates:	Mid-June
Qualifications:	Grades 11 and 12
	This program is limited to outstanding high school women interested in exploring opportunities in science and mathematics.
Housing:	Students are housed in the dormitories and provided with meals.
Costs:	$95 application fee; refundable if the student is not selected for the program. Grants cover the cost of tuition, meals, housing, and materials for all participants selected.
Credits Given:	None
Contact:	Dr. G. Kritsky
	Women in Science and Mathematics Workshop
	College of Mount St. Joseph
	Department of Biology
	Cincinnati, OH 45233-1670
	(513) 244-4411

Designed to introduce participants to opportunities for women in the sciences, mathematics, and related research careers, the workshop brings outstanding students together with professional women scientists and mathematicians. The focus is on the role of women at the cutting edge of science and technology. The program includes presentations by speakers from industry, medicine, education, and small business. Experimental laboratory work is performed in fields such as microbiology, molecular biology, biochemistry, forensic science, and quantitative analysis. Application deadline: May 22.

❖ Ross Young Scholars Program

Host School:	Ohio State University
Type:	Summer study
Location:	Columbus, OH
Duration:	Eight weeks
Dates:	Late June through mid-August
Qualifications:	Grades 9-12 (The majority are entering grade 12.)
	This program is designed for mathematically talented young people who have a strong interest in mathematics and who wish to pursue careers in mathematics, science, or technology.
Housing:	Students are housed in double suites in the dormitories of Ohio State and have 20 meals per week provided.
Costs:	Approximately $1,300, which includes room, board, and tuition. Some limited financial aid is available. Incidental expenses, such as books and laundry, are about $120.
Credits Given:	3 quarter credits
Contact:	Professor Arnold Ross
	Ross Young Scholars Program
	Ohio State University
	Department of Mathematics
	231 West 18th Avenue
	Columbus, OH 43210
	(614) 292-1569

The Ross Summer Program in Science and Mathematics is designed to provide an apprenticeship in mathematical and scientific research. For this reason, the program is intensely mathematical. Participants study discrete mathematics and number theory to provide a basis for problem-solving. Advanced participants (many students return for several years) take a course in combinatorics. Additional courses change from year to year; recent programs have seen courses and seminars on fractal geometry, algebraic coding theory, knot theory, and advanced number theory. Although the program stays almost entirely within the field of mathematics, a capacity for scientific thinking is developed through deep involvement in observation, experimentation, and conjecturing. Application deadline: May 15.

❖ Future Leaders in Science Summer Workshop

Host School:	University of Dayton
Type:	Summer study
Location:	One week
Dates:	Two sessions: middle July and late July
Qualifications:	Grades 11 and 12
	Applicants should have at least a 3.0 (B) average overall, as well as in science and math classes, and should intend to study science or math as college students.
Housing:	Students live on campus in a new, air-conditioned residence hall in four-person suites. An exercise room, multipurpose room, and dining hall are part of the facility.
Costs:	$350 includes tuition, housing, meals, recreational activities, and a closing banquet for all participants and their parents. Limited partial grants of need-based financial aid are available.
Credits Given:	None
Contact:	Amy Sandmann
	Future Leaders in Science Summer Workshop
	University of Dayton
	Office of Admission
	300 College Park
	Dayton, OH 45469-1611
	(513) 229-2002; (800) 837-7433

Students have an opportunity to explore scientific issues in biology, chemistry, computer science, physics, and clinical health sciences while they consider ethical issues, such as risk and personal responsibility, associated with technological advances. Participants interact with University of Dayton professors who make learning both interesting and enjoyable. Hands-on experiences are provided in the university's laboratories and research facilities. Tours of the labs are included in the program. Current college students act as resident advisors and teaching assistants, serving both as friends and role models. Social activities are planned for the participants. College planning discussions are also held. Application deadline: May 31.

❖ Investigations in the Sciences

Host School:	Denison University
Type:	Summer study

Location:	Granville, OH
Duration:	One week
Dates:	Late June
Qualifications:	Grade 12
	Students interested in science and mathematics who want to experience current areas of activity in the sciences and who want to explore possible career options are eligible for the program.
Housing:	All participants are housed in Denison's Shepardson Hall, supervised by student associates who assist the faculty and live in the dormitory. Meals are provided in the college dining hall. Athletic facilities of the university are available to the students.
Costs:	$300 includes room and board and instructional costs. A limited amount of need-based financial aid is available.
Credits Given:	None
Contact:	Dr. George Gilbert
	Investigations in the Sciences
	Denison University
	Department of Chemistry
	Granville, OH 43023
	(614) 587-6492

Investigations in the Sciences provides participants with laboratory experiences and discussions in two different sciences chosen by the student from a number of offerings. The focus of the program is on hands-on investigation of current areas of scientific inquiry. Course selections include studies in astronomy, biology (genetics and embryology), chemistry, geology, mathematics, and psychology (experimental psychology and learning). Research-level equipment, such as spectrophotometers, electron microscopes, lasers, and computers, are used in performing investigations. Evening programs include college and career planning sessions and use of the Swasey Observatory for star gazing. Movies and picnics are planned as part of the social activities. Application deadline: April 23.

❖ Women in the Sciences

Host School:	Marietta College
Type:	Summer study
Location:	Marietta, OH
Duration:	Nine days
Dates:	Middle of June
Qualifications:	Grades 5 through 8
	The program is open to highly motivated students and is especially geared towards involving young women in the sciences.
Housing:	Students live in the college dormitories supervised at all times by trained college students and staff adults. Meals are provided at the Student Center.
Costs:	$195 covers room and board. Instructional fees are supported by a grant from the Merck Foundation. Financial aid is available for students unable to meet the basic fee.
Credits Given:	None

Contact: Dr. George Banzinger
Women in the Sciences
Marietta College
Office of Continuing Education
215 Fifth Street
Marietta, OH 45750-3031
(614) 374-4794

This award-winning program takes a multidisciplinary approach to hands-on science. The goal of the program is to enhance the science, mathematics, and engineering skills of highly motivated children and to interest them in possible careers in science. Separated by grade level into two groups, students explore a variety of disciplines, including biology, earth science, computer science, physics, and psychology. Math strategies and logic, discovery laboratories, cooperative learning, presentations of scientific projects, and sessions on the skills needed for success in math and science are all part of the program. Presentations by women scientists and engineers, field trips, and career guidance help students explore technical career opportunities. A follow-up program during the school year keeps interest alive. Application deadline: April 1.

❖ YMCA Camp Kern: Camp Challenge, The Voyagers, Archaeology Camp, and Science Camp

Type: Science camp
Camper Level: Ages 10 to 17 (Each camp limited to specific age group.)
Location: Oregonia, OH
Duration: One week to ten days
Dates: Weekly throughout summer
Housing: Housing accommodations depend upon program and range from
      wilderness camping to cabins.
Costs: $275 to $515, depending upon program.
Contact: Mr. Larry Maxwell
YMCA Camp Kern
5291 State Route 350
Oregonia, OH 45054-9747
(513) 932-3756

Camp Kern, located on 420 acres in the Little Miami River Valley, offers a number of science-oriented and wilderness-adventure camps geared for preteens and teenagers. Camp Challenge (ages 13 and 14) provides canoeing, rock climbing, windsurfing, and other outdoor activities. The Voyagers (ages 15 to 17) allows campers to experience travel and high-adventure trips that focus on backpacking and rafting, climbing and cycling, white-water kayaking and mountain biking, or canoeing. Archaeology Camp has campers participating in authentic excavations of prehistoric importance while Science Camp has campers (ages 10 to 12) exploring the natural world. Participants may stay for more than one session. Accredited by the American Camping Association.

❖ WISE Academic Camp

Host School: Wittenberg University
Type: Summer study
Location: Springfield, OH

Duration:	One week
Dates:	Late June
Qualifications:	Grades 6-8
	This program is for gifted and talented students who have tested at least at the 95th percentile on standardized tests or who have demonstrated exceptional talent, leadership, or creativity.
Housing:	Campers live in a residence hall, supervised by the head counselor and Wittenberg student assistants. Meals are taken on campus.
Costs:	$375 covers instruction, room, and board. Partial financial aid is available.
Credits Given:	None
Contact:	Dr. Barbara Mackey
	WISE Academic Camp
	Wittenberg University
	Director of Community Programs
	PO Box 720
	Springfield, OH 45501-0720
	(513) 327-7050; FAX (513) 327-6340

Each summer's program is centered around a theme; campers select three classes and participate in an interdisciplinary seminar experience. Class topics include biology, chemistry, computers, and math along with journalism, drama, and visual arts. Academic experiences include lectures, demonstrations, library, and laboratory work. The students use the facilities of Wittenberg University, including the science laboratories, the theater complex, and the recreational facilities. WISE encourages creativity and individual expression. A head counselor supervises evening activities. Application deadline: April 15.

❖ Hughes Summer Science Camp

Host School:	The College of Wooster
Type:	Summer study
Location:	Wooster, OH
Duration:	Two weeks
Dates:	Late June through early July
Qualifications:	Grade 12 (Exceptional juniors will be considered.)
	Students should be interested in and have an aptitude for science. Each applicant must have completed algebra I and at least two high school science courses.
Housing:	Students are provided with housing and meals on the college campus.
Costs:	$25 refundable deposit. Tuition, room, and board for students are paid by a grant from the Howard Hughes Medical Institute. Students are responsible for providing their own spending money.
Credits Given:	None
Contact:	Dr. Gary Gillund
	Hughes Summer Science Camp
	The College of Wooster

Department of Psychology
Wooster, OH 44691
(216) 263-2370

The Summer Science Camp provides instruction in the sciences and integrates mathematics, writing, and critical reading into the curriculum. Laboratory experiences in biology, chemistry, geology, psychology, and mathematics provide students with the skills and techniques needed to carry out scientific research. Students collect data in the laboratory or field and use computers in analyzing their data. Students make extensive use of the college's Macintosh Laboratories for both word processing and data analysis. Instructional sessions of over six hours per day include lab work, reading, writing, and computing sessions. Time is set aside for recreation. Field trips to NASA, Rubbermaid, and the Ohio Agricultural Research & Development Center provide a look at industrial science. Social and cultural events are planned. Application deadline: April 20.

❖ Exploring the Geosciences: Earth, Atmosphere, and Environment

Host School: University of Oklahoma
Type: Summer study
Location: Norman, OK
Duration: Three weeks
Dates: Middle to late July
Qualifications: Grades 9-12
The program is limited to Oklahoma residents very interested in science and mathematics.
Housing: Students live in double occupancy rooms in an air-conditioned university residence hall, supervised by adult counselors. An all-you-can-eat meal plan is provided at the university cafeteria. Students have access to the campus recreational facilities and student union.
Costs: No program costs. All expenses, including room, board, tuition, supplies, books, and field trips, are provided by grants from the Oklahoma State Regents for Higher Education. Students are responsible for transportation to and from the university and for incidental personal expenses.
Credits Given: None
Contact: Exploring the Geosciences: Earth, Atmosphere, and Environment
University of Oklahoma
Precollegiate Programs: Summer Academy
1700 Asp Avenue
Norman, OK 73037-0001
(405) 325-6897

Student participants have a unique opportunity to explore Oklahoma as seen through the eyes of three scientific disciplines: geology/geophysics, geography, and meteorology. Students take field trips to the Arbuckle and Wichita Mountains to collect geological samples, and then section and examine specimens in the laboratories. Studies involving tornadoes, lightning, hail, and climate changes along with trips to the National Severe Storms Lab and the National Weather Service Forecast Office aid in the understanding of Oklahoma's weather. The field of geography is explored through satellite images, air photos, and maps as well as field surveying. Special activities and events are planned for the evenings and weekends. Application deadline: March 1.

❖ Futures in Science

Host School:	Oklahoma State University
Type:	Summer study
Location:	Stillwater, OK
Duration:	Four weeks
Dates:	Early June to early July
Qualifications:	Grades 9 and 10
	The program is open to exceptional students interested in science and mathematics. Minority students are encouraged to apply.
Housing:	Students are housed in double rooms in supervised campus residence halls. Meals are served in adjoining cafeterias. A qualified counseling staff will chaperone and tutor participants.
Costs:	No program costs. All expenses, including room, board, tuition, books, and field trips, will be provided through a grant from the National Science Foundation. Students are responsible for their own transportation to and from campus and for personal expenses.
Credits Given:	None
Contact:	Dr. W.D. Warde
	Futures in Science
	Oklahoma State University
	301 Math Sciences
	Department of Statistics
	Stillwater, OK 74078
	(405) 744-5684

Students chosen for Futures in Science will better understand how scientists think and work and will learn about the many opportunities in the fields of science and technology. Participants gather each morning for lectures, presentations, field trips, and discussions, all designed to enrich the students' background in the sciences. Afternoons are devoted to study/laboratory experiences, with one week devoted to each of the scientific disciplines of physics, biology, and chemistry. Evening lectures by distinguished scientists, conversations with mentors, and time to work on individual research projects are also built into the program. Each participant is assigned a project to be completed during the school year. Students also participate in recreational activities. Application deadline: April 16.

❖ Apprenticeships in Science and Engineering (ASE) Program

Host School:	Saturday Academy
Type:	Internship
Location:	Sites in Oregon, dependent on placement
Duration:	Dependent upon placement
Dates:	Summer
Qualifications:	Grades 9-12

The program is limited to highly motivated high school students from Oregon and southern Washington State who are interested in participating in a scientific research experience. Selection is competitive.

Housing: Housing arrangements depend upon placement. Contact program for specific information.

Costs: No program costs. Students are paid for their work.

Contact: Dr. Bill Lamb
Apprenticeships in Science and Engineering (ASE) Program
Saturday Academy
Oregon Graduate Institute of Science & Technology
19600 NW von Neumann Drive
Beaverton, OR 97006
(503) 690-1190

Students work side by side with professional scientists and engineers, gaining inquiry skills and making real contributions to the ongoing research of their mentors. Students are placed with researchers in sites that include universities, government agencies, and private industry. The students apply for positions based on their area of interest. Recent placements have included assisting with DNA research at Oregon Health Services University and working for the US Forest Service on an archaeological dig in the Umatilla Forest. Apprentices are assigned background reading to learn about their assigned project and also participate in workshops, seminars, and leadership development activities. Students share their experiences with each other through a conference in August and through use of a computer bulletin board system. Application deadline: February 5.

❖ Hancock Natural Science Field Study and Research Program

Host School: Oregon Museum of Science and Industry/Hancock Field Station

Type: Field experience

Location: Fossil, OR

Duration: Two weeks

Dates: Late June through early July

Qualifications: Ages 14 to 18
This program is for students with interest in a field experience program focusing on the natural history, geology, and ecology of the central Oregon Cascade region.

Housing: Hancock Field Station provides A-frame cabins for students and has a dining hall, library, darkroom, and laboratories, as well as recreational facilities.

Costs: $485 for Oregon Museum of Science and Industry members; $510 for nonmembers. A limited amount of need-based financial aid is available.

Credits Given: College credits may be offered for high school juniors and seniors.

Contact: Dr. Joseph Jones
Hancock Natural Science Field Study and Research Program
Oregon Museum of Science and Industry/Hancock Field Station
1945 S.E. Water Avenue
Portland, OR 97214
(503) 797-4571

Students taking part in this program have an opportunity to participate in a series of group and individual research projects encompassing such disciplines as geology, biology, paleontology, archaeology, astronomy, and arid and alpine ecology. The program begins at the Hancock Field Station with a study of the rich geologic history and fossil wealth of the John Day Valley. From the station, participants travel to Mt. Saint Helens National Monument to study this large volcano and its varied plant and animal communities. The last two days of the program find the students back at the Hancock Field Station using computers to write up the results of their research. Time for swimming, fishing, volleyball, and campfires, along with other camping activities, is built into the program. Application deadline: May 15.

❖ Pacific Marine Science Camp & Northwest Natural Science Camp

Host School:	Oregon Museum of Science and Industry
Type:	Field experience
Location:	Sites in Oregon, dependent on program
Duration:	Six days
Dates:	Various dates, late June through August
Qualifications:	Ages 10 to 18 (Grouped by age into specific camp programs.) Students should be interested in a field experience program in marine science or environmental studies.
Housing:	This is a camp-based program. Students are responsible for their own camping equipment. Campers at Hancock Field Station live in A-frame cabins.
Costs:	$295 for OMSI members; $320 for nonmembers. Cost includes transportation, food, instruction, charter fees, scientific equipment, and numerous field trips. Limited amounts of need-based financial aid are available. Application deadline for financial aid: May 1.
Credits Given:	None
Contact:	Dr. Jeffry Gottfried
	Pacific Marine Science Camp & Northwest Natural Science Camp
	Oregon Museum of Science and Industry
	Outreach Department
	1945 S.E. Water Avenue
	Portland, OR 97214-3354
	(503) 797-4571

Based in Newport, Oregon, the Pacific Marine Science Camp of the Oregon Museum of Science and Industry (OMSI) offers students the opportunity to experience firsthand the field of marine science research. On shore, students investigate Oregon's coastline, including the intertidal zones, sand dunes, salt marshes, and the Yaquina estuary, studying the organisms and physical makeup of these marine ecosystems. Students also work aboard a research vessel, collecting specimens and performing experiments in the lower Yaquina River, and sail on the open ocean to locate a pod of California gray whales that summer along the coast. Participants get a realistic look at careers in marine science research. OMSI also offers a variety of other field-based programs for students. The Northwest Natural Science Camps are based at Hancock Field Station in central Oregon's John Day River Valley. Campers select specific disciplines such as the Astronomy Camp, the Naturalist Program, or the Geology and Fossils Program. Van-based camps take students to Mt. Saint Helens to study the volcano, while the Ancient Forests Camp participants travel from the coast to central Oregon. Application deadline: May 15.

❖ The Dan Fox Youth Scholars Institute

Host School:	Lebanon Valley College
Type:	Summer study
Location:	Annville, PA
Duration:	One week
Dates:	Two sessions: late June and mid-July
Qualifications:	Grades 10-12
	The program is open to exceptional high school students who desire a preview of college life.
Housing:	Participants live in an air-conditioned campus dormitory, supervised by the college residence-hall staff. Meals are eaten in the college dining hall. Students have access to all of the college facilities, including the recreational and athletic complex.
Costs:	$310 covers room, board, and extracurricular activities. Tuition and fees are provided by Lebanon Valley College. Limited additional financial aid is available through a grant from the Hershey Educational Foundation.
Credits Given:	None
Contact:	Mrs. Susan Greenawalt
	The Dan Fox Youth Scholars Institute
	Lebanon Valley College
	Biology Department
	Annville, PA 17003-0501
	(717) 867-6213

Students take an intensive course in one of 18 subject areas chosen from the fields of science, the social sciences, and the humanities. Science selections include classes in animal physiology, microbes and genetics, computer graphics, developmental or general psychology, sound recording technology, experimental microscopy, psychobiology, and actuarial science. Participants work closely with college faculty members and make use of the college's well-equipped science laboratories and computer rooms. Evenings and free time are devoted to supervised social events and field trips, including activities such as sports, parties, dances, movies, and an outing to Hershey Park. Students must be nominated for the program by a teacher or guidance counselor. Nomination deadline: February 19.

❖ Young Scientists Program

Host School:	University of Pittsburgh at Bradford
Type:	Summer study
Location:	Bradford, PA
Duration:	One week
Dates:	Mid-July
Qualifications:	Grades 11 and 12 and first year of college
	Talented science students interested in further explorations in science are eligible for the program.

Housing:	Students are housed in the university's apartment-style residence hall supervised by adults as well as residence hall counselors. Meals are served in the college cafeteria. Although most participants live on campus, commuting students can be included in the program and are given lunch.
Costs:	$395 for resident students, which includes science experiences, housing, meals, and recreational activities; $295 for commuting students. A limited number of full and partial scholarships are available on an as-needed basis.
Credits Given:	None
Contact:	Professor Sharon Woodruff Young Scientists Program University of Pittsburgh at Bradford Fisher Hall Room 209 300 Campus Drive Bradford, PA 16701-2898 (814) 362-7542

Students choose science experiences from offerings in five areas of science: biology, chemistry, computer science, geology, and physics. Students participate in two intensive science experiences daily. Some areas of interest include the conversion of solar energy to fuel and the mapping of the Milky Way Galaxy using radio waves. Participants also have a full program of recreational and social activities available. Application deadline: May 1.

❖ Science Quest

Host School:	Seton Hill College
Type:	Science camp
Camper Level:	Grades 6–8 (Any middle school girl interested in exploring science.)
Location:	Greensburg, PA
Duration:	One week
Dates:	Late July
Housing:	Students live in a college dormitory supervised by a resident assistant. Meals are provided.
Costs:	$300 covers the cost of tuition, room and board, and fees. Scholarships may be available.
Contact:	Science Quest Seton Hill College Office of Continuing Education Seton Hill Drive Greensburg, PA 15601-1599 (412) 838-4208

Dedicated to the premise that science is fun, Science Quest exposes middle school girls to a variety of hands-on activities. Participants are presented with a view of the many career opportunities for women in the fields of science and technology. Girls work together in a noncompetitive atmosphere, participate on a number of field trips, and meet career women actively working in a variety of scientific fields. Recreational activities include tennis, volleyball, basketball, swimming, and use of an exercise room. Participants also attend a local theater performance, hike, and picnic. Application deadline: rolling admissions.

❖ Camp Watonka

Type:	Science camp
Camper Level:	Ages 7 to 15 (Boys only.)
Location:	Hawley, PA
Duration:	Four weeks or eight weeks
Dates:	Late June through late July, and/or late July through late August
Costs:	$1,995 for four-week program. $3,850 for eight-week program. Fees are all-inclusive; the only extra is transportation to and from the camp.
Contact:	Mr. Donald Wacker
	Camp Watonka
	Box 127
	Hawley, PA 18428
	(717) 226-4779

This unique camping program combines laboratory science activities with a full traditional summer-camp recreational and sports program. Camp Watonka is located at the edge of the Pocono Mountains. Campers select up to two laboratory sciences at a time chosen from selections including astronomy, biology, chemistry, computer science, electronics, ham radio, geology, and robotics. Science programs are supervised by certified teachers. Two other activity periods each day are devoted to activities such as sailing, swimming, tennis, and windsurfing. A complete American Red Cross water program is offered on the camp's private lake. Evening programs are varied. Camp Watonka is accredited by the American Camping Association.

❖ Young Scholars Program

Host School:	Saint Vincent College
Type:	Summer study
Location:	Latrobe, PA
Duration:	Three weeks
Dates:	Late June through mid-July
Qualifications:	Grades 9 and 10
	The program is open to high-ability students, those who have achieved grades of at least 90 in science and math classes over the last two years, and high-potential students, those with grades of at least 80% in science and mathematics over the last few years who are seriously interested in science.
Housing:	Students live in double occupancy dormitory rooms, and eat in the college dining hall. Participants have access to the sports and recreational facilities on campus.
Costs:	$50 for field trips. A grant from the National Science Foundation covers tuition, room, and board. Students are also responsible for transportation to and from the college and for personal spending money. Financial aid is available.

Credits Given: None
Contact: Dr. Elizabeth Balser
  Young Scholars Program
  Saint Vincent College
  Latrobe, PA 15650-2690
  (412) 537-4569

Participants select one of three areas of study and experience hands-on, research-based science activities in their area of interest. Workshop choices include Environmental Chemistry, Computer Graphics with Software Engineering, and Physics of the Earth's Atmosphere. In each discipline, students will learn basic principles along with scientific methods and ethical standards, as they participate in extensive research and laboratory workshops. Students also may participate in an "Ethics in Science Forum" and investigate career opportunities in the sciences. Field trips and presentations by guest speakers also add to the educational component of the program. Recreational, cultural, and sports activities round out the program, and special activities and day trips occupy weekend time. Application deadline: April 16.

❖ Penn Summer Science Academy

Host School: University of Pennsylvania
Type: Summer study
Location: Philadelphia, PA
Duration: Four weeks
Dates: Mid-July through early August
Qualifications: Grades 10-12
  Students should have an outstanding academic record and the ability to do creative work.
Housing: Resident students live in three- or four-person suites, supervised by resident advisors. Meals are provided Monday through Friday. Residents have access to recreation facilities, and evening and weekend social/recreational activities are planned.
Costs: Approximately $2,350 for resident students. This includes tuition, room and board, and activity fees. Commuting students pay $1,415 to cover instructional costs, lunches, and transportation for field trips. Need-based full and partial scholarships are available.
Credits Given: None
Contact: Dr. David Reibstein
  Penn Summer Science Academy
  University of Pennsylvania
  College of General Studies
  3440 Market Street, Suite 100
  Philadelphia, PA 191044-3335
  (215) 898-5809; FAX (215) 573-2053

This challenging program allows students interested in science and math the opportunity to participate in intensive guided and independent lab projects, math projects, computer labs, and seminars by faculty. Each student chooses either a science or math concentration. The science concentration includes lab projects in environmental sciences or in molecular biology. Students in the molecular biology concentration explore topics that include molecular genetics, neurotransmitters, metabolic enzymes, and hormones. The math concentration features small-group hands-on labs on current math research topics. All students participate in seminars featuring problem solving in math and computer science (including programming languages Pascal or C), issues in science, research papers, and site visits. Application deadline: April 15.

❖ Careers in Applied Science and Technology (CAST)

Host School:	Carnegie Mellon University
Type:	Summer study
Location:	Pittsburgh, PA
Duration:	Six weeks
Dates:	Late June through early August
Qualifications:	Grade 12 or age 16
	Students should have an interest in exploring possible careers in applied science and technology.
Housing:	Precollege students are housed together in several residence halls, supervised by resident counselors. The dining plan provides 19 meals per week. Students have access to recreational, academic, cultural, and social activities on and near the campus.
Costs:	None. This program is supported by the National Science Foundation.
Credits Given:	None
Contact:	John Papinchak
	Careers in Applied Science and Technology (CAST)
	Carnegie Mellon University
	Pre-College Programs; Summer Studies Office
	5000 Forbes Avenue
	Pittsburgh, PA 15213-3890
	(412) 268-6620; FAX (412) 268-7838

The Careers in Applied Science and Technology (CAST) program is designed to expose participants to the human side of science and technology. Two central workshops stress the connections between science and life: Presenting Specialized Information helps students improve their communication skills; Science, Technology, and Society explores the interrelationships between technical and social issues. Two-week tracks allow participants to increase their laboratory research or science writing skills. A series of visits to state-of-the-art laboratories and meetings with scientists in the field broadens students' understanding of research and its place in modern life. CAST members also have access to all other extracurricular activities presented for precollege students, including sports, social, and college admissions workshops. Application deadline: May 1.

❖ Pennsylvania Governor's School for the Sciences

Host School:	Carnegie Mellon University
Type:	Summer study
Location:	Pittsburgh, PA
Duration:	Five weeks
Dates:	End of June through early August

Qualifications:	Grade 12
	The program is open to students with outstanding ability in science and math. Applicant's parents or guardians must be fulltime residents of Pennsylvania. Student may not have previously attended any of the six Pennsylvania Governor's Schools.
Housing:	Students live in the Carnegie Mellon dormitories, supervised by college student counselors, and have their meals at the university's dining facilities. Participants have access to recreational and athletic facilities of the university.
Costs:	No program costs. Full scholarships are provided to all participants covering instructional costs, supplies, room and board, and activities. Students are responsible for transportation costs to and from the university and for incidental expenses.
Credits Given:	None
Contact:	Professor Albert Caretto
	Pennsylvania Governor's School for the Sciences
	Carnegie Mellon University
	Doherty Hall 2201
	Schenley Park
	Pittsburgh, PA 15213
	Information hotline: (717) 524-5244; (412) 268-6669

This program provides outstanding students with an advanced curriculum and unique research experiences. Students take core courses including molecular biology, chemistry, physics, discrete mathematics, and computer science. Additional elective classes in astrophysics, biochemistry, nuclear chemistry, mathematics, and the philosophy of science are also offered. Students select one laboratory course from a number offered and work as a member of a research team on a project of their choice. The program also includes workshops, interaction with guest scientists, and field trips. Recreational and social activities complete the experience. Application deadline: February 12.

✦ Science & Engineering Research Academy (SERA)

Host School:	Penn State University
Type:	Internship
Location:	University Park, PA
Duration:	Four weeks
Dates:	Early to end of July
Qualifications:	Grades 11 and 12
	High-achieving or high-potential students interested in engineering, mathematics, or science are eligible for the program. Applications from minority students, women, rural, and handicapped students are strongly encouraged.
Housing:	Students are housed in supervised campus residence hall and are provided with meals.
Costs:	No program costs. The program is supported through a grant from the National Science Foundation. Students are responsible only for incidental personal expenses and transportation to and from campus.
Credits Given:	None

Contact: Dr. Robert Pangborn
          Science & Engineering Research Academy (SERA)
          Penn State University
          227 Hammond Building
          University Park, PA 16802
          (814) 863-0721; FAX (814) 863-7967

Students work in eight-person teams supervised by a practicing scientist-engineer who advises, guides, and instructs the team as they work on a research project. Students are matched in their own field of interest with teams investigating cryptography, computer vision, acoustical holograms, polymers, food technology, remote sensing, and materials research. Participants learn basic research techniques, discover how to use the library's data bases, and interact with practicing scientists and graduate students. Discussions on topics ranging from ethics to cutting-edge research to ways of paying for college provide students with valuable information needed to make career decisions. The athletic and recreational facilities of Penn State are available for student use during free time. Application deadline: March 30.

❖ W. Alton Jones Camp: Teen Expeditions
The Environmental Education Center of the University of Rhode Island

Type: Science camp
Camper Level: Ages 12 to 16 (Trips limited to specific age groups.)
Location: West Greenwich, RI
Duration: Six to ten days
Dates: July and August
Housing: Low-impact wilderness camping is practiced on expeditions.
               Campers help prepare meals.
Costs: $245 to $425, depending upon program chosen. Need-based full
               and partial camperships are available.
Contact: Mr. Joseph Blotnick
               W. Alton Jones Camp: Teen Expeditions
               Environmental Education Center
               401 Victory Highway
               West Greenwich, RI 02817-2158
               (401) 397-3304

The W. Alton Jones Environmental Center is situated on 2,300 acres of forests, lakes, and old farm lands that provide an ideal setting to study and enjoy the natural world. A variety of trips concentrate on different wilderness experiences. Campers can choose canoeing, backpacking, hiking and survival skills, both beginner and more intensive wilderness challenge trips highlighting rock climbing and low-impact camping, or a variety of waterways programs that feature canoeing and marine study. All programs begin at the base camp where campers acquire skills needed for the trip. On expedition, participants camp along the trail. The camp is accredited by the American Camping Association.

❖ Summer Science and Engineering Enrichment Program

Host School: Clemson University
Type: Summer study

Location:	Clemson, SC
Duration:	One week, two weeks, or three weeks (Length of session increases with increasing grade.)
Dates:	June and July
Qualifications:	Grades 7-12
	Students must have an IQ of at least 120 or rank in the top 10 percent of their class.
Housing:	Students are housed in double rooms at a Clemson dormitory, supervised by qualified instructors and counselors. Meals are taken in a university dining hall.
Costs:	One week: $375. Two weeks: $735. Three weeks: $975. Cost includes room and board, tuition, materials, field trips, recreational programs, insurance, and health services.
Credits Given:	None
Contact:	Dr. Spurgeon Cole
	Summer Science and Engineering Enrichment Program
	Clemson University
	310 C Brackett Hall
	Clemson, SC 29634-5105
	(803) 656-5849

Clemson offers three different types of programs depending upon grade level and interests of the students. One-week sessions, designed especially for students entering grades 7 through 9, allow students to choose two areas of study from choices that include biology, chemistry, computer science, psychology, physics and astronomy, and earth science. Two-week sessions, for students entering grades 9 through 11, present choices similar to those of the one-week sessions and also include electronics and communication skills. The three-week sessions, for the oldest students, are the most rigorous and include the basic choices as well as regular university offerings. All students take part in evening and weekend activities, small-group discussions with faculty, and career and educational guidance activities. Application deadline: May 1.

❖ Research in Science at Erskine (RISE): Scientific Application of Technology

Host School:	Erskine College
Type:	Summer study/Internship
Location:	Due West, SC
Duration:	Four weeks
Dates:	Early July through end of July
Qualifications:	Grades 10-12
	The program is open to high ability students with at least a B in high school science and math courses. Admissions are competitive.
Housing:	Students will be housed in air-conditioned dormitories on the Erskine campus. Meals are provided in the dining hall. Students have access to Erskine's lab, athletic, computer, and library facilities.
Costs:	$620 for room and board. Course fees, including tuition, lab

supplies and equipment, and field trips, are paid for by the
National Science Foundation grant. Funds are available to assist
those with financial need.

Credits Given: None
Contact: Dr. William Junkin III
RISE: Scientific Application of Technology
Erskine College
Department of Chemistry and Physics
Due West, SC 29639
(803) 379-8822

Research in Science at Erskine, RISE, funded by the National Science Foundation,
introduces its participants to the scientific applications of technology. Half of the students
concentrate on investigations in biotechnology, learning the techniques of cloning, genetic engineering, and radiotelemetry. Students use these technologies to design and
carry out investigations in genetics, plant physiology, ecology, and animal behavior. The
rest of the participants concentrate on computer interfacing, learning how to use computers to collect data and control scientific apparatus. These techniques are used in investigations in meteorology, physics, robotics, chemistry, and acoustics. Students have access
to modern equipment in the labs. Evening and weekend activities, as well as field trips,
are planned. Application deadline: May 15.

❖ HHMI High School Science Scholars Program

Host School: King College
Type: Summer study
Location: Bristol, TN
Duration: Four weeks
Dates: Early June through early July
Qualifications: Grade 12
The program is open to students interested in pursuing careers in
the sciences, mathematics, or related fields. Applicants must
have at least three years of high school mathematics and at least
one year of chemistry. Women, minorities, and disadvantaged
students are encouraged to apply.
Housing: Mainly a commuter program, on-campus housing is available only
for those participants who cannot commute to campus. Only a
limited number of students can be accommodated.
Costs: About $60 for books and supplies. The program offers stipends of
$50 per week plus free textbooks to 15 economically
disadvantaged students. Housing and meal cost for residential
students is about $375.
Credits Given: 4 college credits
Contact: HHMI High School Science Scholars Program
King College
Office of Admissions
1350 King College Road
Bristol, TN 37620-9976

The program, supported by a grant from the Howard Hughes Medical Institute (HHMI), seeks to attract talented students to careers in research and/or teaching in the fields of medicine and the biological sciences. Participants take one of three introductory laboratory science classes for college credit. Students choose an area of specialization from courses in general biology, introduction to chemistry, and introduction to computer science (Pascal). Special seminars, demonstrations, and field trips to visit area laboratories are all part of the program. Application deadline: April 1.

❖ Summer Science Program for Gifted and Talented Students

Host School:	Tennessee Technological University
Type:	Summer study
Location:	Cookeville, TN
Duration:	One week
Dates:	Two sessions: middle July and late July
Qualifications:	Grades 6-9
	Applicants must be high-ability students, either scoring high on IQ or achievement tests or having had an average of B+ or better in all subjects during the last school year.
Housing:	Boys and girls live in reserved sections of the university's dormitories under the close supervision of a resident advisor. Students are supervised 24 hours a day. Meals, with the exception of Sunday breakfast, are provided in the university's cafeteria.
Costs:	$350 includes all costs except spending money and transportation to and from Tennessee Tech.
Credits Given:	None
Contact:	Dr. Tom Willis
	Summer Science Program for Gifted and Talented Students
	Tennessee Technological University
	Department of Curriculum and Instruction
	Box 5042
	Cookeville, TN 38505
	(615) 372-3458

The program seeks to identify high-ability students who have both scientific interest and aptitude and to provide them with challenging science and computer science activities as well as an opportunity to interact with professional scientists and a stimulating peer group. Session I, for grades 6 and 7, emphasizes the major areas that explain the physical world. Lessons in computers, physics and chemistry, and math are followed up by lab investigations. The biological sciences are explored through hands-on laboratories and lecture meetings along with library research. Session II, for grades 7 through 9, is similarly structured but provides different concepts for study. Recreational activities are planned, and students have access to the university's athletic facilities. A theater trip, dinner out, and social events complete the program. Application deadline: June 1.

❖ Tennessee Governor's School for the Sciences

Host School:	University of Tennessee, Knoxville
Type:	Summer study
Location:	Knoxville, TN
Duration:	Four weeks

Dates:	Mid-June through mid-July
Qualifications:	Grades 11 and 12
	Tennessee residents only are eligible.
Housing:	Students live in a dormitory on the University of Tennessee, Knoxville, campus, supervised by resident assistants. Meals are provided.
Costs:	None. All expenses are provided by the Tennessee State Department of Education, the Alcoa Foundation, and the University of Tennessee.
Credits Given:	None
Contact:	Director
	Tennessee Governor's School for the Sciences
	University of Tennessee, Knoxville
	Suite 191 Hoskins
	Knoxville, TN 37996-4120
	(615) 974-0756

The Governor's School program seeks to provide intensive instruction in one area of science or mathematics, to teach the methods used by practicing scientists, and to expose students to current thinking in the sciences. Classes are held Monday through Friday and Saturday morning. One of the morning sessions is devoted to the art of thinking mathematically. A writing component explores writing to develop ideas and to effectively communicate them to others. Computing classes help students deal with volumes of data effectively. Afternoon sessions are devoted to intensive study in the area of students' choice; these sessions emphasize research and problem solving. Evening discussions cover philosophy, ethics, and current concerns. Social and recreational activities are also planned. Application deadline: December. Contact program for more information.

❖ Summer Resident Scholars Program

Host School:	Rhodes College
Type:	Summer study
Location:	Memphis, TN
Duration:	Two weeks
Dates:	Late June through mid-July
Qualifications:	Grades 11 and 12
	The program is open to students interested in pursuing college-level study while in high school.
Housing:	Students live in air-conditioned residence halls. Meals are served in the college cafeteria. Labs, athletic facilities, and libraries are available to the students.
Costs:	$800 includes tuition, room, board, supplies, and all extracurricular activities.
Credits Given:	2 college credits
Contact:	Ms. Beth Kamhi
	Summer Resident Scholars Program
	Rhodes College
	Director of Programs, Special Studies
	2000 North Parkway
	Memphis, TN 38112
	(901) 726-3825; FAX (901) 726-3919

Small classes involving intensive academic work along with three to four hours of out-of-class study are featured. All classes offer class study and hands-on activities in the form of labs and field trips. Students select one of the following two-credit courses: Chromosomes, Heredity, and Evolution focuses on cytogenetics, the structural basis of heredity and variation; lab studies focus on techniques used while lectures center on use. Society and the Human Condition introduces key sociological concepts and shows how they may be used to explain social phenomena such as poverty and crime. Artificial Intelligence and Robotics studies operating systems, artificial intelligence, and robotics techniques. Evening programs on multiculturalism, college admissions, and other topics round out the program. Application deadline: April 30.

❖ Minority High School Student Research Apprenticeship Program

Host School:	Tennessee State University
Type:	Internship
Location:	Nashville, TN
Duration:	Six weeks
Dates:	Late June through end of July
Qualifications:	Grade 12 and first year of college
	The program is limited to high-ability minority students—those identifying themselves as being Black, Hispanic, American Indian, Alaskan Native, or Pacific Islander/Asian. Applicants must be in the top third of their high school class with an average of B+ or better.
Housing:	Students are housed in dormitories on campus and take their meals in the campus dining facilities.
Costs:	None. Each student receives financial support of approximately $2,000. Part of this support is in the form of room and board fees.
Credits Given:	Credits are available for students who choose to take a college class.
Contact:	Dr. Robert Newkirk
	Minority High School Student Research Apprenticeship Program
	Tennessee State University
	3500 John A. Merritt Boulevard
	Nashville, TN 37209-1561
	(615) 320-3462

The program is designed to encourage students to consider careers in scientific research in a health-related field. Each participant spends six weeks conducting a research project under the guidance and direction of a faculty scientist. Students may also enroll in a class in chemistry, zoology, or psychology in addition to their involvement in laboratory research. At the conclusion of the program, each student participates in a summer science symposium. Application deadline: April 30.

❖ Young Scholars Program in Life Sciences & Biochemistry, Chemistry & Physics with Research Participation

Host School:	University of Texas, Austin
Type:	Summer study/Internship
Location:	Austin, TX
Duration:	Nine weeks
Dates:	Early June through early August
Qualifications:	Grade 12 (Some exceptional juniors may be accepted.)
	This program is for outstanding students (in the top 5 percent of their class in science and mathematics) interested in a science program that emphasizes research participation. Minorities, women, and the disabled are especially encouraged to apply.
Housing:	Students are housed in a special area of the university dormitories, supervised by counselors. Meals are provided in the university cafeterias.
Costs:	About $870 for room and board for the nine week program. No tuition or academic fees are charged to participants. Books and instructional materials are provided. Financial assistance is available for needy students to cover room and board, as are a few stipends.
Credits Given:	None
Contact:	Dr. Irwin Spear
	Young Scholars Program in Life Sciences & Biochemistry, Chemistry & Physics
	University of Texas, Austin
	Box 7640, University Station
	Austin, TX 78713-7640
	(512) 471-8630

The program seeks to present students with a look at the new frontiers of biology, biochemistry, chemistry, and physics through a program of research participation, guest lectures, course work, and field trips. During the first five weeks, students attend classes in the morning and are involved in research in the afternoon. The first week's course is interdisciplinary and for all participants; during the remaining weeks of course work, students attend classes in their selected field. Each course stresses current areas of study and includes guest lectures and computer work. After the initial five weeks, the entire day is spent in research under the guidance of a faculty mentor. Assignments are made in a variety of related fields. Cultural, recreational, and athletic facilities are available to participants. Application deadline: April 1.

❖ TAG (Talented and Gifted) Science Program

Host School:	Southern Methodist University
Type:	Summer study
Location:	Dallas, TX
Duration:	Three weeks
Dates:	Middle through end of July
Qualifications:	Grades 8-10

The program is open to talented and gifted students as demonstrated by SAT or ACT results taken as part of the five, national, talent-search programs or as independent registrants.

Housing:	Residential students live in an air-conditioned residence hall reserved for TAG students and are supervised by resident advisors who provide academic and nonacademic guidance. Boys and girls are housed on separate floors. All TAG students eat together in a university cafeteria.
Costs:	Approximately $1,520 covers the cost of tuition, room and board, recreational program, and books for residential students. Commuter students pay $1,000 for tuition and recreation and about $70 for books. A limited number of need-based partial scholarships are available.
Credits Given:	3 college credits for some courses
Contact:	TAG (Talented and Gifted) Science Program Southern Methodist University Pre-College Programs SMU Box 382 Dallas, TX 75275-0382 (214) 768-5437

Academically gifted students spend three weeks in intensive study while enjoying the intellectual stimulation of their peers. Students take two courses; some courses may be taken for college credit by selected students. Morning sessions include choices of study in computer science, mathematics, robotics, anthropology, and logic among others, while afternoons are devoted to the study of paleontology, astronomy, applied physics, medical science, or engineering and design. All courses include hands-on learning. A wide assortment of supervised cultural and recreational activities is offered in the evenings and on weekends. Intramural sports, talent shows, movies, and field trips complement the program. Application deadline: April 15.

❖ Access to Careers in the Sciences (ACES) Camps

Host School:	Texas Woman's University
Type:	Summer study
Location:	Denton, TX
Duration:	Two weeks
Dates:	Two sessions: late June to early July and middle July to late July
Qualifications:	Session 1: Grades 7 and 8; session II: Grades 9-12 The program is open to female students with a B+ or better average who are interested in career opportunities for women in the sciences.
Housing:	Students are housed in the residence halls and take their meals in the dining facilities.
Costs:	$575 includes room, board, tuition, lab fees, and field trips. Students must provide their own transportation to and from campus. An additional charge of $100 is made for the four-day field trip for 11th- and 12th-grade girls to Galveston, Texas. Limited financial aid is available.

Credits Given:	None
Contact:	Access to Careers in the Sciences (ACES) Camps
	Texas Woman's University
	Science and Mathematics Center for Women
	PO Box 22785
	Denton, TX 76204
	(817) 898-2769

Access to Careers in the Sciences (ACES) camps provide young women with the experiences necessary to make realistic career choices. In addition, participants are introduced to professional women who are successful in scientific careers and who act as role models for the participants. Scientific knowledge is gained through hands-on experiences in the fields of anatomy and physiology (through comparative dissections and experimentation), chemistry, genetics, logic, marine biology, microbiology, physics, probability and statistics, and zoology. An SAT-prep course introduces test-taking strategies and problem-solving techniques. About half of all class time is spent in the laboratory, providing extensive firsthand experience. Field trips highlight people using math and science in their jobs. Application deadline: April 23.

❖ Science and Summer at Trinity

Host School:	Trinity University
Type:	Summer study
Location:	San Antonio, TX
Duration:	Three weeks
Dates:	Late June through mid-July
Qualifications:	Grade 12
	Motivated students interested in science with a record of academic achievement are eligible for the program.
Housing:	Students are housed in Trinity's modern, air-conditioned residence halls located on its 104-acre, hilltop campus. Meals are provided at the dining halls. The university's library, computer labs, extensive recreational facilities, and Student Center are available to students.
Costs:	$1,400 includes tuition, room and board, and application and lab fees. A limited amount of need-based aid is available, particularly for minority students.
Credits Given:	None
Contact:	Dr. Charles White
	Science and Summer at Trinity
	Trinity University
	Associate Vice President for Academic Affairs
	715 Stadium Drive
	San Antonio, TX 78212-9934
	(210) 736-8201

The program offers a summer experience emphasizing an interdisciplinary approach to science and nature. The main focus is on environmental systems, specifically the aquatic systems of the Greater San Antonio area. The subject is approached from geological, biological, and chemical points of view as students, working independently and in teams with university faculty, study and compare different systems. Field observations, sample collection, laboratory analysis, and computer modeling are used to discover the factors involved in keeping these systems in dynamic equilibrium. Students learn to use such sophisticated techniques as spectroscopy and electron microscopy. Participants also have a full range of cultural, athletic, and recreational activities available, including rafting and field trips. Application deadline: April 3.

❖ High School Summer Science Research Fellowship Program

Host School:	Baylor University
Type:	Internship
Location:	Waco, TX
Duration:	Six weeks
Dates:	Early June through early July
Qualifications:	Grade 12
	Outstanding students interesting in a scientific-research experience must be nominated by their schools.
Housing:	Students are housed in the dormitories of Baylor University. They may choose one of two meal plans; one provides 20 meals per week; the other, 13 meals per week.
Costs:	$372 or $327 for the cost of the meal plan selected and $13 student fee. Students are responsible for their transportation to and from the campus. Participants are provided with housing and all instruction at no cost. A limited number of need-based stipends are available.
Credits Given:	1 college credit
Contact:	Dr. Thomas Charlton
	High School Summer Science Research Fellowship Program
	Baylor University
	PO Box 97286
	Waco, TX 76798-7286
	(817) 755-3437

During the course of this six-week fellowship program, participants are involved in ongoing research with Baylor professors and their research groups. Opportunities are available for research participation in fields that include anthropology, astronomy, biology, biochemistry, chemistry, computer science, environmental studies, geology, museum studies, nutrition, physics, and psychology. Through their involvement, students develop working relationships with scientists and other gifted students who have similar interests. Participants learn to use tools and techniques not available to them in their home schools. In addition, students participate in weekly seminars on topics focusing on the history and philosophy of science and take part in group social and recreational events. Application deadline: April 15.

❖ Keewaydin Wilderness Canoe Trips

Type:	Science camp
Camper Level:	Ages 15 to 19 (Groups may be all boys or co-ed.)
Location:	Middlebury, VT, and central Quebec
Duration:	Five weeks

Dates:	Trip dates vary throughout summer.
Housing:	Participants camp along the trail and help to prepare meals.
Costs:	Costs vary depending upon itinerary. Average cost for five-week program is about $2,650 plus plane and train fares (if applicable). A few partial-fee reductions are usually available based on need.
Contact:	Mr. Seth Gibson
	Keewaydin Wilderness Canoe Trips
	The Keewaydin Foundation
	PO Box 626
	Middlebury, VT 05753
	(802) 388-2556

Keewaydin Wilderness Canoe Trips are expeditions in central Quebec during which the campers paddle anywhere from 250 to 350 miles. The trips gather in Vermont for three days of intensive training in whitewater canoeing and portaging before busing to Canada. In Quebec, nine trippers, two leaders, and a Cree Indian guide paddle together, experiencing the challenges inherent in depending upon themselves to meet their needs, comforts, and enjoyments. The physical challenges include the winds and the rapids and portages from lake to lake; living and working together in a small group provides other challenges. The selection of rivers and trips available changes each year. Keewaydin is accredited by the American Camping Association.

❖ Summer Scholars Program

Host School:	Pacific Lutheran University
Type:	Summer study
Location:	Tacoma, WA
Duration:	Three weeks
Dates:	Early to late July
Qualifications:	Grades 11 and 12 (Occasionally, very gifted 10th-grade students are accepted.)
	The program is open to academically gifted students interested in science or writing. Most applicants rank in the top five percent of their high school class.
Housing:	Summer Scholars live in the college dormitories and eat in the dining hall. Many students find the close interaction with bright peers to be one of the most important aspects of the program.
Costs:	$900 includes tuition, room, and board. Textbooks may cost up to another $50. Limited need-based financial aid, to a maximum of $400, is available.
Credits Given:	4 college credits
Contact:	Dr. Judith Carr
	Summer Scholars Program
	Pacific Lutheran University
	Special Academic Programs
	Tacoma, WA 98447
	(206) 535-7130; FAX (206) 535-8320

Students in the Summer Scholars Program select either a science or writing workshop and become totally immersed in the subject through both morning and afternoon sessions. The focus of the science workshop may change from year to year. Selections in the past have included a natural science course on The Puget Sound Environment and a natural science class titled The Cellular and Molecular Aspects of Biological Diversity. The science course always includes lectures, class discussions, field trips, and extensive use of the laboratory. Through laboratory activities, students become familiar with various scientific techniques and with the use of standard laboratory equipment. Each student performs an independent laboratory project and presents the results in the format required for scientific journals. Application deadline: April 15.

❖ National Youth Science Camp (NYSC)

Type:	Summer study/Science camp
Location:	Near Bartow, WV
Duration:	Three and a half weeks
Dates:	Late June through late July
Qualifications:	First year of college
	Two graduating seniors from each state are chosen annually, based on academic achievements, leadership abilities, well-rounded interests, and intent to pursue a career in science or mathematics. Selection is competitive.
Housing:	Delegates live at a rustic camp near Bartow in the eastern part of West Virginia's Potomac Highlands. The camp is located within the wilderness areas of the Monongahela National Forest.
Costs:	No cost to participants. All expenses, including transportation, are provided by the National Youth Science Foundation, Inc., funded through contributions from technological corporations. Apply through school guidance counselor and the State Department of Education.
Credits Given:	None
Contact:	National Youth Science Camp (NYSC)
	National Youth Science Foundation, Inc.
	PO Box 3387
	Charleston, WV 25333
	(304) 342-3326

National Youth Science Camp (NYSC) provides a truly unique educational forum, held in a beautiful rustic camp setting in the eastern highlands of West Virginia. Scientists from across the nation present lectures on the most current topics, including the human genome project, ozone depletion, AIDS, robotics, and the fate of rain forests. Participants pursue their own research projects in the camp's laboratories and field research stations and engage in informal discussions with prominent scientists. Free time and weekends find the delegates involved in a wide range of athletic activities including fishing, rock climbing, kayaking, caving, and backpacking. A highlight of the program is a three-day trip to Washington, DC, where participants lunch with senators and tour cultural sites as well as scientific facilities such as the NASA/Goddard Space Flight Center. Application deadline: Contact program or your State Department of Education for information.

❖ Oglebay Institute Junior Nature Camp

Type: Science camp
Camper Level: Ages 11 to 15; ages 16 and 17 for Counselor in Training (CIT)
program
Location: Wheeling, WV
Duration: One week or two weeks
Dates: Early to mid-August
Housing: Housing and meals are provided at the camp.
Costs: $140 for one week; $275 for two weeks. Scholarships are awarded
as funds permit.
Contact: Mr. Ford Parker
Oglebay Institute Junior Nature Camp
Oglebay Institute
A.B. Brooks Nature Center
Wheeling, WV 26003
(304) 242-6855

Held at Camp Giscowheco, Oglebay Institute Junior Nature Camp is for those young people who love the outdoors and approach it with curiosity and interest. At this camp, each camper picks from a variety of activities including concept adventures exploring natural history, special speakers talking about the natural world, as well as all of the traditional camping activities such as swimming and campfires, birding and volleyball. On Saturday, an optional canoe trip takes campers down an exciting stretch of the Yough (short for Youghiogheny) River. This spectacular journey takes participants through a river gorge and ends with a barbecue. Theme nights add to everyone's enjoyment.

❖ Summerscience

Host School: Lawrence University
Type: Summer study
Location: Appleton, WI
Duration: Two weeks
Dates: Late June through early July
Qualifications: Grades 11 and 12
Students with a strong interest in math or science are eligible for
the program.
Housing: Students live in Lawrence University residence halls supervised by
upperclassmen who act as residence counselors. All meals are
served in the campus dining hall.
Costs: $795 includes tuition, room and board, laboratory supplies, and
recreational activities. Limited financial aid is available.
Credits Given: 2 college credits
Contact: Ms. Diana Janssen
Summerscience
Lawrence University
Special Programs Coordinator
PO Box 599
Appleton, WI 54912-9986
(414) 832-6500; (800) 227-0982

Motivated high school students are given a chance to explore topics in science and math that are not generally available in high schools. This includes advanced topics in biology, chemistry, geology, psychology, and anthropology. Interaction with Lawrence faculty and with peers with similar interests broadens students' knowledge. Participants identify preferred areas of study; independent lab work, classroom lectures, problem solving, and research assignments are all part of the academic program. Students have access to campus libraries, computer facilities, athletic complex, and science labs. Off-campus recreational activities, including river rafting, canoeing, bowling, and roller skating, are also planned. Application deadline: May 15.

❖ Science World

Type:	Science camp
Camper Level:	Grade 8 (Limited to Wisconsin public and private school students.)
Location:	Near Drummond, WI
Duration:	One week
Dates:	Six sessions: last week in June through first week in August
Housing:	Housing and meals are provided at the Field Station.
Costs:	$50 registration fee. Room and board are provided at no cost to the students. Campers are responsible for transportation to and from the camp site.
Contact:	Ms. Mary Kay York
	Science World
	Department of Public Instruction
	PO Box 7841
	Madison, WI 53707-7841
	(608) 267-9270

Sponsored by the Wisconsin Department of Public Instruction, Science World is a science camp experience for the state's students and is designed to encourage able students to take more science courses in high school and perhaps pursue a career in science. Schools nominate students to attend. Open-ended science activities developed and supervised by Master teachers are presented each day; the campers are actively involved in hands-on learning in labs and field study. Activities center around life science, physical science, earth and space science, and computer science. Campers also work in the Exploratorium, a classroom filled with over 40 experiments designed to challenge all students. Each evening, guest scientists talk to students about careers in the sciences. Recreational activities including hiking, swimming, and canoeing are also part of the camp experience. The camp is held at Pigeon Lake Field Station in the middle of the Chequamegon National Forest, a natural laboratory for intensive environmental study.

❖ Modeling Acid Deposition: An Introduction to Scientific Methods, A Young Scholars Program

Host School:	University of Wisconsin, Superior
Type:	Summer study
Location:	Superior, WI
Duration:	Five weeks
Dates:	Late June through late July

Qualifications:	Grades 11 and 12
	High-ability and high-potential students interested in science and mathematics are eligible for the program. Students must have completed classes in geometry, intermediate algebra, chemistry, and biology.
Housing:	Participants are housed in double rooms in a university dormitory. Meals are provided in the cafeteria during the week. Participants are generally responsible for their own weekend meals.
Costs:	No program costs. Grants from the National Science Foundation cover tuition, room, and weekday and some weekend meals. Students are responsible for their own transportation to and from campus. Students who successfully complete the program receive a $100 stipend. Some additional aid is available.
Credits Given:	None
Contact:	Dr. Francis Florey
	Modeling Acid Deposition: An Introduction to Scientific Methods
	University of Wisconsin, Superior
	Sundquist 334
	1800 Grand Avenue
	Superior, WI 54880
	(715) 394-8289 or 394-8321

Students are introduced to scientific methodology through participation in a project studying acid rain deposition. The program includes lecture, laboratory, and field-trip activities. Classroom lectures address relevant topics in biology, chemistry, and statistics. Laboratory work in biology and chemistry is combined with extensive computer work. Through statistical methods, small groups of participants study acid rain data and develop predictive models for acid rain. Field trips take participants to a coal-burning plant, to the Midwest Energy coal facility, and on a three-day camping trip to Vilas County to enjoy the beauty of northern Wisconsin. Recreational trips include a canoe trip, picnics, park visits, and a trip on a Lake Superior research vessel. Evening and weekend social and educational events are planned. Application deadline: April 19.

❖ Youthsummer

Host School:	University of Wisconsin, Superior
Type:	Summer study
Location:	Superior, WI
Duration:	One to four weeks
Dates:	Four one-week sessions: mid-June to mid-July
Qualifications:	Ages 13 to 18
	This program is for students interested in learning without the pressures of tests and grades.
Housing:	Students will be housed in a campus dormitory, supervised by dormitory counselors who live with students and participate in all evening activities. Weekday meals are provided; weekend meals are the student's responsibility.
Costs:	$275 per session for resident students includes course fee, all materials, housing, three meals per day for five days, and

evening activities. Weekend stays are an additional $14.
Commuters pay $150 per session. Wisconsin minority students
may qualify for full scholarships. Other limited aid is also
available.

Credits Given: None

Contact: Dr. Albert Dickas
Youthsummer
University of Wisconsin, Superior
Old Main, Room 203
1800 Grand Avenue
Superior, WI 54880-2898
(715) 394-8311 or 394-8173

Youthsummer offers students choices of five-day courses, each consisting of about 30 hours of instruction and/or lab and field experiences. Participants can select courses of interest from such offerings as Aerospace Opportunities—career exploration, aviation theory, and flight experience; Veterinary Medicine—career opportunities, ethical issues, veterinary practice; a Wilderness Science Canoe Trip—an exploration of the physical history and biological treasures of the northeastern Wisconsin area; Medical Careers— options in the field of health; botany; astronomy; and psychology. Students may attend as many of the sessions as they choose, participating in planned social and recreational events along with the academic portion of Youthsummer.

❖ Research and Engineering Apprentice Program (REAP), Academy of Applied Science

Type: Internship

Location: Nationwide

Duration: Dependent on program

Dates: Summer

Costs: No costs. REAP is funded by a grant from the U.S. Army.
Participants receive a stipend for their work.

Contact: Ms. Susan Zhender
Research and Engineering Apprentice Program (REAP)
Academy of Applied Science
1 Maple Street
Concord, NH 03301
(603) 225-2072; FAX (603) 228-0210

The Research and Engineering Apprentice Program (REAP) program was developed to give disadvantaged students and minority students the opportunity to learn firsthand about research careers in math, science, or engineering. Each student chosen works directly with a university mentor who provides guidance on day-to-day activities. Local schools nominate appropriate students who are then interviewed by the mentor. The criteria for being chosen for this program vary by opportunities available in each region. High school guidance counselors or the Academy of Applied Science can be contacted for information about opportunities for apprenticeships that are available in a particular locale. Application deadline: Contact program for information.

❖ Volunteer for Science, U.S. Geological Survey

Type: Internship
Location: Nationwide, dependent on project
Duration: Dependent on project
Dates: Available throughout the year; arranged by mutual agreement
Qualifications: This program is for people of all ages who are interested in aspects of the work done by the U.S. Geological Survey, the nation's largest earth-science research organization.
Costs: Costs vary for incidental expenses such as training, transportation, lodging, subsistence, equipment, and supplies. Some stipends are available for those expenses.
Contact: Ms. Maxine Jefferson, Program Coordinator
Volunteer for Science
U.S. Geological Survey
215 National Center
Reston, VA 22092
(703) 648-7439

Volunteers can use their talents and gain valuable experience while working in the field of earth-science research. Participants may donate their services for a few hours a day or a few days a year, or volunteer over an extended period like a summer vacation or winter break. Duties may vary according to need and personal interest; they could include assisting in geologic or hydrologic field, lab, or office projects; gathering water-quality data; performing computer and graphic analysis of data; being involved in administrative or library services; or working with map and informational services. Recorded information is available by calling (415) 329-5003 for the western region or (703) 648-7440 for all other regions. The volunteer program coordinator can be contacted for more information.

❖ Wilderness Ventures Inc.

Type: Science camp
Camper Level: Ages 13 to 18
Location: Dependent on trip
Duration: 24 to 44 days
Dates: Dates depend upon trip chosen. Trips run all summer.
Housing: Participants live in the wilderness, sleeping under the stars or in mountain tents. Campers help to prepare meals.
Costs: About $2,300 to $3,900, depending on trip chosen
Contact: Mr. Mike Cottingham
Wilderness Ventures Inc.
PO Box 2768
Jackson Hole, WY 83001
(307) 733-2122

The entire trip of a Wilderness Venture expedition is spent outdoors. Participants engage in activities such as backpacking, white-water rafting, mountain climbing, sea kayaking, or canoeing, each for several days at a time. Camp leaders seek to provide a cooperative, noncompetitive atmosphere where each individual contributes to and learns from the group experience and enhances his or her own self-confidence through direct involve-ment in challenging and rewarding activities. Participants gain an understanding of the natural world and people's effects upon it. Trips are centered in the Northwest region, the Rocky Mountains, and Alaska. Biking expeditions are also available.

❖ Wilderness Southeast Camps: Mountain Trek, Mountain Adventure, Coastal Experience, and Tropical Venture

Type:	Science camp
Camper Level:	Ages 12 to 17, depending upon program chosen
Location:	Dependent on program
Duration:	Eight to ten days
Dates:	Several sessions, beginning in early July and running through mid-August
Housing:	Dependent on program. Most programs include wilderness camping.
Costs:	Mountain Trek: $690. Mountain Adventure: $570. Coastal Experience: $545. Tropical Venture: $1,125. A limited number of partial scholarships are available.
Contact:	Mr. Ted Wesemann
	Wilderness Southeast Camps
	711 Sandtown Road
	Savannah, GA 31410
	(912) 897-5108

Mountain Trek and Mountain Adventure are wilderness backpacking experiences that emphasize safe backcountry skills and wildlife ecology learned in an atmosphere condu-cive to teamwork and fun. The programs stress ways of enjoying and protecting the environment. Participants investigate stream and forest habitats, observe wildlife, and construct and use a Native American sauna while backpacking about 30 miles over 10 days in Pisgah National Forest in western North Carolina. Mountain Trek participants also spend time learning technical rock climbing. The shorter and less rigorous Mountain Adventure program for younger campers includes a day of white water rafting. Coastal Experience campers combine camping with environmental science activities. This pro-gram begins in the labs at Skidaway Marine Institute and continues with a camping and marine study experience on a barrier island. Tropical Venture participants study the ecology of the coral reefs, tropical forest, rocky shores, and mountain tops of Tortola, in the British Virgin Islands.

❖ Foundation for Field Research: Research Expeditions

Type:	Field experience
Location:	Dependent on expedition chosen
Duration:	One or more weeks, depending on expedition chosen and desire of participant
Dates:	Dates vary throughout year, depending on project chosen
Qualifications:	Adults and students age 14 and older
	Participants have to have a desire to be an active member of a scientific research team. No other special skills are necessary.
Housing:	Volunteers need to be prepared for possible hardships in the field—

these are not disguised vacations. Base camps either have tents or are permanent research stations. Enclosed toilets and hot-water showers are provided at the camps. Meals are provided.

Costs: Each volunteer shares in the cost of the expedition. Fees for weeks after the initial week are generally much less than those for the initial week. Scholarships ranging from 10 percent to 50 percent of the cost are available.

Credits Given: Credit can sometimes be arranged with home school.

Contact: Foundation for Field Research: Research Expeditions
Foundation for Field Research
PO Box 910078
San Francisco, CA 92121
(619) 450-3460; (619) 452-6708

For people who have dreamed about trying out a career as an archaeologist, a naturalist, an oceanographer, or other environmental researcher, this is their chance! Participants join other volunteers, who have ranged in age from 14 to 86, as both a labor and a funding source for a scientific expedition. This is a hands-on experience—participants who join an archaeological expedition dig and screen; those on an oceanography expedition dive and collect specimens. The projects take place all over the world including current projects studying archaeology on a Zuni Indian Reservation; one discovering the astronomers of ancient Arizona; another saving marine turtles at Baja, California, or the giant leatherback turtles of Michoacan, Mexico; or studying the African monkeys in the Caribbean or chimps and baboons in Mali, to name just a few of those available.

❖ University Research Expeditions (UREP)

Host School: University of California, Berkeley

Type: Field experience

Location: Dependent on expedition

Duration: Two weeks

Dates: Dates vary; most programs run between May and September, depending upon chosen expedition.

Qualifications: Upper high school grades through adults
No special expertise is necessary other than curiosity, adaptability, and a willingness to share expenses and work as an active participant on a scientific expedition.

Housing: UREP expeditions are located throughout the world and accommodations vary greatly. Participants may be housed in modest hotels or in wilderness camps. Living standards and medical facilities vary from site to site. Many expeditions are physically demanding.

Costs: Each participant contributes an equal share of the costs of the expedition, ranging from about $900 to $1,500, part of which is a tax-deductible contribution to UREP. Travel costs and personal expenses are not covered. Partial student scholarships are available; scholarship application deadline: March 13.

Credits Given: None

Contact: University Research Expeditions (UREP)
University of California, Berkeley

Berkeley, CA 94720
(510) 642-6586

The University Research Expedition Program (UREP) matches people of all ages and from all walks of life with scientists from the University of California in need of assistance on field expeditions worldwide. Each participant becomes an active member of the field team and is counted on as the teams seek to answer specific questions that may have global consequences. In 1992, teams interested in animal behavior studied the monkeys of the Kenyan rain forest; archaeological teams in the South Pacific explored the ancient households of the Polynesians; and environmental teams studied global warming in northeast United States and Canada and the biodiversity of the dry tropical forest in Costa Rica. Fields of study include archaeology, environmental studies, paleontology, and the social sciences.

❖ Earthwatch Expeditions: EarthCorps Volunteers

Type: Field experience
Location: Worldwide, dependent on project
Duration: Dependent upon project and dates chosen
Dates: Year round
Qualifications: Participants are usually adults, but high school students are welcome.
No special skills are needed besides a willingness to work and learn.
Housing: Housing varies depending upon project chosen and its location. Field conditions are described in the magazine and in more detail in the Expedition Briefings that can be ordered about each available expedition.
Costs: Fees vary depending upon project chosen. All costs for the participant are included in the fee, except for transportation to and from the staging area. Competitive grants to offset costs are available to high school students. Write for information.
Credits Given: Through prior arrangements, schools may grant credit for these experiences.
Contact: Earthwatch Expeditions: EarthCorps Volunteers
Earthwatch
680 Mount Auburn Street
PO Box 403
Watertown, MA 02272-9924
(617) 926-8200; (800) 776-0188

EarthCorps volunteers participate as members of scientific expeditions based all over the world that study a full range of environmental issues. Each participant helps to fund the project chosen through his or her participation fees. Programs currently in operation include a glaciological study in Russia, a coastal hydrology study in Florida, flood control in the Negev Desert in Israel, an archaeological study in Greece, and a study of ice age mammoths in South Dakota, as well as others too numerous to mention. The Earthwatch Magazine describes current expeditions as well as procedures for joining. These are scientific expeditions, not tours, and participants must be prepared for a range of conditions.

❖ International Mathematics and Science Summer Institute, International Educational Network

Type:	Summer study
Location:	Long Island, NY, and Washington, DC, and/or Moscow and St. Petersburg, Russia
Duration:	Three weeks in Long Island with an optional six days in Washington, DC, or four weeks in Russia
Dates:	New York: end of June to mid July; Washington, DC: middle of July; Russia: early July through early August
Qualifications:	Grades 10-12
	The program is open to students interested in both science and cultural exchange.
Housing:	Students live on the campus of LaSalle Academy in Oakdale, Long Island, NY, and at Georgetown University in Washington, DC. In Moscow, participants live at Moscow State University.
Costs:	$1,825 for Long Island portion. $495 for optional Washington trip. $1,975 for Moscow-St. Petersburg portion. This does not include New York-to-Moscow roundtrip airfare of approximately $1,100. Some partial financial aid is available.
Credits Given:	None
Contact:	Dr. Edward Lozansky
	International Mathematics and Science Summer Institute
	International Educational Network
	3001 Veazey Terrace, NW
	Washington, DC 20008
	(202) 362-7855; FAX (202) 364-0200

In a unique program sponsored by the International Educational Network in cooperation with the National Science Teachers Association, the Russian Academy of Sciences, and sponsoring universities, 35 U.S. and 35 international students participate in an educational, scientific, cultural program in either the United States or Russia. The U.S. session begins in Oakdale, Long Island, New York and includes morning classes in either mathematics or physics problem solving or in molecular biology, followed by lectures by American and Russian scientists and mathematicians, visits to labs, cultural exchanges, and social events. An optional six-day program offers a cultural visit to Washington, DC. In Russia, students take classes (in English) at Moscow State University and tour historical sites. A five-day cultural program in St. Petersburg follows. Application deadline: May 15.

❖ International Summer Science Institute

Host School:	Weizmann Institute of Science
Type:	Summer study/Internship
Location:	Rehovot, Israel
Duration:	One month
Dates:	Early July through early August
Qualifications:	First year of college (Participants come from the United States, Europe, Asia, South America, and Israel.)
	This program is for excellent science students interested in working

alongside top researchers as well as learning something about life in Israel today. All instruction is in English.

Housing: Participants live at a special campus on the Institute grounds. Meals are provided at the Institute restaurants. Libraries, computer center, and recreational facilities of the Institute are all available to the participants.

Costs: $2,850 includes room and board, tuition, and tours. It does not include transportation to and from Israel. Over the past four years, all U.S. students accepted for the program have received full scholarships.

Credits Given: None

Contact: Ms. Margaret Brewer
International Summer Science Institute
Weizmann Institute of Science
American Committee for the Weizmann Institute of Science
51 Madison Avenue, Suite 117
New York, NY 10010
(212) 779-2500

A unique opportunity is provided students that enables them to spend three weeks at the Institute, participating in lectures and laboratories. Students may study biology, chemistry, physics, computer science, or mathematics. The laboratory work centers on current research topics, including cancer, laser applications, and computer modeling. Each participant chooses a subject of interest and works in a small research group; at the conclusion of the program, each participant presents a seminar on the work done. At the end of the initial three weeks, the group moves to a field school in the Negev, a desert in southern Israel, where students focus on methods of field inquiry. Social activities, tours, and discussions are part of the program. Applications are available in November. Application deadline: March 1.

❖ Sci-Tech: Technion's International Science and Technology Research Program

Host School: Technion—Israel Institute of Technology
Type: Research
Location: Technion City, Haifa, Israel
Duration: One month
Dates: Mid-July through mid-August
Qualifications: High school students ages 16 and 17
Science-oriented students who have demonstrated an exceptional interest in science and technology are eligible for the program.
Housing: Students live in dormitories on the Technion campus and take meals in the university dining rooms. All food is strictly kosher.
Costs: $2,000 includes room and board, tuition, and tours. Health insurance and transportation to and from Israel are not included. Partial scholarships are available.
Credits Given: None
Contact: Ms. Elissa Lieberman
Sci-Tech: Technion's International Science and Technology Research

Technion—Israel Institute of Technology
American Society for Technion
810 Seventh Avenue, 24th floor
New York, NY 10019
(212) 262-6200; FAX (212) 262-6155

The Technion, Israel's first university, educates about 70 percent of all Israeli-trained scientists and engineers. Situated in the Carmel mountain range, the campus overlooks the Bay of Haifa and the lower Galilee. Each summer, 80 students from the United States, Europe, Asia, and Israel come together for a scientific research program. Groups of two to four students carry out research projects under the supervision of faculty members. Project areas include robotics, aerospace, CAD/CAM, cryptography, neural networks, industrial psychology, chaos, lasers, superconductivity, and biomedical engineering, among other choices. Seminars by Technion faculty address cutting-edge topics in science. Visits to historic sites and recreational and sports activities round out the experience. Application deadline: March 1.

CHAPTER 2

Academic Year Adventures

A wide variety of science programs awaits students during the academic school year. The experience gained from these programs can greatly expand students' understanding of science as it is practiced in the real world. Academic year programs are especially important for those students whose home schools provide limited exposure to hands-on science.

Academic year adventures may take various forms. In this chapter, the programs are grouped under general headings, each of which presents students with interesting opportunities for learning:

Internships

Enrichment Classes

Distance-learning Opportunities

Volunteer Involvement

School-break Programs

Specialized Science Schools

A word of caution first: Students contemplating involvement with an academic year experience need to realize that the time to participate in these programs must be carved out of the student's already busy week. Good time-management skills are necessary to juggle school work with extracurricular, social, and recreational as well as science activities. Is it worth it? For those interested in science and possibly in a career in science and/or technology, making time for academic year programs will pay off handsomely in terms of both experience and knowledge gained.

INTERNSHIPS

Internships provide the most intensive of all hands-on experiences. During an internship, the student is paired with a mentor, generally a research scientist or engineer. The mentor provides guidance, advice, and support to the student. Often, the student joins an established research team and studies one segment of an ongoing research project. Alternatively, the student can initiate his or her own study and work independently on a project; the student relies on the mentor for guidance as needed. Research projects generally involve library research as well as laboratory experimentation. Usually, students use their mentor's laboratory facility to conduct their studies.

How does a student get involved in a science internship? Often, the student's home school will have an established internship program. The school may participate in organized programs, such as those sponsored by "Executive High School Internships of America," or it may have established its own community-based program. A student should consult a science teacher or a guidance counselor for help in becoming involved in a high school's program.

Mentors for school-based programs are usually found through college and university contacts and by association with local industries and nearby science laboratories. Regional hospitals, national laboratories, and professional career organizations also serve as a source of mentors. School-sponsored internships provide students with more than just an intensive science experience. Participants also have the advantage of receiving high school credit as well as released time for their research investigations. Schools often sponsor a symposium in which student interns share their research findings with their peers and may facilitate entrance into science competitions, such as Westinghouse Science Talent Search and Science Fair. If a school does not offer a science internship program, a student might place a call to the Science Supervisor at the State Board of Education or contact the science coordinator for his or her school district for help in locating a local internship. A young woman or a member of an underrepresented minority group can check with the appropriate local organization to see if they sponsor internships for members. Many groups, such as the Mid-America Consortium for Engineering and Science Achievement (MACESA), provide student internship opportunities. (See Appendix A for more information about opportunities for women and minorities.) Local chapters of professional organizations such as medical and dental societies, the American Chemical Society, and professional engineers' groups as well as regional organizations such as 4-H and environmental concerns may also support student research participation programs. The American Academy for the Advancement of Science or the National Academy of Science may be able to provide the names of local affiliates who might sponsor such a program. The volunteer coordinator of local hospitals, animal welfare organizations, health agencies, or the U.S. Geological Survey may also know about programs in the student's field of interest. Still another alternative is to check with regional laboratories and research facilities. Private industry is another source of internships; IBM, through its "Problem-solving Project Mentor's Program," provides mentors, a laboratory site, and materials for student research.

Students can also initiate their own studies. They can read articles in scientific journals that address their field of interest and, if possible, write to the author and express that interest. Often, researchers are happy to encourage young people who share their interest and can serve as sources of advice and support even if they are located far away from a student's home. Long-distance mentorships can be established with student and mentor communicating through letters, phone calls, or electronic mail. Alternatively, the scientist may know of other researchers working on similar projects who are geographically close to the student.

When taking part in an internship, it is very important that both the student and mentor be realistic in their expectations about the relationship. Students should expect to be at the research site at the agreed-upon times and to conduct themselves in a business-like manner. Students can be expected to contribute to the ongoing work of the laboratory. Often, the student's research project is an offshoot of the central work being pursued by the mentor. Internships provide a firsthand look at the life of a research scientist. Taking part in an internship relationship is perhaps the best way for a student to know if a career in scientific research is right for him or her.

ENRICHMENT CLASSES

Although some high schools offer an array of science electives, many schools provide only the basic sciences courses including biology, chemistry, physics, earth science, or marine biology. Larger high schools may also offer special elective courses including advanced placement courses as well as specialized electives like bioethics, forensic medicine, or oceanography. To supplement the classes available at their home schools, students might consider participating in alternative study opportunities.

Local colleges and universities often allow qualified students to take college-level courses through dual high school/college enrollment. In addition, these institutions may provide special workshops like those offered by the West Virginia School of Osteopathic Medicine on Cholesterol Determination or the Aquatic Studies Field Day provided by Southwest Texas State University. Still others provide hands-on sessions for secondary school students such as the Saturday Academy of Bennett College.

In a similar vein, area museums and science centers may offer short courses and intensive workshops in specialized areas. Museums may also provide special services like the Science Kit Rentals available through the Boston Museum of Science or provide opportunities for science research participation.

DISTANCE-LEARNING OPPORTUNITIES

Distance learning provides still other opportunities to enrich a student's science experiences. The Boston Museum of Science offers a unique "Science-by-Mail" program linking student teams with volunteer scientist pen pals. The scientists provide encouragement and advice to small groups of students attempting to find solutions to a scientific challenge. This program can be initiated through schools or individual teachers or may be organized by parents or youth group leaders. More technologically advanced programs can be found through the use of interactive (two-way) communication via computers and modems or through interactive television. Students with access to a system such as Internet can set up communication with scientists throughout the world or may use the data base to search out information on their field of interest.

Access to a satellite dish provides still more opportunities for distance learning. Talcott Mountain Science Academy in Avon, Connecticut, has initiated several distance-learning programs, including "On Shoulders of Giants," which presents eminent scientists explaining their work. Even those young people who only have access to regular television can broaden their base of knowledge through offerings on network television and PBS. In recent seasons, ongoing PBS programs have included "Scientific American's Frontiers" and "The New Explorers," profiling scientists working at the cutting edge of discovery.

VOLUNTEER INVOLVEMENT

Students can get firsthand experience in science through volunteer work with community-based or national organizations. Environmental groups such as Greenpeace and Earthwatch welcome student volunteers. Besides providing these organizations with much-needed help, students meet other members who share similar interests and have an opportunity to develop a network of professional supporters. Students may also draw on the knowledge and experience of professional scientists through student membership in area chapters of career organizations such as the American Medical Association, horticultural clubs, or engineering societies. The U.S. Geological Survey also has openings for student volunteers interested in the earth sciences.

SCHOOL-BREAK ADVENTURES

Vacation periods and long weekends during the school year provide time for more intensive science experiences. A number of universities and science institutes offer short science workshops and courses during winter or spring break. The Oregon Museum of Science and Industry offers school-vacation adventure camps; the Chewonki Foundation provides challenging wilderness experiences for students interested in nature/ecology. Other wilderness adventure programs and field experience programs listed in the index also offer school-break trips.

SPECIALIZED SCIENCE SCHOOLS

For even more exposure to science during the academic year, students can take advantage of available school-associated programs that run from less than a week to fulltime. Programs such as Newfound Harbor Marine Institute in Big Pine Key, Florida, and the Environmental Education Programs at the Central Wisconsin Environmental Station can provide intensive field experiences to school groups. Active archaeological digs often offer school-year programs to organized groups. The Fernbank Science Center provides quarter-year programs for selected students from the DeKalb, Georgia, school system. To participate in such a program, a student should first check out local options. If there are no local programs that meet a student's needs, he or she might choose to take part in a residential program like the Chewonki Foundation's "Maine Coast Semester." This program provides high school students with a challenging, semester-long, environmentally based high school curriculum.

A final alternative for the academic year is to attend a school that specializes in science education. Science-oriented middle schools and high schools provide all required subjects along with an extensive array of science classes and electives. Since the focus of these schools is science, the classes are more likely to be hands-on and to offer experiences with instrumentation and modern technology. Science schools like the Bronx High School of Science are generally research-oriented and may require students to be involved in their own scientific investigations. Bronx Science has, for many years, been a leader and innovator in science education in the United States.

More recent additions to the science school ranks have come about through the development of magnet schools. Magnets were originally conceived as a way of achieving racial integration by offering special programs at neighborhood schools that served minority students. The creation of a technologically advanced, science-oriented program at these schools attracted the children of the more affluent, white middle class. Today, magnet schools may be built in any area and serve children through the school district. The High School for Science and Engineering in Ft. Worth, Texas, and the MAST (Maritime and Science/Technology) Academy in Miami, Florida, are two examples of successful science magnet schools.

Attending a magnet school or a specialized school like the Bronx High School of Science provides many positive benefits for science-oriented students. These young people are actively encouraged to consider careers in the sciences and engineering and are more likely to come in contact with professional scientists who serve as role models. The schools generally have access to the most modern technology and actively encourage scientific inquiry. Students are also more likely to be kept aware of opportunities available to them for precollege programs. There are some drawbacks to attending a science-oriented school, however. There is usually less elective opportunity for students who discover that science is not their field of choice and less exposure to non-science-oriented programs and activities. On balance, though, these schools do graduate young people who are better qualified to succeed in a technologically advanced society.

The listings that follow include a representative sample of programs that operate during the academic year. In addition to those listed, many wilderness expeditions provide school trips, even designing custom trips for specific groups. Minority organizations and women's groups also sponsor school-year activities (see listings in Appendix A). The listings are arranged alphabetically by state.

❖ U.S. Space Academy

Sponsor:	U.S. Space and Rocket Center
Type:	School-break science camp
Location:	Huntsville, AL
Qualifications:	Programs are available for middle-school and high school students interested in learning about career possibilities in the field of aerospace science. This is the program for young people who dream about becoming an astronaut.
Dates/Duration:	Five to eight days in length. Several different programs are presented throughout the calendar year and are designed for students with different levels of knowledge.
Housing:	Program participants are housed in the Space Habitat Complex or on the campus of the University of Alabama. Campers are fully supervised at all times. Meals are provided in the dining facilities.
Costs:	$525 to $650 for Space Camp level I; $725 for Space Camp level II; $525 to $650 for Aviation Challenge. Costs are determined by time of year and duration and type of program chosen.

Credits Given: None
Contact: U.S. Space Academy
    U.S. Space and Rocket Center
    One Tranquility Base
    Huntsville, AL 35807
    (800) 63-SPACE

The U.S. Space Academy presents two levels of Space Camp, as well as a program called Aviation Challenge. Each camper takes part in a simulated space shuttle mission and gets hands-on experience along with academic knowledge. Space Camp, level I, participants experience the excitement of astronaut training, learning about shuttle operations and equipment, mission control operations, and the jobs of each member of a shuttle mission. Space Camp level II campers choose a scientific track to study; choices include technology, engineering, and aerospace. Technology students design and conduct shuttle experiments; engineering students receive training in extra-vehicular activities. Students in both of these areas participate in entry-level scuba training. The aerospace students train in space-shuttle piloting and mission-control activities. The Aviation Challenge program is patterned on actual, military, jet-pilot programs.

❖ A Hands-On Archaeological Experience

Sponsor: White Mountain Archaeological Center
Type: School-break field experience
Location: St. Johns, AZ
Qualifications: People of all ages interested in archaeology may attend, whether individuals, family groups, school groups, or special interest clubs.
Dates/Duration: Programs range from day trips and overnight visits to week-long field experiences. Available from mid-April through mid-October.
Housing: Bunkhouse lodging and meals are provided on-site for multi-day programs. RV and tent camping as well as motel accommodations are also available nearby.
Costs: Day rates: Students (to age 17)–$24; adults–$42. Includes program and lunch.
    Overnight rates: Students–$44; adults–$66. Includes lodging, meals, and program.
Credits Given: None
Contact: A Hands-On Archaeological Experience
    White Mountain Archaeological Center
    HC 30
    St. Johns, AZ 85936
    (602) 333-5857

White Mountain is operated as an archaeological field school and is dedicated to the research, preservation, and protection of prehistoric Southwest Indian sites. Current excavation takes place at the Raven Site Ruin, a five-acre site overlooking the Little Colorado River. Artifacts at this site are from the Mogollon and Anasazi Indian cultures and date back over 800 years. Participants help in excavation, working alongside professional archaeologists as they analyze, document, and restore the sites. Visitors hike or ride horseback into the canyons to survey and explore the surrounding area to better understand how the total environment was used by the prehistoric cultures living in the area. Some participants may choose to restore prehistoric ceramics, while others are adept at finding new petroglyph areas. Those visitors who stay for a week or more receive intensive archaeological field responsibilities and may choose to participate in more laboratory restorations. Staff archaeologists present evening lectures describing work in which they have been engaged or explain archaeological techniques. This is a good experience for students considering careers in archaeology.

❖ The Astronomy Camp of Steward Observatory

Sponsor:	University of Arizona
Type:	School-break and specialized science school programs
Location:	Tucson, AZ
Qualifications:	School groups
Dates/Duration:	Programs and dates are by special arrangement during the school year.
Housing:	Dormitory housing and meals can be provided by the program.
Costs:	Costs are arranged depending upon length and type of program desired.
Credits Given:	None
Contact:	Don McCarthy
	The Astronomy Camp of Steward Observatory
	University of Arizona
	Steward Observatory
	Tucson, AZ 85721
	(602) 621-4079

Steward Observatory offers an astronomy experience to students both during the summer and during the school year. Academic-year programs are by special arrangement and are designed to meet the needs of the participants. Opportunities available at the Observatory include the operation of large telescopes to explore planets, stars, and galaxies. Students can learn about computers, optics, and engineering as they use the tools of professional astronomers. Interaction with professors, astronomy students, and researchers, coupled with field trips, guest lectures, and demonstrations, provide participants with a firsthand understanding of the field of astronomy.

❖ Talcott Mountain Academy of Science, Mathematics, and Technology

Sponsor:	Talcott Mountain Science Center
Type:	Specialized science school
Location:	Avon, CT
Qualifications:	This school is for "intellectually excited" students in grades 4–8. Students at the Academy demonstrate overall above-average ability, are frequently academically advanced, and enjoy challenging learning experiences. More than 80 percent have qualified as seventh graders for the Johns Hopkins University Talent Search.
Dates/Duration:	Regular school year
Costs:	Contact Talcott Mountain for information.

Credits Given: School year credits for grades 4–8
Contact: Dr. Donald LaSalle
Talcott Mountain Academy of Science, Mathematics, and
Technology
Talcott Mountain Science Center
Montevideo Road
Avon, CT 06001
(203) 677-0035

Talcott Mountain Academy seeks to prepare students for "a full, productive life in a technologically oriented world." The program is designed to encourage the development of problem solving, creativity, and critical-thinking skills. A full range of academic courses are presented at the Academy. Science, mathematics, and technology are approached through hands-on investigations using the facilities of Talcott Mountain Science Center, including laboratories, observatories, and a planetarium. Students learn to use programming languages, software, interactive CDs, and videodiscs as part of the computer curriculum. Language arts and social studies curricula promote literacy and provide experience with all forms of communication, as well as an understanding of economic, social, political, and geographic changes. Art, music, physical science, and health complete the curricula offerings. Enrichment courses, clubs, and extracurricular activities are also offered.

❖ Talcott Mountain Science Center Programs

Sponsor: Talcott Mountain Science Center
Type: Enrichment classes for students, teachers' workshops, interactive
distance-learning programming, consultant services, and a
variety of other programs
Location: Avon, CT
Qualifications: Programs are open and available for any students, teachers,
individual schools and school districts.
Dates/Duration: Programs are offered periodically throughout the school year and
during the summer.
Costs: Costs depend upon programs and services chosen.
Credits Given: Depends upon programs chosen.
Contact: Dr. Donald LaSalle
Talcott Mountain Science Center Programs
Talcott Mountain Science Center
Montevideo Road
Avon, CT 06001
(203) 677-8571

The Talcott Mountain Science Center is a nonprofit, educational and research facility that provides programs dedicated to helping students better understand their physical world. Science enrichment classes for students in grades K through 12 are offered each day at the Science Center. Students receive instruction in areas that include astronomy, chronobiology, geology, meteorology, and space communications. Special programs for gifted students are also available. Evening classes are open to students from grade 5 to adult. The Center also provides teacher training in the form of workshops and inservice training. Schools and school districts may avail themselves of services that include consultation, speakers, educational curricula, and innovative videotapes. SCISTAR, interactive educational television, is a program of Talcott Mountain that links teachers and students all across the nation with eminent scientists working at the cutting edge of science. Through this program, students learn about the latest developments in science long before they are reported in texts. Project PROMMISE, supported by a grant from the National Science Foundation, focuses on role models for female and minority middle school students. This project includes videotapes, curriculum support materials, teacher training workshops, and a computer network to provide interactive support. Contact the Center for more information.

❖ Science Demonstration Program

Sponsor: National Air and Space Museum
Type: Parttime employment
Location: Washington, DC
Qualifications: The program is limited to students residing in Washington, DC; Virginia; or Maryland. Students must be available to work six hours per week (weekends or weekdays) and be able to demonstrate to visitors that science can be fun. Students must be enthusiastic about science and possess good communications skills.
Dates/Duration: Positions available during the academic year and/or summer vacations.
Costs: No program costs. Beginning Demonstrators are paid $6.75 an hour. The rate increases to $8.50 per hour with experience.
Credits Given: None
Contact: Christopher Stetser
Science Demonstration Program
National Air and Space Museum
Education Division
6th and Independence Avenue, SW
Washington, DC 20560
(202) 786-2106

The National Air and Space Museum recruits enthusiastic high school and college students from the metropolitan Washington, DC, area to work as Science Demonstrators. Applicants need to be good communicators and able to present material in a way that is both informative and fun for visitors. Work schedules are flexible. The Science Demonstrators have an opportunity to really get to know the Air and Space Museum.

❖ STT (Scientific Tools and Techniques) Independent Study Program

Sponsor: Fernbank Science Center
Type: Specialized science school: Intensive science and math study program. The Independent Study Program is an enrichment program.
Location: Atlanta, GA
Qualifications: Grades 9 and 10
Students must be enrolled in the DeKalb County, Georgia, School

System. Competitive selection is based on grades, recommendations, scores on the CAT, extracurricular activities that indicate an interest in science, and a personal statement from the applicant.

Dates/Duration: Students selected for STT (Scientific Tools and Techniques) spend one-quarter of the school year studying at Fernbank for 9 A.M. to 2:15 P.M. Subjects not available at Fernbank are provided by the home schools. The Independent Study Program serves DeKalb, Georgia, high school students who choose from enrichment classes offered during the fall, winter, and spring quarters.

Costs: No cost to the students. Transportation to and from the students' home schools is provided along with lunch.

Credits Given: 25 quarter hours of science and mathematics credits can be earned in the STT program. The Independent Study Program also carries credit.

Contact: STT (Scientific Tools and Techniques)
Fernbank Science Center
156 Heaton Park Drive, NE
Atlanta, GA 30307
(404) 378-4311

Fernbank offers a rigorous program in the fundamentals of science and mathematics to interested, qualified, high school students. Students are given the opportunity to develop the skills of inquiry, creativity, and critical analysis. Math classes range from algebra I to advanced geometry; 5 quarter hours of credit in math can be earned. The physical sciences offered include astronomy, aerospace, chemistry, geology, meteorology/seismology, and physics; students earn 15 quarter hours of credit. Students may also earn 10 quarter hours of credit in the life sciences, choosing from courses that include animal and plant ecology, electron microscopy, microbiology, ornithology/ethology, and physiology. Students are provided with individualized laboratory materials and make extensive use of the 19,000 science volumes in the Fernbank library. Field trips are also a part of the STT Program. The Independent Study Program provides other students with the opportunity to investigate specific areas of science that are of interest to them. Advanced Placement courses in chemistry and physics, Physical Sciences Study Committee (PSSC) Physics, and specialized classes in animal behavior, scanning electron microscopy, aeroscience, astronomy, and coastal studies are but a few of the choices available.

❖ Wilderness Adventures

Sponsor: Wilderness Southeast
Type: School-break wilderness trips
Location: Dependent on trip
Qualifications: Trips are open to students, families, or individual adults who desire a wilderness experience.

Dates/Duration: Trips are scheduled throughout the calendar year. Special dates can be arranged for group trips of 12 to 16 participants. Contact Wilderness Southeast for information.

Costs: From $310 to nearly $2,000, depending upon duration and destination. A scholarship program offers financial assistance to people of all ages who would otherwise be unable to join one of the wilderness adventures. Call to request a scholarship application.

Credits Given: None

Contact: Wilderness Adventures
Wilderness Southeast
711 Sandtown Road
Savannah, GA 31410-1019
(912) 897-5108

Founded in 1973, Wilderness Southeast is a nonprofit, outdoor-education school. It specializes in natural history through wilderness camping trips that provide participants with a firsthand look at some remarkable ecosystems. Small groups of individuals under the direction of naturalist guides practice minimal impact camping as they experience a break from life's daily hustle and bustle. The classrooms of Wilderness Southeast range from the Okefenokee Swamp to the Great Smoky Mountains to the Amazon Basin. Participants may enjoy, for example, a five-day canoe trip in the Okefenokee Wilderness of Georgia and Florida, spend ten days hiking or backpacking in the jungles of Costa Rica, travel by riverboat on the Rio Negro in the Amazon Basin of Brazil, snorkel in the Bahamas or the Virgin Islands, or hike the Great Smokies of North Carolina. Wilderness Southeast handles all the logistics and provides staff, camping gear, and food.

❖ The Chewonki Foundation Wilderness Trips

Sponsor: The Chewonki Foundation

Type: School-break wilderness trips

Qualifications: Students interested in a challenging wilderness experience and in nature/ecology.

Dates/Duration: Trips are held at different times during the school year and vary in length from three to ten days.

Costs: $120 to $675, dependent on trip. Any needed airfare is additional. Some limited scholarship aid may be available.

Credits Given: None

Contact: Dick Thomas
The Chewonki Foundation Wilderness Trips
The Chewonki Foundation
Wiscasset, ME 04578
(207) 882-7323; FAX (207) 882-4074

The Chewonki Foundation offers for teens and adults coed wilderness adventures that provide participants with an appreciation for nature in all its forms. A variety of unusual experiences are offered during the school year. One weekend trip to northern Maine and New Hampshire finds participants snowshoeing, skiing, and learning winter camping skills while living in the comfort of a yurt; this trip is also available for an extended time during school vacation. On another offering, campers spend eight days canoeing the Okefenokee Swamp in southeastern Georgia. Students on this trip get to experience the back country, living in the realm of alligators and sandhill cranes, while camped on wooden platforms above the swamp. Canoe trips are available on the St. John River, the Allagash Wilderness Waterway, and on the west branch of the Penobscot River in Maine. Participants on all of these adventures spend their days paddling, exploring, and discovering wildlife. Still another trip finds its participants camping on secluded islands and sailing along the coast of Maine.

❖ The Maine Coast Semester

Sponsor: Chewonki Foundation
Type: Specialized science school
Location: Wiscasset, ME
Qualifications: Capable and motivated high school students who want to spend one-half of their junior year in a challenging college preparatory program held in a unique living and learning environment.
Dates/Duration: Two sessions are held each year. The fall semester runs from early September to mid-December. The spring semester begins in late January and runs through the end of May.
Costs: $8,250 per semester for tuition, room, and board. Another $400 covers the cost of books, travel, entertainment, and personal supplies. Financial aid is available.
Credits Given: One semester of high school credit
Contact: Scott Andrews
The Maine Coast Semester
Chewonki Foundation
Wiscasset, ME 04578
(207) 882-7323

Student participants in the Maine Coast Semester use their surroundings, including pine forest, farm pasture, and a tidal estuary, for an exploration of the relationship between people and their environment. The goal of the program is to give students the skills they need to effect change in the way people understand and use their environment. Thirty students and nine faculty members share responsibility for all aspects of the program, including working the farm, cutting wood, cooking food, and maintaining the facilities. Students are encouraged to think creatively and to approach problems from an interdisciplinary point of view. The core curriculum, English and Natural Science, focuses on the interrelationships between people and their world. Courses in American history, foreign language, and mathematics parallel those of honors level classes from the sending schools. Optional classes in Art and the Natural World and in Environmental Issues and Ethics are also available. College counseling and advising plus necessary college admissions testing are available to participants. Application deadline: March 1.

❖ Science-By-Mail

Sponsor: Boston Museum of Science
Type: Distance-learning opportunity
Qualifications: Grades 4–9
Dates/Duration: The program consists of three mailings during the school year. Actual work on the challenges takes as much or as little time as students and/or teachers wish to devote to it.
Costs: $44 for the school year for all materials for a team of four students.
Credits Given: None
Contact: Science-By-Mail
Museum of Science
Science Park
Boston, MA 02114-1099
(617) 589-0437; (800) 729-3300

In an innovative, international, science-outreach program, volunteer scientists are teamed with small groups of school children as the children attempt to creatively solve scientific challenges. Science-By-Mail sends challenge packets to teams of four students three times during the school year. The packets include background information about that month's subject (photography, cartography, and simple machines were the subjects of recent mailings), activities, puzzles, and a central problem. The student groups work on activities included as they attempt to solve that mailing's "Big Challenge." If they need expert advice, they can correspond with their scientist pen pal. Teachers act as coaches; parents can also serve in this role if the program is used as an extracurricular activity. Solutions to problems are sent to the volunteer scientist; they may be presented in writing, on videotape, or in any other form the students desire. The volunteer scientists have a chance to share their enthusiasm with young minds while students, teachers, and parents gain a new perspective on science. Everybody wins! Application deadline: November 1.

❖ Marine Labs

Sponsor:	University of New Hampshire
Type:	Specialized science school field experience
Location:	New Hampshire coast
Qualifications:	Grades 7–12
	This program is for school groups interested in exploring the marine habitat.
Dates/Duration:	The Great Bay Living Lab is a four-hour program presented during the last week in September and the first week in October. The three-hour Coastal Floating Lab is held twice a day during May.
Costs:	$280 per school group of 25 students and 2 or more adults.
Credits Given:	None
Contact:	Marine Labs
	University of New Hampshire
	Sea Grant Extension Program
	Kingman Farm
	Durham, NH 03824
	(603) 749-1565

The Sea Grant Extension of the University of New Hampshire presents several programs designed to increase the sensitivity of middle school and high school students towards the marine environment and to expose students to the possibilities of careers in marine science. The Great Bay Living Lab includes a tour of the university's Jackson Estuarine Laboratory, a research cruise on Great Bay, and an exploration of several Adams Point habitats. Students sample the estuary bottom, do plankton tows, and run water tests. The Coastal Floating Lab program introduces students to the riches of the coastal environment and is designed to get students thinking about the need for environmental protection. The students observe and perform a variety of marine-related studies from the dock area and Hampton Harbor and while traveling on a 70-foot research vessel along the New Hampshire coast. Activities include sampling planktonic and benthic communities; testing water samples for oxygen content, acidity, salinity, and temperature; and testing water turbidity. Students also have an opportunity to learn basic navigation techniques and to catch fish and invertebrates.

❖ Sargent Camp Internship in Environmental Education

Sponsor: Boston University's Sargent Camp
Type: Internship
Location: Peterborough, NH
Qualifications: Interns must be at least 18 years old, committed to the environmental education of children, enjoy being outdoors, willing to work long hours, and have a sense of humor, enthusiasm, and a flexible personality.
Dates/Duration: Fall internship: late August to early December. Spring internship: early January through April.
Costs: None. Interns receive a stipend of $200 per month plus room and board. Weekend work is occasionally available at the rate of $55 per day.
Credits Given: Credits may be available from the student's school or college.
Contact: Mr. Bill Frankel
     Sargent Camp Internship in Environmental Education
     Boston University's Sargent Camp
     RD #3 Windy Row
     Peterborough, NH 03458
     (603) 525-3311

This is a practical training program in the many facets of outdoor environmental education. The internships begin with two-week training programs that include adventure tasks and group problem-solving activities, ropes course techniques, a study of land and water environments, outdoor skills, orienteering, sensory awareness, and night activities. During the program, each intern, paired with a group leader, works with a group of about 10 school children in age groups ranging from grade 4 through high school. The groups and programs vary from week to week depending upon theme and grade level. On weekends, interns may participate in workshops held at Sargent Camp in subjects such as canoeing, rock climbing, cross-country skiing, and outdoor safety.

❖ The Bronx High School of Science

Sponsor: New York City Public School System
Type: Specialized science school
Location: Bronx, NY
Qualifications: The program is for intellectually gifted students who reside within the five boroughs of New York City. Admission is competitive. Students are selected by means of a citywide examination.
Dates/Duration: Grades 9–12
     The school serves students throughout their high school years.
Costs: No cost to admitted students; this is a specialized public high school.
Credits Given: High school credits
Contact: The Bronx High School of Science
     New York City Public School System
     75 West 205th Street
     Bronx, NY 10468
     (212) 295-0200

Founded in 1938, Bronx Science quickly gained a tradition of academic excellence and has maintained that tradition throughout its history. The basic core of required courses is supplemented by electives in the area of the individual student's interest; students take at least five majors plus required minors each semester. Many junior-year students also take a sixth major, choosing from science-related courses such as bioethics, computer-assisted drafting, computer-generated music, marine ecology, astronomy and astrophysics. Project research courses in biological and physical science, mathematics, technology, and the social sciences are also available to juniors; many students enter their projects in competitions that include the Westinghouse Science Talent Search. Besides numerous offerings to attract science-oriented students, students may also choose from 10 different foreign languages and take classes in heroic literature, constitutional law, the African-American experience, or Asian literature, to name only a few. Students may choose from a full range of advanced placement courses and participate in numerous extracurricular activities.

❖ New York Academy of Sciences Educational Programs

Sponsor: The New York Academy of Sciences

Type: A variety of programs are offered including a science research training program, a science expo, science seminars for teachers, and the Art of Science competition.

Location: New York, NY

Qualifications: Some of the programs of the Academy are limited to students and teachers from the New York City area and its surrounding communities. Programs are applicable for students in elementary grades through high school. Other sponsored programs function in other parts of the state and nation.

Dates/Duration: Programs are offered throughout the academic year and during the summer months.

Costs: Most programs are available without cost to participating students. Some programs may provide a stipend and/or cash or scholarship awards.

Credits Given: Depends upon program chosen

Contact: New York Academy of Sciences Educational Programs
The New York Academy of Sciences
2 East 63rd Street
New York, NY 10021
(212) 838-0230

The Academy presents programs designed to enhance both students' and teachers' understanding of science. Sponsored programs include the New York City School Science and Technology Expo at which students in grades 7–12 present science projects and compete for awards, scholarships, and cash prizes. The Science Research Training Program (SRTP) places middle school and high school students as interns with research scientists at a variety of distinguished institutions. The Junior Academy of Science is open to any student in grades 8–12 who wants to learn more about science and its applications. Support services for teachers include Science Seminars for middle and high school science teachers and a program bringing scientists from a variety of fields directly into elementary and secondary school classrooms. The Academy also sponsors the Art of Science Competition for students in grades 10–12 and participates in the National Science Bowl.

❖ Saturday Scholars Program

Sponsor:	Rensselaer Polytechnic Institute
Type:	Enrichment classes
Location:	Troy, NY
Qualifications:	Grades 7–10
	Minority, disadvantaged, and/or gifted and talented students are eligible for the program. Separate programs are held for "entry level" students (grades 7 and 8) and "intermediate level" students (grades 9 and 10).
Dates/Duration:	Six consecutive Saturdays, from 9 A.M. to 12 P.M. Sessions are held from October through June.
Costs:	None
Credits Given:	None
Contact:	Mark Smith
	Saturday Scholars Program
	Rensselaer Polytechnic Institute
	Troy Building
	Troy, NY 12180-3590
	(518) 276-6272

The Saturday Scholars Program provides selected students with the opportunity to explore topics in science and mathematics at greater depth. Separate instructional units focus on areas that include the Physics of Motion and Machines, the Art of Architecture, Computer Skill Building, Chemical Mysteries, and Aeroscience Technology, among other choices. Each instructional unit presents participants with hands-on, project-oriented laboratory experiences in which students learn to improve their problem-solving and learning skills while attempting to solve real-world problem situations. Students are encouraged to depend on each other for peer support as a way of increasing the success of students in secondary mathematics and science coursework. Saturday Scholars are challenged with scientific and mathematical projects to stretch their imaginations and creativity and to increase their knowledge.

❖ The Saturday Academy

Sponsor:	AM-BC/Bennett College
Type:	Enrichment classes
Location:	Greensboro, NC
Qualifications:	Grades 4–8
	The program is open to minority students recommended by school counselor or teacher for participation. Selection is on a first-come, first-served basis.
Dates/Duration:	Twelve Saturday morning sessions are held each semester. The Academy runs from 9 A.M. to 12:10 P.M.
Costs:	Participant fees are kept at a minimum through the support of Bennett College and North Carolina A&T State University. Community organizations also provide scholarships for needy students.
Credits Given:	None
Contact:	Dr. Nellouise Watkins

The Saturday Academy
AM-BC/Bennett College
900 East Washington Street
Greensboro, NC 27401-3239
(919) 370-8684

The Saturday Academy emphasizes building student confidence while increasing compe-
tence. Students are provided with role models in science, and parents are enlisted to
provide support. Regular university faculty work with young minority students in a
college setting providing science enrichment activities. Students gain firsthand experience through laboratory experimentation in the fields of chemistry, physics, and biology.
Students may have a chance to work with lasers, to dissect pig embryos, to study
pendulum motion, or to compare metric units. Mathematics concepts are taught to
improve computational and reasoning skills. In a computer science class, students learn
to program in LOGO and BASIC. Special communication skills classes build skills
through vocabulary workshops, interview practice, debates, and poetry writing.

❖ Saturday Academy

Sponsor:	Oregon Graduate Institute of Science & Technology
Type:	Enrichment classes
Location:	Beaverton, OR
Qualifications:	Grades 4–12
	This program is for students who want to learn more about the topic presented. In some cases, courses require prerequisites.
Dates/Duration:	Workshops range from one to eight sessions in length and are presented on Saturdays, Sundays, and on selected weekday evenings during the school year. Each individual session may last from one hour to an entire day, although most are two to three hours long per session.
Costs:	A fee is charged for each workshop, but these programs are heavily subsidized by grants and contributions. Tuition assistance is available upon request. No student is turned away on the basis of inability to pay tuition.
Credits Given:	None
Contact:	Saturday Academy
	Oregon Graduate Institute of Science & Technology
	19600 NW von Neumann Drive
	Beaverton, Or 97006
	(503) 690-1190

The Saturday Academy presents a variety of programs in a range of subject areas but with
a strong emphasis on science, mathematics, and technology. The classes are informal and
are project oriented. Most of the classes are held at the site of the instructor's work,
allowing the participants to work with the equipment and facilities used by professionals
employed in this field of study. Recent offerings have included workshops in Computer-
Aided Design at Hewlett-Packard, in which students learned to use a computer to design
mechanical parts, and Reptiles and Amphibians held at the Metro Washington Park Zoo.
Other interesting classes include a Nuclear Science Workshop at the Reactor Facility of
Reed College and an Aviation Workshop at Portland International Airport. Students of

the Academy get a chance to "test out" careers while having learning experiences that are impossible to duplicate in their home schools.

✦ OMSI Spring Break Safari, Whale Camp, and Naturalist Camp

Sponsor:	Oregon Museum of Science and Industry (OMSI)
Type:	School-break adventure camps
Location:	Various sites in Oregon
Qualifications:	Ages 10 to 13 and 14 to 18
Dates/Duration:	Several sessions are held each year during the spring break period. Contact the program for available dates. Programs are five to six days in length.
Housing:	Housing for the Spring Break Safari and the Naturalist Camp is provided at the Hancock Field Station. Whale Camp participants live in heated cabins at the B'nai B'rith Camp near Lincoln City, Oregon. Meals are provided.
Costs:	$295 for OMSI members; $320 for nonmembers. All instruction, room and board, fees, and transportation while on the program are included.
Credits Given:	None
Contact:	OMSI Spring Break Safari, Whale Camp, and Naturalist Camp Oregon Museum of Science and Industry 1945 SE Water Avenue Portland, OR 97214 (503) 797-4547; FAX (503) 797-4500

Students aged 14–18 can spend their spring break investigating the geology, wildlife, and plants found in the central Oregon region. After stopping to explore the Columbia River Gorge on their way to Hancock Field Station, students work on research projects under the guidance of professionals from the National Park Service and the Oregon Department of Fish and Wildlife. Trips to collect rocks and fossils and to explore Lava River Cave and the Cove Palisades are some highlights of this program. Students aged 10 to 13 may choose a Naturalist Camp at Hancock Field Station that focuses on geology, paleontology, fire ecology, and historical archaeology or may choose to study the largest of all mammals in a Whale Camp adventure. Whale Camp participants work alongside scientists from the Hatfield Marine Science Center and spend time investigating tidepools and estuaries.

✦ Enrichment Programs at the Allegheny Square Annex

Sponsor:	The Carnegie Science Center
Type:	Enrichment classes for grades 7 and 8; apprenticeship programs for grades 10–12; science academy for grades 9–12.
Location:	Pittsburgh, PA
Qualifications:	The Spectroscopy program accepts seventh- and eighth-grade students from the Pittsburgh area who have been nominated by their teachers. The Apprenticeship program is for older students.
Dates/Duration:	Four Saturdays in the spring for Focus on Spectroscopy. The apprenticeship program takes place over five school days at selected times.

Costs: None
Credits Given: None
Contact: Enrichment Programs at the Allegheny Square Annex
The Carnegie Science Center
One Allegheny Avenue
Pittsburgh, PA 15212-5850
(412) 237-3360

The Carnegie Science Center sponsors a variety of academic year programs for elementary, middle school, and high school students. One such program is Focus on Spectroscopy in which middle school students explore the properties of light and discover its uses in the various scientific and technological fields. Another program pairs qualified students in grades 10–12 with practicing professionals in the fields of astronomy, oceanography, or meteorology. The student-researchers spend five school days at the Carnegie Science Center and the Annex working alongside scientists in their chosen fields and gain a firsthand look at possible career choices. Still another option is the Science Academy for high school students, a precollege science club that offers science-oriented students a variety of experiences that include field trips, lectures, and internships.

❖ Spring Field Biology Camp

Sponsor: South Dakota State University
Type: School-break science camp
Location: 25 miles north of Brookings, SD
Qualifications: Ages 12 to 15
This program is for students who have a serious interest in hands-on field biology.
Dates/Duration: End of May through early June. The camp lasts one week.
Housing: Campers are housed in supervised bunkhouses; meals are provided.
Costs: $175 covers program costs, meals, and housing.
Credits Given: None
Contact: Professor Gerald Myers
Spring Field Biology Camp
South Dakota State University
Biology/Microbiology Department
PO Box 2207B
Brookings, SD 57007
(605) 688-4566 or 688-6141

Spring Camp provides students with an opportunity for firsthand experience in the fields of environmental and biological science. Explorations at the camp cover aspects of science unavailable in the classroom. The camp seeks to develop a concern for the environment in its participants through an understanding of the impact of people on the environment. The camp is held at the beautiful Oak Lake Biology Field Station, located 25 miles north of Brookings, SD, on the Minnesota/South Dakota state line. Campers are involved in activities that focus on woodland ecology, meteorology, water-quality studies, small mammals, plant identification, insect collection, parasitology, nature photography, and astronomy among other offerings. Recreational activities, including canoeing, swimming, softball, and volleyball, are also available to participants. All applicants will be notified of acceptance by May 15.

❖ The Exxon Energy Cube

Sponsor: Exxon Corporation
Type: Curriculum enrichment resource
Qualifications: Secondary school
The Energy Cube is provided without costs and as a permanent acquisition to secondary schools that send one teacher to attend a six-hour training workshop. Currently, the Cube is available in Florida, South Carolina, Texas, Alaska, California, and Louisiana. It is expected to become available in an additional 18 states by 1998.

Dates/Duration: The Cube can be used at the teacher's discretion to supplement the existing curriculum or as a separate, interdisciplinary unit.
Costs: The Exxon Energy Cube is provided without cost to secondary schools.
Credits Given: None
Contact: The Exxon Energy Cube
Exxon Corporation
225 East John W. Carpenter Freeway
Irving, TX 75062-2298
(214) 444-1104; FAX (214) 444-1139

The Energy Cube contains a variety of learning resources including videotapes, lesson plans, data files, wall charts, student activities, and a classroom simulation. These tools are designed to help secondary students understand the scientific principles that govern energy choices and to encourage consideration of the social implications of these choices. The videotapes present key concepts, relating energy use to real-world experiences. Activities are designed to be open-ended and problem-solving in approach. A classroom simulation involves students in making their own decisions about energy use on an imaginary planet.

❖ Volunteer for Science

Sponsor: U.S. Geological Survey
Type: Science internship
Location: Dependent on job
Qualifications: The program is open to students of all ages interested in earth science research.
Dates/Duration: Time spent is at the discretion of the volunteer. Students may devote anything from a few hours a day, a few days a year, or extended time such as a school vacation break to working in the field of earth science research.
Costs: Some stipends are available for incidental expenses such as training, transportation, lodging, equipment, and supplies, when needed.
Credits Given: None
Contact: Ms. Maxine Jefferson
Volunteer for Science
U.S. Geological Survey
215 National Center
Reston, VA 22092
(703) 648-7439

Participants in Volunteer for Science may find themselves assisting in a geologic or hydrologic laboratory, working in the field gathering data, or assisting with computer- or graphic-data analysis, depending upon the interest of the volunteer and the needs of the local Geological Survey office. Other volunteers provide administrative, library, map, or informational services. All of these internship positions give students a firsthand look at possible career opportunities in the field of earth science research.

❖ OPTIONS in Science, Sharing Science with Schools Program

Sponsor:	Pacific Northwest Laboratory
Type:	Enrichment classes and presentations at schools
Location:	Oregon and Washington
Qualifications:	OPTIONS targets northwestern (Washington and Oregon) middle schools that have large populations of minority students. Sharing Science with Schools is available to high schools in Washington and Oregon.
Dates/Duration:	Programs are scheduled throughout the school year at times mutually convenient to the Laboratory and individual schools.
Costs:	None
Credits Given:	None
Contact:	Ms. Irene Hays
	OPTIONS in Science
	Pacific Northwest Laboratory
	Science Education Center
	PO Box 999
	Richland, WA 99352
	(509) 375-2800

OPTIONS, an enrichment program presented by Pacific Northwest Laboratory (PNL), teams individual middle schools with the Laboratory to support the science education goals of that particular school. Students explore options in science, mathematics, and technology, learning about a wide variety of scientific disciplines. On OPTIONS days, Laboratory researchers present demonstrations on topics that range from robotics to computer modeling to metallography. Field trips around Washington State and to the Laboratory allow students to explore hands-on science in areas that include marine biology, geology, and space. Special projects are jointly developed by school and Laboratory staff to enhance student learning. Additional teacher enrichment and support activities are offered as part of OPTIONS; these include teacher workshops and funding for equipment and materials to support curricula. To continue to motivate students from populations traditionally underrepresented in the sciences, OPTIONS also offers educational awards at community college and university levels, as well as grants covering tuition, fees, and books for students interested in pursuing degrees in science, mathematics, or technology. The Sharing Science with Schools Program sends scientists from the Laboratory's staff into schools to talk about current research developments. The program complements school classes and establishes connections with real-world science.

❖ Environmental Education Programs

Sponsor:	Central Wisconsin Environmental Station
Type:	Specialized science school; Environmental education camp

Location:	Amherst Junction, WI
Qualifications:	Central Wisconsin students in grades K–12
Dates/Duration:	One-, two-, and three-day programs are available and are held throughout the school year.
Housing:	Housing and meals are provided on site for multiday programs.
Costs:	Costs are dependent upon program chosen. A fee schedule will be sent upon inquiry.
Credits Given:	None
Contact:	Environmental Education Programs
	Central Wisconsin Environmental Station
	7290 County MM
	Amherst Junction, WI 54407
	(715) 824-2428

The Central Wisconsin Environmental Station is a nonprofit educational facility supported by the University of Wisconsin-Stevens Point Foundation, the College of Natural Resources, and the Portage County United Way. Located 18 miles east of Stevens Point, the Station land consists of pine and hardwood forests, lakes, ponds, marshlands, and fields. The physical facilities at the Station include a dining hall, dormitories and cabins, classrooms, library, an amphitheater, waterfront, and several miles of walking trails. Teachers plan programs for their students in conjunction with the Station staff. Activities emphasize ecological concepts and are designed to develop an awareness in and sensitivity to the environment. Students investigate environmental issues and are involved in determining appropriate actions. School groups are scheduled in May for the following year. Reserve by May 1.

CHAPTER 3

Challenge Yourself: Science Contests and Competitions

"Science Fair"—The words alone can bring dread to the hearts of parents and cause anxious moments for their children. Since science fairs, spelling bees, history competitions, and academic bowls have been a part of the American educational system for many years, it should be asked if there is value to be found in participating in competitive academic events.

Polling educators and science professionals would probably result in answers that run the gamut from "Yes, definitely, they motivate students to achieve" to "They're of no value whatsoever." As seen through the eyes of this experienced science teacher, science competitions can provide motivation, stimulate curiosity, and might lead participating students to consider careers in science and technology. Athletic competitions occupy the time and energy of hundreds of thousands of young Americans. A student member of a sports team gains a sense of being part of a team, learns about group cooperation, and is instilled with the desire to push just a bit harder to achieve. In a similar fashion, science competitions can provide students with the same sense of accomplishment, promote teamwork, and motivate young people to stretch themselves mentally just as the athlete stretches physically.

INDIVIDUAL EVENTS

Perhaps the most familiar type of science competition is the science fair. Through participation in school fairs, students are encouraged to choose a scientific problem of personal interest and to attempt to find a solution by applying the steps of the scientific method. If correct procedures are followed, students learn to hypothesize, to design procedures for testing their hypothesis, to follow through with a controlled experiment—making observations, gathering data, and drawing conclusions. All of these experiences serve students well in the future, as they learn to apply a scientific approach to solving any life challenge.

Science fair participants can gain as much from entering a project as from winning. Certainly, award-winning projects motivate students, rewarding them with prizes, trophies, scholarships, and increased self-esteem. Presenting a project to a panel of judges improves the student's ability to organize information and may result in an exchange of ideas with practicing scientists. Student competitors, too, are stimulated by their contact with each other and may find their scientific curiosity piqued by a competitor's project.

Too often, however, student science projects degenerate into adult challenges, cause family stress, and turn into contests in which one adult-created project competes with another. Reducing parental involvement makes the experience more meaningful for students.

Science fairs, although the most familiar, are not the only type of science competition available to students. Competitive events include both individual and team competitions. The Westinghouse Science Talent Search, the Thomas Edison/Max McGraw Scholarship Program, the Agriscience Student Recognition Program, and the Junior Science and Humanities Symposium all recognize and reward individual students for sustained study and their attempts to solve scientific problems. Projects entered in these competitions are often the product of a student's participation in a research internship. Participants increase their ability to organize thoughts, design and conduct experiments, interpret data, and draw conclusions. Student communication skills are enhanced through symposia and research-paper presentations at which the students share their findings with others. Although significant tangible rewards may be gained, including scholarships and prizes, the intangible rewards of participation may be far greater.

Other individual competitions challenge the inventiveness and creativity of young people. Contests such as the International Bridge Building Contest, the Estes Rocket Contests, and the Duracell Scholarship Competition motivate students to think about and create a device that meets certain requirements. Their efforts might result in rewards, such as scholarships and prizes, and a feeling of accomplishment in meeting a challenge and might also signal the start of a career in engineering or science.

TEAM COMPETITIONS

More and more of the newer science competitions generate the atmosphere and benefits of team athletics. Competitions such as the Chemistry, Physics, and National Science Olympiads and the Foundation for Scholastic Advancement's Science Invitational pit teams of students against each other. Instead of physical strength, students utilize brain power to answer questions that test their knowledge of the various scientific disciplines. Other contests encourage groups of students to work together to solve scientific challenges. Student teams may be asked to invent a working machine, as in the U.S. First competition, or to creatively solve problems, as in the Odyssey of the Mind competitions. These events generate the same excitement found at any athletic competition and provide student participants with the benefits of association as part of a team.

Other team competitions challenge students to brainstorm ideas as they attempt to solve an environmental or scientific problem of interest to the group. The Seiko Youth Challenge motivates young people to consider local environmental issues and to attempt solutions to community-based problems. Besides the obvious benefits to the participants, the students' communities also gain from their children's efforts. The SuperQuest Computer Competition encourages students to use the computational ability of the most modern supercomputers to solve problems. Toshiba's ExploraVision Program encourages teams of students to use their imagination in concert with research, artistic, and writing abilities to create a view of future technology. When students engage in creative thinking, everyone benefits.

The listings that follow provide information about science competitions, both individual and team events, in which students can participate. Individual students can enter appropriate competitions by writing to the contact listed for more information and entry materials. Teachers, sponsoring groups, and/or parents might choose to organize team competitions and can write to inquire about regional as well as national events. The listings are arranged alphabetically by name of the competition.

Considering both the tangible rewards (college scholarships, trophies, prizes, trips) as well as the intangible benefits (interaction with others interested in science, increased self-esteem and creativity, heightened ability to communicate, cooperative behaviors learned through teamwork), science competitions provide young people with benefits far greater than the effort expended in competing. In answer to the question originally posed, "Is there value in participating?"—yes!

❖ The DuPont Challenge Science Essay Awards Program

Sponsors: DuPont, General Learning Corporation, and the National Science Teachers Association

Contestants: Students in grades 7–12 enrolled in public and private schools in the United States and its territories and in Canada and in U.S. sponsored schools abroad. Junior division includes grades 7–9. The senior division includes grades 10–12.

How to Enter: Submit essay according to official rules either individually or in a packet of essays submitted by a science teacher.

Entry Date: All entries must be postmarked by the date noted in the official rules. This date is in late January.

Location: Entries are mailed to the address noted in contact information.

Awards: First place winners in each division, along with a parent and sponsoring science teacher, receive an all-expense-paid trip to Space Center Houston plus an educational grant of $1,500. In each division, second place winners receive grants of $750, third place receive $500, while 24 honorable mentions receive $50 awards. Sponsoring teachers of first place winners also receive educational awards of $500.

Contact: The DuPont Challenge Science Essay Awards Program
General Learning Corporation
60 Revere Drive
Northbrook, IL 60062-1563

Students compose and submit individual essays that describe a significant challenge in science. The topic may reflect a scientific problem, development, achievement, or effort that has captured the interest and imagination of the contestant and may be drawn from any of the scientific disciplines. Essays must be between 700 and 1,000 words in length and conform to the competition rules available from the sponsor.

❖ Duracell/NSTA Scholarship Competition

Sponsors: Duracell and the National Science Teachers Association (NSTA)

Contestants: Open to all students in grades 9–12.

How to Enter: Participants create and design their device and test that it functions as desired. The official entry form is used to enter the contest; students can obtain one from their school counselor or directly from the contact below. The entry form describes the items needed for the initial judging including the criteria for the descriptive essay, the wiring diagram, and photographs required. The student then mails the entry (but not the device) to NSTA Headquarters for initial judging.

Entry Date: Initial entries are due by mid-January.

Location: Entries are mailed to the NSTA Headquarters in Washington, DC.

Awards: There are 41 student awards. One first place winner receives a $10,000 college scholarship for use at any four-year college, two-year technical school, or community college. Five second place winners receive $3,000 college scholarships; 10 third place winners receive $500 college scholarships; 25 fourth place winners receive cash awards of $100 each. In addition, the first and second place winners, their parents, and teachers are honored at an awards ceremony at the NSTA national convention. Transportation to the site of the convention is provided.

Contact: Duracell/NSTA Scholarship Competition
National Science Teachers Association
1742 Connecticut Avenue, NW
Washington, DC 20009
(202) 328-5800

This competition rewards imagination, mechanical ability, and student ingenuity. To enter, students individually design and build a working device that is powered by Duracell brand batteries. Devices should be practical and may be used to educate, entertain, or make life easier. An entry consists of a two-page description of the device, a wiring diagram, photos of the completed product, and an official entry form. One hundred finalists are selected from the initial entries; these finalists are asked to send their devices to Duracell Headquarters for final judging. The 41 prize-winners are selected from this group of finalists.

❖ ExploraVision Awards

Sponsors: Toshiba/National Science Teachers Association

Contestants: Open to U.S. students in grades K–12, the program offers four levels of competition: Primary (K–3), Upper Elementary (4–6), Middle (7–9), and High School (10–12). Students compete in teams of four, along with a teacher/advisor and an optional community advisor.

How to Enter: Entry form, project description, and ten storyboard frames must be sent to the contact listed below by February 1. Regional judging takes place in each of the National Science Teachers Association's 12 districts; 48 semifinalist teams are selected at the regionals. Each of these teams receives $500 to produce a five-minute videotape presentation of their project to be submitted for final judging by mid-April.

Entry Date: Entries must be received by February 1.

Location: There are both regional and national judgings held.

Awards: Every student-team member (and teacher) who submits a complete entry receives a gift and certificate. Twelve finalist teams, their parents, and teacher/advisors are awarded all-expense-paid trips to Washington, DC, to attend the awards ceremony. Student members of the four winning teams each receive a $10,000 savings bond. Their advisors receive Toshiba products. The 48 regional winners' schools receive TVs and VCRs, while those of the 12 finalist teams receive choices of FAX machines, copiers, and computers.

Contact: Toshiba/NSTA
ExploraVision Awards
1742 Connecticut Avenue, NW
Washington, DC 20009

Designed to excite students about the potential of science and technology, ExploraVision allows students to use their imagination in concert with their artistic, research, and writing abilities to create a view of a future technology. Each team selects a current technology (such as a light bulb, FAX machine, or gene splicing), researches its development and how it works, and then projects what that technology might look like 20 years from now. This view is conveyed by both a written description and a storyboard, a series of frames from a would-be movie.

❖ Foundation for Scholastic Advancement Science Invitational Competition

Sponsor: Foundation for Scholastic Advancement (FSA)

Contestants: High school students compete in small groups. Three separate contests are held testing students on knowledge and comprehension of topics covered on the Advanced Placement curricula of biology, chemistry, and physics (mechanics).

How to Enter: Teachers should enter their students in the competition by contacting the sponsors and registering by early March.

Date of Event: The contest is held during a week designated in late March or early April each year.

Location: The competition is held at the students' school and results are sent in to the organizers.

Awards: Each school receives certificates and ribbons for its top students. Students ranked nationally receive medals, trophies, or plaques. In addition, the FSA awards a $500 scholarship to an outstanding high school senior each year. Applications for the scholarship are available by writing to the contact below. Deadline for scholarship applications is February 15.

Contact: Mr. Kenneth Chern
Foundation for Scholastic Advancement
PO Box 3340
Iowa City, IA 52244
(312) 484-4812

The purpose of this contest is to challenge students and to strengthen their problem-solving skills. Material covered in each subject area ranges from basic knowledge to advanced thinking. Small groups of students work together on the questions; the competition is designed to foster teamwork and cooperation. Each test is a 45-minute multiple-choice exam. The biology contest includes questions on plant and animal physiology, photosynthesis, DNA, and cell organelles. The chemistry contest includes the topics of equilibria, gas laws, electrochemistry, acids and bases, and atomic structure. The physics competition is limited to mechanics and includes questions on Kinematics, rotational motion, universal gravitation, energy, and collisions.

❖ International Bridge Building Contest

Sponsor: The International Bridge Building Committee and the Illinois Institute of Technology

Contestants: High school students

How to Enter: Contact the organizers below for information about the nearest regional contest. If no contest is held in your region, instructions for holding your own are available. Students design and construct their own bridges, which are then tested at regional contests. The top two students from each region become contestants at the International Contest.

Entry Date: The International event is held at the beginning of May. Intermediate regional events are held prior to this date to determine entrants for the International competition. Information about regional events is available from contact below.

Location: Regional contests are held within a 150-mile radius. The International competition is held every other year at the Illinois Institute of Technology in Chicago and at other sites in the alternate years.

Awards: The top three students are awarded prizes such as cameras and computers. A partial scholarship to the Illinois Institute of Technology may also be awarded. Each school receives a trophy for participating in the International competition, and each student participant receives a certificate.

Contact: Mr. Earl Zwicker
    Department of Physics
    Illinois Institute of Technology
    3301 S. Dearborn Street
    Chicago, IL 60616
    (312) 567-3375

The object of this contest is to see who can design, construct, and test the most efficient bridge. Model bridges, of a maximum mass of 25 grams, are constructed of basswood following the specifications available from the contest committee. Completed bridges are tested for the maximum load that can be applied; successful bridges are likely to support more than 50 pounds of weight. The bridge with the highest structural efficiency is the winner of the International Bridge Building Contest. Efficiency equals load supported in grams divided by the mass of the bridge in grams.

❖ International Science and Engineering Fair (ISEF)

Sponsor: Science Service, Inc.

Contestants: Contestants include students from grades 9–12. Two students are selected to represent their regions from each of the nearly 400 affiliated fairs that take place across the United States and in foreign countries. All expenses of attending the International Fair are paid by the sponsoring fairs.

How to Enter: Students participate by entering original research projects in local or regional fairs affiliated with the International Fair. The top two projects from each affiliated fair represent their region in the International event.

Date of Event: The International Science and Engineering Fair is held in May of each year.

Location: The location of the Fair changes each year. All expenses involved in attending the Fair, including transportation and housing, are borne by the sponsoring fairs.

Awards: More than 600 competitive awards are given. Each finalist receives a silver medal and certificate. The ISEF Grand Awards are presented to those students who place first through fourth in each of thirteen scientific disciplines. First place awards may be as much as $5,000. Two first place winners are selected for an all-expense-paid trip to the Nobel Prize ceremonies and lectures in Sweden and two represent the United States at the European Community Contest for Young Scientists. Special Awards of cash, scholarships, and summer jobs are also awarded at the Fair.

Contact: International Science and Engineering Fair
Science Service
1719 N Street, NW
Washington, DC 20036
(202) 785-2255

The "World's Fair" of science fairs, the International Science and Engineering Fair, is the final step for student participants who have been selected for their outstanding projects presented earlier in the year at their regional fairs. More than just a competitive event, the International Fair provides significant educational experiences for the participants. Students are interviewed by judges renowned in their fields and have the opportunity to tour universities, scientific research centers, and industries, as well as cultural and historical sites in the hosting region.

❖ Junior Science and Humanities Symposium

Sponsor: The Academy of Applied Science and the U.S. Army Research Office

Contestants: Open to all high school students with a serious interest in science, the Junior Science and Humanities Symposium annually attracts more than 10,000 students and teachers who attend regional symposia. Participants are nominated by their schools based on the student's interest in scientific research coupled with other factors, including academic achievements.

How to Enter: The students choose a topic, research it, design and conduct an experiment, write up results, write a scientific paper following the given guidelines, and present their results at the appropriate regional event.

Date of Event: Regional symposia are held at times determined by each region. The National Symposium is held in early May.

Location: Each region chooses its own location, usually at a state university. The National Symposium is held at the U.S. Military Academy at West Point, NY, every other year and at other locations on the alternate years.

Awards: Five winners at regional events are awarded all-expense-paid trips to the National Symposium. One student from each region is designated as Regional Speaker and presents a paper at the National Symposium. The Regional Speaker is also awarded a college scholarship from the National Academy of Applied Science; the sponsoring teacher receives a $300 grant toward the purchase of materials. Seven national winners receive all-expense-paid trips to London for the International Youth Science Fortnight. Other scholarships are also awarded.

Contact: Ms. Doris Ellis
Junior Science and Humanities Symposia National Office
Academy of Applied Science
98 Washington Street
Concord, NH 03301
(603) 228-4520

The objectives of the Symposia are to promote the study of science and mathematics and to develop an appreciation for the role of the humanities in the development of scientists. Talented youth are supported in their efforts to do scientific research and are assisted in investigative procedures. Participants choose a topic, do a library search to guide their work, and design and perform laboratory experiments. The results of the research are written up for presentation at the 46 annual, regional symposia. A percentage of the students is selected at the regional symposia to give scientific talks on their research projects. The top five students go on to participate in the National Symposium; one winner is selected to represent the region in the competition for a spot at the London International Youth Science fortnight. The regional symposia also involve participants in laboratory visits and tours of scientific installations.

❖ Model Rocket Contests

Sponsor: Estes Industries

Contestants: The contest is open to anyone—children, teenagers, or adults—interested in designing and launching model rockets. Any group may sponsor their own model rocket competition, or students may participate in activities of established aerospace clubs in their local area.

How to Enter: Write to Estes to obtain information on beginning your own program.

Entry Date: Determined by individual clubs.

Location: Determined by individual clubs.

Awards: Determined by individual clubs.

Contact: Mary Roberts
Estes Industries
Educational Marketing Services
1295 H Street
Penrose, CO 81240
(719) 372-6565

Estes Industries provides planning and support materials for groups interested in beginning model rocketry programs or in sponsoring competitive events. Estes provides leaders with a Model Rocketry Manual. The manual is designed for educators and includes an introduction to model rocketry, a teacher's guide, and a student guide book, as well as catalogs of materials and a newsletter. Also provided are a guidebook for aerospace clubs and a model rocket contest guide. The Estes kit even contains a beginner's model rocket that the leader can use to begin a club.

❖ The National Engineering Aptitude Search (NEAS)

Sponsor: Junior Engineering Technical Society (JETS)

Contestants: Tests are available for two levels of students—grades 9 and 10 and grades 11 and 12.

How to Enter: Students complete the application obtained from a high school counselor or from the contact listed below. The test registration fee is $30.

Date of Event: The test is given on selected Saturdays throughout the school year.

Location: Area testing sites are listed in the application brochure. Special testing sites can be arranged through high school counselors or a school administrator.

Awards: High scores on the NEAS may help in admission to selective engineering programs.

Contact: American College Testing
NEAS Registration (8Z)
PO Box 168
Iowa City, IA 52243
(319) 337-1256

Not a contest, the NEAS is a guidance-oriented examination for students who are considering careers in engineering. The three-hour exam measures a student's ability in technical areas, including mathematical understanding, science reading and comprehension, and problem-solving skills. Students who score well on the NEAS are likely to be successful in college engineering programs. Students often use score reports from the NEAS as supporting documents when applying to engineering schools and colleges.

❖ National FFA Agriscience Student Recognition Program

Sponsor: Monsanto Agricultural Company and the National Future Farmers of America Foundation, Inc.

Contestants: Student members of the Future Farmers of America (FFA) who are in their junior or senior year in high school, or in first year of college majoring in agriculture. Students should be planning for a career in agriculture or agribusiness that requires at least a bachelor's degree. Students must have excellent grades in an academically demanding program and be certified by local school leaders.

How to Enter: Each local chapter of the FFA can submit applications to the state office. State winners compete for regional/national awards. Eight finalists are chosen, one from each of four regions and four from the nation at large. A national winner and a national runner-up are chosen from this group.

Entry Date: Chapter applications must be submitted to the state FFA office by dates determined by the state. The state winner's applications are due at the National FFA Center on or before July 15.

Location: State event is determined by the state FFA office. The eight finalists construct a project exhibit as part of the National Agricultural Career Show in Kansas City, Missouri.

Awards: Local participants each receive a certificate. Each state winner is awarded a $1,000 scholarship to the college or university of his or her choice, as well as a state plaque. The finalists are awarded $2,500 scholarships and plaques. The national winner receives an additional scholarship worth $5,000, while the national runner-up receives an additional $3,000 scholarship.

Contact: Ms. Carol Duval
National Future Farmers of America Center
5632 Mt. Vernon Memorial Highway
PO Box 15160
Alexandria, VA 22309-0160
(703) 360-3600; FAX (703) 360-5524

This program recognizes students interested in agriculture or agribusiness who choose challenging academic programs focused on the application of scientific principles and technology to agricultural endeavors. Students plan and perform an agriscience project that can be categorized as biological science, environmental science, food science, or engineering science. A project report of up to 10 pages, including title, abstract, introduction, design and procedure, data collection, results, conclusions, and references, is submitted along with the application. Judging criteria for the awards include 50 percent based on the agriscience project, 35 percent on the student's academic achievements, and 15 percent on school and community activities.

❖ National Junior Horticultural Association Projects and Contests, Senior Division Projects

Sponsor: National Junior Horticultural Association (NJHA)

Contestants: The competitions are open to students ages 15 to 18 and 18 to 22 who are interested in horticulture, the environment, and other related areas. Students must be members of NJHA—membership is free.

How to Enter: Students may enter either through an existing program, such as those sponsored by extension services, 4-H, Future Farmers of America, Scouts, or other organized groups, or through independent association in which individual students participate directly in NJHA. There is no charge for membership or participation. Write for information. Application deadline: generally by October 1.

Date of Event: State contests are held to select regional winners. These students then compete at the National Convention. The National Convention is generally held during the last weekend of October. Contact program or state NJHA for date of state competition.

Location: State competitions are decided by regional NJHA chapters. The national competition takes place at the site of the annual convention.

Awards: The majority of awards include pins, plaques, certificates, trophies, and gift certificates. Some competitions also provide trips and/or cash awards both at the state and national level.

Contact: National Junior Horticultural Association
401 North Fourth Street
Durant, OK 74701-4101
(405) 924-0771

Students compete in an area of their choice. Competitive events available to students include a demonstration contest that concerns itself with the how and why of production practices, soil-improvement methods, and marketing procedure, as well as an extemporaneous speech contest. Students may also compete in an experimental horticulture project, a production and marketing project, or an environmental beautification project.

❖ National Science Olympiad

Sponsor: National Science Olympiad/Continental Mathematics League

Contestants: Separate contests are held in 13 areas for students ranging from elementary through grade 12.

How to Enter: Teams register through their schools. Applications are due in early October. Schools may register two teams for the $55 entrance fee; additional teams may be registered for $25 each.

*Date of Event:*Schools choose any day from dates in late April to early May.

Location: Competition takes place at home school.

Awards: Each school team receives a medal and 10 certificates. Individual and team awards are also provided on a national level.

Contact: National Science Olympiad
PO Box 5477
Hauppauge, NY 11788-0121
(516) 265-4792

Participants take multiple-choice tests in a selected subject area at their home school. Junior high school competitions in life science and general science (grades 7 and 8), general science (grade 9), and physical science, as well as high school level earth science, biology, chemistry, and physics contests are held. The contest includes a few difficult questions requiring creative thought, but most questions are suitable for the majority of students. The cumulative scores of the top 10 students equal the team score. Competition is among students at the same grade level or taking the same science course.

❖ The Odyssey of the Mind Program

Sponsor: OM Association, Inc.

Contestants: Teams enter in one of four divisions—Division I: K–grade 5; Division II: grades 6–8; Division III: grades 9–12; Division IV: college and military. Teams consist of five to seven members and have an adult designated as coach. Teams are sponsored by schools that must become members of the OM Association in order to participate in competitions.

How to Enter: Schools join the OM Association ($90) in order to have the option of competing in the program. Each member school receives the program Handbook, copies of the long-term problems for each division, a subscription to the OM Newsletter, and creative problem-solving guides provided by IBM.

Date of Event: Teams sponsored by the same school may compete intramurally at the school's discretion to determine the best team to enter in sanctioned competition. Many state OM Associations run regional events, with the winning teams participating in the World Finals. Contact program for specific dates.

Location: Regional and national competitions are held. The World Finals location changes each year.

Awards: Team members who are high school seniors or college students are eligible for OM scholarships.

Contact: Odyssey of the Mind
PO Box 547
Glassboro, NJ 08028

The Odyssey of the Mind Program promotes divergent thinking by team members who strive to creatively solve problems while honing their independent- and critical-thinking skills. Teams work on long-term problems and are judged in three areas. Each team must prepare solutions to the long-term problems that are brought to the competition; the solutions are judged as to style, and the teams must also solve a spontaneous problem that is posed to them on the day of competition. Long-term problems cover a wide range of interests including engineering and design problems, performance-oriented problems, and nonlinguistic problems. The spontaneous problems generally take only a few minutes to solve. The program is sponsored by IBM.

❖ Science Olympiad

Sponsor: Science Olympiad, Inc.

Contestants: Students enter in one of four grade-level divisions: K–3, 3–6, 6–9, 9–12. Most events require team competition and cooperation.

How to Enter: School teams of up to 15 students per team enter the first level of competition; winning teams continue to the next level. Teams may participate in selected or all events within their division. Schools send in $50 memberships to enter; some states have local memberships.

Date of Event: Decided by regional organizers. The national tournament is generally held in May.

Location: Local, regional, and national events.

Awards: Athletic-style medals are awarded for each event. Championship trophies are awarded to high school and middle school teams from each Olympiad. The American Honda Foundation awards scholarships to selected upper division gold medal winners at the National Olympiad.

Contact: Science Olympiad
5955 Little Pine Lane
Rochester Hills, MI 48306
(313) 651-4103

Science Olympiad seeks to "elevate science education and learning to a level of enthusiasm and support normally reserved only for varsity sports." Thirty-two events are held representing the three broad goals of science education: concepts and knowledge, processes and thinking skills, and scientific application and technology. Included are events such as bridge building, egg-drop technology, computer programming, and balancing equations. All of the scientific disciplines are featured in team events. Four divisions ensure appropriate questions for students from K through 12. Local, regional, and national events are held.

❖ Seiko Youth Challenge

Sponsor: Seiko Corporation of America

Contestants: Each team is composed of 2–4 students from grades 9–12 in the same school and is supervised by a faculty advisor. Schools may enter as many teams as they wish.

How to Enter: Teachers register their teams by writing to the contact below. Teams may be encouraged to brainstorm possible problems to be solved and may be guided in carrying out research on their chosen topics; but all work must be done by the student team members only. Entries are submitted according to the rules available from Seiko.

Entry Date: Presentations must be received by late February for regional competition. Videotaped presentations from the Regional Finalists must be received by mid-April for final judging.

Location: All entries are sent to the Seiko Youth Challenge in Stamford, CT.

Awards: All entrants receive certificates of participation. The team members of the 25 Regional Finalist teams and their advisors each receive a special limited edition Seiko Youth Challenge watch. The members of the five Regional Winning teams divide $5,000 college scholarships between team members; a $1,000 grant is awarded to their school. The members of the National Winning team divide a $25,000 college scholarship; a $5,000 grant is awarded to their school. In each region, the school that submits the most entries is awarded a Seiko Youth Challenge wall clock.

Contact: The Seiko Youth Challenge
DRB Communications
1234 Summer Street
Stamford, CT 06905
(800) 323-1550

In the Seiko Youth Challenge, teams of students are asked to identify a specific environmental problem that faces their home community and to then investigate, analyze, and propose a solution to this problem. Each entry is composed of a one-page summary and up to ten pages of main text. The entry also should include an appendix containing charts, exhibits, and reference sources. Five teams are selected as Regional Semifinalists from each of five geographic regions: Northeast, Southeast, Midwest, Central, and West. Semifinalist winners are selected on the basis of imagination and originality of approach, depth of research, methodology, practicality of implementation, and magnitude of environmental impact. Five Regional Finalists are then selected from each region to submit videotaped presentations for final selection of the top five National winners.

❖ Student Energy Research Competition (SERC)

Sponsor: New York State Energy Research and Development Authority/Energy Office

Contestants: The competition is open to New York students in grades 9–12 from public and private schools, as well as students who have been home-schooled. Students may work as individuals or in teams of up to three.

How to Enter: Teams of students or individuals write a proposal that includes an abstract, hypothesis, statement of project goals, a project description, and a project budget. Students must have a faculty advisor who provides guidance and advice only. All actual project work must be done by the students.

Entry Date: Round I proposals are due by late October. Round I winning students complete their projects and travel to Albany for the Round II Competition in mid-May.

Location: Round I written proposals are sent to the Energy Authority/Energy Office for judging. Round II judging takes place over three days in Albany, NY.

Awards: Round I winning students and teachers receive certificates. Round II winners receive medallions and savings bonds, and their schools receive plaques. Meals and lodging are provided for students and advisors in Albany for Round II.

Contact: Student Energy Research Competition
New York State Energy Research and Development Authority
2 Rockefeller Plaza
Albany, NY 12223
(518) 465-6251 ext. 238

Through this competition, New York State students are encouraged to explore innovative solutions to the energy problems that face New York State. Students focus their research on one of four areas: Energy-Efficient Buildings, Manufacturing Processes, Transportation for Computers or Freight, or Technology Transfer. Students or teams propose a project to study one aspect of an energy issue. The projects must include the gathering of data through experimentation, surveys, or energy audits and must consider potential environmental impacts and benefits. There are 105 proposals chosen as Round I winners, which are awarded up to $500 to help complete the project for Round II.

❖ SuperQuest Computer Competition

Sponsor: Cornell Theory Center in conjunction with the National Science Foundation

Contestants: Teams are composed of four high school students (only one member of each team may be in grade 12) advised by one or two teacher-coaches. Entries may be submitted as either individual or team projects.

How to Enter: Student teams select project topics that are as specific as possible. Background information is researched using available sources of help. Working with the guidance of the teacher-coaches, the students develop a prototype code to solve the computational problem, using any available computer equipment. Teams submit the registration form along with a 200-word project description by March 1. Project report applications are due in early April.

Entry Date: Teams register by March 1. Project reports must be received by early April for review. Results of the competition are reported by early May.

Location: Students work at their home school and send in reports to the national organization.

Awards: Winning teams participate in an all-expense-paid, three-week, supercomputing summer institute at one of five supercomputing centers. Mentors at the institutes guide students in exploring areas of mutual interest. Students receive a stipend of $1,000 each; teacher-coaches are awarded stipends of $3,000. Advanced computing workstations are awarded to the winning teams' schools along with a year's access to the National Internet Network. All teams also receive a scientific video for use at their school.

Contact: Cornell Theory Center: SuperQuest
422 Engineering and Theory Center Building
Cornell University
Ithaca, NY 14853-3801
(607) 254-8614

SuperQuest is a national high school science competition in which students are asked to develop computational solutions for scientific problems that require the use of a high-performance computing facility. The problem may be drawn from any of the following disciplines: behavioral and social sciences, biochemistry, botany, chemistry, computer science, earth and space science, engineering, environmental science, mathematics, medicine and health, microbiology, physics, and zoology.

❖ Technology Student Association Competitive Events

Sponsor: Technology Student Association

Contestants: Students compete at two levels—level I: grades 7–9; level II: grades 9–12. Contestants must be members of the Technology Student Association in order to compete at the national level. Students may compete in the events at the chapter, state, or national level.

How to Enter: Students must be members of the Technology Student Association. Each local chapter receives rules for holding events and for student participation. Contact the national Association for more information.

Entry Date: School chapters hold their competitions in March, and state-level events are held each April. The National Competitive Events take place at the National Conference in June.

Location: The National Conference is held in a different city each year. Sites of state and local events are at the discretion of the sponsoring organizations.

Awards: Students who place in the top three of each event at the National Conference receive trophies. Scholarships are also awarded to level II winners in a number of the competitive events.

Contact: Ms. Rosanne White
Executive Director
Technology Student Association
1914 Association Drive
Reston, VA 22901
(703) 860-9000

The Technology Student Association Competitive Events include a number of science-related competitions. Students may enter a maximum of six events at the National Conference. Events include areas such as technology problem solving, computer-aided drafting and design, electricity/electronics, radio-control transportation, construction technology, aerospace technology, and a technology bowl, among other events. Some of the competitions are for individual members, while others require a team effort.

❖ Thomas Edison/Max McGraw Scholarship Program

Sponsor: The Max McGraw Foundation & the National Science Supervisors Association

Contestants: Students in grades 7–12 who are interested in science or engineering are eligible from all public, private, and parochial schools in the United States, Canada, or other participating nation.

How to Enter: Student submits two typed copies of a proposal and a letter of recommendation. A cover sheet containing title of entry, student's name, home address, home telephone number, student's grade level, teacher/sponsor name, name of school, school address, school telephone number, and name of local utility company MUST be included.

Entry Date: Entries must be postmarked by December 15, Finalists are notified around February 15. Final judging takes place in April or May.

Location: The final judging and a ceremonial program are held in Chicago. All expenses for transportation, lodging, and meals are paid for the finalists.

Awards: The two Grand Award Scholars are chosen from the 10 finalists. The senior division winner receives a $6,000 scholarship; the junior division winner receives a $3,000 scholarship. Each of the four remaining senior division finalists receives $1,500; the junior division finalists receive $750. Each finalist is also eligible for one of two $1,000 Energy Awards from the Edison Electric Institute and the U.S. Energy Association.

Contact: Dr. Kenneth Roy
Edison/McGraw Scholarship Program
NSSA Executive Director
PO Box 380057
East Hartford, CT 06138-0057
(203) 827-7981

This program recognizes the students "who most nearly demonstrate the inventive genius of both Thomas Edison and Max McGraw." Students submit two copies of a proposal (limited to 1,000 words or five pages) that describes either an already completed experiment or an idea for a project that deals with a practical application of some facet of science and/or engineering. Included with the proposal is a letter from the student's teacher/sponsor that describes how the student exemplifies the creativity of the inventors Edison and McGraw. Ten finalists are selected, five each in senior and junior divisions. These students present their projects before a panel of judges in Chicago in the spring. Two Grand Award Scholar Finalists (one in each division) are chosen at this time. In addition to the national program, some local utility companies sponsor similar programs for students living in the area served by their company.

❖ U.S. FIRST Competition

Sponsor: U.S. FIRST

Contestants: The competition is open to high school students in association with professional scientists and engineers from their sponsoring corporation or university.

How to Enter: Local schools form partnerships with sponsoring businesses, industries, or universities. Teams of students meet with professional scientists and engineers from the sponsoring companies to design and build a competitive machine that meets the specifications stated by the contest organizers. Payment of a $5,000 registration fee guarantees the team a slot in the competition and includes all materials needed. Application deadline: June 30.

Entry Date: Dates have not been finalized as of this time. Past competitions have been held in February.

Location: Location has not been finalized at this time. Both regional and national events are expected to be held. Past national competitions took place in New Hampshire.

Awards: Winning teams are awarded trophies and prizes. Scholarships are also awarded as a result of the competition. Winning teams are invited to the White House to be presented with the National Medals of Science and Technology by the President of the United States.

Contact: U.S. FIRST
340 Commercial Street
Manchester, NH 03101
(603) 666-3906; FAX (603) 624-0573

U.S. FIRST is a not-for-profit alliance of industry, governmental agencies, and schools that seeks to create a demand for science and mathematics education among secondary school students. One method of creating this demand is through the U.S. FIRST Competition, an engineering design competition. Student teams, in association with sponsoring businesses or universities, design and build radio-controlled "robo-athletes" from a supplied kit of parts. The machines are pitted against each other in a "final four" type of athletic event. Through their association with professionals, students learn engineering design in a creative way that approaches technology as fun.

❖ U.S. National Chemistry Olympiad (USNCO)

Sponsor: American Chemical Society

Contestants: Each year over 10,000 high school chemistry students compete in a series of qualifying events yielding the "final four" who will represent the United States in the International Chemistry Olympiad (IChO).

How to Enter: Contact your local American Chemical Society organization, or write to the contact listed below for information on how to participate in local screenings.

Entry Date: Local sections of the American Chemical Society choose their own dates for screenings; these usually occur in March. The National exam is held each April.

Location: Local events are held in locations chosen by the section.

Awards: The top 20 contestants receive an all-expense-paid trip to the National Chemistry Olympiad Study Camp held in Colorado each June. The "final four" who comprise the U.S. team receive an all-expense-paid trip to the city where the international event is held. Gold, silver, and bronze medals are awarded at the International Olympiad.

Contact: Ms. Denise Creech
U.S. National Chemistry Olympiad
American Chemical Society: Education Division

1155 Sixteenth Street, NW
Washington, DC 20036
(202) 872-6169

Nominees are selected by local sections of the American Chemical Society through the use of the USNCO prepared exams, locally made exams, laboratory practicals, teacher recommendations, or regional competitions between local school teams. Five students per section sit for the national exam that covers a broad range of chemical topics. Part I is a 70-question, multiple-choice exam. Part II requires students to explain the meaning and/or use of chemical models and theories behind chemical phenomena. Twenty students are selected to attend the 10-day Olympiad Study Camp held in June at the U.S. Air Force Academy. After rigorous training and competitions at the study camp, the "final four" team members are selected to represent the United States at the International Chemistry Olympiad held each July.

❖ United States Physics Team for the International Physics Olympiad

Sponsor: American Association of Physics Teachers

Contestants: The competition is open to outstanding high school physics students, nominated by their school or selected through locally-held contests. Contestants must be less than 19 years of age, U.S. citizens or permanent residents who have completed at least three years of schooling in a U.S. high school, and are presently enrolled in high school.

How to Enter: Physics teachers nominate outstanding students who file applications by January 15. Preliminary exams are administered by teachers in early February and include both multiple-choice and free-response questions. Semifinal exams, composed of free-response questions, are given to the highest scorers in March. Twenty students are selected from this group and are invited to participate in the training camp.

Entry Date: The training camp is held in late May. The International Physics Olympiad takes place in mid-July.

Location: This is a traveling competition. The U.S. training camp is held at the University of Maryland; the International Olympiad rotates among different countries.

Awards: The 20 members of the U.S. team have the opportunity to attend the 10-day training camp with all expenses paid. Laboratory work, intensive training in physics, and recreational activities are part of this experience. The top five members who represent the United States travel to the site of the competition with all expenses paid. Gold, silver, and bronze medals are awarded to the highest scorers at the International Olympiad.

Contact: U.S. Physics Team
American Association of Physics Teachers
5112 Berwyn Road
College Park, MD 20740-4100
(301) 345-4200

The International Physics Olympiad is a 10-day competition held for precollege students from about 40 different countries. The event seeks to encourage excellence in physics education and to reward outstanding physics students. Contestants are asked to solve challenging problems in theoretical and experimental physics. To qualify as a member of the 20-person U.S. team, locally nominated students take two competitive tests. The team members are invited to a 9-day training camp held in late May to work on problem-solving skills. The top five team members represent the United States at the international event. All expenses are paid by the team sponsors.

❖ Westinghouse Science Talent Search

Sponsor: Westinghouse Electric Corporation and Science Service

Contestants: The competition is open to U.S. students in their last year of secondary school.

How to Enter: Read and follow all directions on the application booklet. Assemble all entrance materials, including final project report, and mail them to Science Service. The complete entrance packet must be received by December 1.

Entry Date: The deadline for entry and receipt of all materials is December 1.

Location: Materials are mailed to Science Service in Washington, DC.

Awards: Forty finalists receive an all-expense-paid trip to the five-day Science Talent Institute held in March in Washington, DC. Projects are brought to the Institute for display. Finalists visit historic and scientific sites, meet with prominent scientists and public officials, and have many opportunities to interact with other scientifically talented youth. During the Institute, a board of judges selects the top 10 winners. They will receive scholarships ranging from $10,000 to $40,000. All other finalists will receive $1,000 scholarships.

Contact: Westinghouse Science Talent Search
Science Service
1719 N Street, NW
Washington, DC 20036

The Science Talent Search seeks to discover those young people whose scientific talent, skills, and ability indicate the potential for creative original work in science. Each student chooses an area of study, performs original independent research, and prepares a written report (maximum of 20 pages) on the results of their study. The project may be from any of the scientific disciplines including the physical, biological, medical, behavioral and social sciences, mathematics, or engineering. The rules of the competition must be followed carefully and can be obtained from a high school counselor, science teacher, or from the contact listed above. From the students entering the competition, 300 are named as Semi-finalists; from this group 40 are chosen as Finalists.

❖ Young America Horticultural Contests

Sponsor: National Junior Horticulture Association (NJHA)

Contestants: Junior division contestants are divided into three groups: ages 8 and younger, ages 9 to 11, and ages 12 to 14. Students may compete individually through direct participation in NJHA or through an existing group such as 4-H,

Future Farmers of America, or Scouts. Projects may be individually done or group projects.

How to Enter: All entrants must be members of NJHA. Membership is free. Students may join individually or through an existing sponsoring organization. Write to the National Association for more information on getting started.

Entry Date: Reports must be submitted before October 15.

Location: Completed project reports are sent to the national chairperson for judging.

Awards: The majority of awards include certificates, pins, plaques, trophies, and gift certificates. The purpose of the awards is to encourage student interest in horticulture.

Contact: National Junior Horticultural Association
401 North Fourth Street
Durant, OK 74701-4101
(405) 924-0771

Individual or group projects may be submitted in any of four areas: gardening, plant propagation, environmental beautification, or experimental horticulture. After completing their projects, students send in project reports to the appropriate project chairperson.

❖ Young Inventors' Contest

Sponsor: Foundation for a Creative America

Contestants: The contest is open to students enrolled in public, private, or parochial senior high schools. Entries may be submitted by individuals or by teams of up to three students in one or more categories. Schools may submit only one entry per category but are not required to enter all categories.

How to Enter: Students or teams design and build an invention. Each participating school may select one winner in each category for consideration in the state contest. There is a $5 fee per project entry. The state selects and notifies two state winners whose entries are sent to Washington, DC, for the national competition.

Entry Date: High schools submit entries by May 1 for consideration in the state contest. Two state winners are entered in the national contest by August 1. Eight national winners are invited to Washington, DC, in late October for awards.

Location: Projects are judged by state or region. State winners' projects are sent to Washington, DC, for further competition. The awards ceremony is held in Washington for winners and their teachers.

Awards: All state winners receive certificates of merit and tee shirts. Each national winner receives a medal, certificate, and a $250 savings bond. The teacher/advisor for national winners receives $100. Transportation and lodging for a two-day historic tour of Washington are also provided for the national winners and their teachers.

Contact: Young Inventors' Contest
Foundation for a Creative America, Virginia Office
1755 Jefferson Davis Highway, #400
Arlington, VA 22202
(703) 413-4491

Students or student teams design and build an invention that falls into one of eight categories. Inventions may be in the fields of health, business, household and food, agriculture, new technology, leisure and entertainment, transportation and travel, or the environment. Judging criteria include originality, usefulness, and marketability. Illustrative material (drawings, photos, videotapes of the invention) as well as written descriptions are used in judging.

CHAPTER 4

Rewards for Young Scientists: Science Scholarships

College costs continue to increase dramatically. A year at college today may range from about $1,500 for a student studying at local community college and living at home to over $25,000 for a student attending a private, residential institution. The cost of attendance includes tuition, room and board, fees, books, and personal and travel expenses. With educational expenses that can total well over $100,000 for four years of undergraduate study, some students (and their families) will need to carefully consider costs and seek out whatever help is available.

Although this chapter is focused primarily on specialized science scholarships, it is helpful to understand how the college financial aid system operates in the United States today. Financial assistance takes two forms:

- Need-based aid: awarded to students who qualify because of their family's financial circumstances.

- Merit aid: awarded for special achievements in academics, athletics, or extracurricular activities.

NEED-BASED AID

Most college financial assistance is awarded to students whose families are unable to pay the full cost of their child's college education. These awards are made through a process known as the Congressional Methodology—assistance is determined using formulas established by Congress. Students first apply to the colleges that they wish to attend. Those individuals who also want to apply for need-based aid then complete the forms required by their prospective colleges. Two forms are currently in use. All students applying for aid must fill out the FAFSA—the Free Application for Federal Student Aid. Some colleges and universities ask students to complete additional forms: the college's own financial aid application and/or a national or state FAF—Financial Aid Form. All these forms gather information pertaining to the financial situation of the student and his or her parent(s). The information required includes income, assets, expenses, and family data such as the number of family members attending college and the age of the older parent. This information is used to determine financial need.

The FAF and FAFSA may be completed any time after January 1 of the year in which financial aid will be sought. Generally, a completed federal tax return for the preceding year as well as estimates of income and expenses for the coming year for both the student and the parent(s) are needed in order to work on the forms. Since many colleges and universities award aid on a rolling basis, it is advisable to apply as soon as possible after January 1. Assembling tax information early may pay handsome dividends.

Four to six weeks after the forms are completed and submitted to the processing agency indicated, the student and the colleges selected by the student receive a Student Aid Report, or SAR. The SAR summarizes data and indicates "expected family contribution." This is the amount the formula has determined that the family can be expected to contribute toward the student's educational expenses for the coming school year. The student confirms the accuracy of the information or has an opportunity to make corrections at this point.

The financial aid administrator at the student's college now uses the "expected family contribution" figure to determine how much (if any) additional money will be needed. "Established need" is the difference between the total cost of one year of schooling at that institution and the expected family contribution. The school's financial aid officer proceeds to put together a package that hopefully will enable the student to attend the college.

A financial aid package generally consists of three parts:

- Grants and scholarships: gift aid to the student that does not need to be repaid

- Loans: money that will be repaid by the student and/or his/her parent(s) after graduation

- Work-study: parttime employment that will be provided by the college or university to enable the student to earn money to help defray college costs

Depending upon the policy and endowment of the institution, the package may meet part or all of the established need. Financial aid administrators also have some leeway in providing more aid for students whose families have unusual expenses or in providing a higher percentage of grant aid for students who are especially desirable because of unusual achievements (the Merit Scholar, star quarterback, award-winning poet, or accomplished oboe player). Other students may be especially sought after to contribute to ethnic or geographic diversity; these students, too, may receive more advantageous financial aid packages.

New financial aid forms must be completed each year to qualify the student for need-based aid for the next academic year. Although the process seems complicated, the system is designed to enable students to attend colleges they might otherwise be unable to afford. Completing the needed forms by the deadline dates may provide you with considerable financial help towards meeting the costs of higher education.

MERIT AID

Merit aid is awarded on the basis of achievement. Financial need is generally not considered in making these awards. Colleges and universities offer merit scholarships as a way of attracting the brightest students or students interested in studying a specific field. Merit awards are also made to students who demonstrate outstanding abilities in areas such as athletics, music, or art. The "Minority Scholarship Program for Research Careers in Math and Science" at Allegheny College is an example of a specialized merit award, supported by the National Science Foundation and designed to attract capable minority students to study science or math at Allegheny. Students interested in pursuing degrees in science should request information about science scholarships from the colleges they are considering attending. If a student has already determined a major (such as biomedical engineering or chemistry), he or she should check with the department chairperson to learn about specialized scholarships that are available.

In addition to merit aid awarded by individual colleges and universities, private organizations and career councils may also offer merit scholarships. In some cases, applicants are asked to write an essay, and the program may request family financial information. Occasionally, the sponsoring organization may have other requirements such as club membership or ethnic group membership. Other scholarships are earmarked for students planning to major in specific fields, such as electrical engineering or horticulture.

Still other science scholarships require students to enter a contest or competition. More information about competition-based scholarships will be found in Chapter 3. The following programs offer scholarships; Chapter 3 describes qualifications and entrance procedures for each of these scholarship programs.

- Duracell/NSTA Scholarship Competition
- Foundation for Scholastic Advancement Science Invitational Competition
- International Science and Engineering Fair
- Junior Science and Humanities Symposium
- National FFA Agriscience Student Recognition Program
- The Odyssey of the Mind Program
- Seiko Youth Challenge
- Thomas Edison/Max McGraw Scholarship Program
- Westinghouse Science Talent Search

Each listing provides basic information about the program described. Students who think they might qualify should write to the contact listed and request an application as soon as possible. Students must complete all requirements by the deadline dates in order to validate their application.

Professional organizations also award scholarships to deserving students; the listings describe ways in which the reader can qualify for consideration. Students can write to professional organizations in their field of interest and request information about scholarships that organization might sponsor. Often, professional groups sponsor awards for students who have completed one or two years of college. Obtain this information directly from the program's sponsors.

Minority student and women's professional organizations also offer both need-based and merit aid to members of their special populations. These awards are made to encourage students from populations traditionally underrepresented in science and engineering to consider careers in these technical fields. Qualified students can apply for other scholarships noted in the minority and women's listings in Appendix A.

The listings that follow are a representative sample of the kinds of scholarships available to students interested in pursuing careers in science and/or technology. They are arranged in alphabetical order by name of the scholarship program.

❖ AGI Minority Geoscience Scholarships

Sponsor: American Geological Institute (AGI) funded by a grant from the National Science Foundation

Type of Award: Renewable scholarships of up to $10,000 per year for geoscience majors who are members of ethnic minority groups underrepresented in geoscience

Qualifications: Applicants must be U.S. citizens and members of a minority group that includes Blacks, Hispanics, or Native Americans (American Indian, Eskimo, Hawaiian, or Samoan). Recipients must enroll at an accredited institution as a geoscience major, studying one of the geosciences such as geology, geophysics, hydrology, meteorology, physical oceanography, planetary geology, or earth science education. Only fulltime students with demonstrable financial need are eligible.

Award Specifics: Scholarship awards of up to $10,000 per year are available for qualified minority students. The program seeks to increase the participation of minority individuals in the geosciences by providing financial support and counseling. Applicants are judged on their potential for professional success. Students should have a strong academic background. The awards are renewable if performance (based on GPA) remains satisfactory.

How to Apply: Complete applications include a financial profile, an essay, official academic transcripts, standardized test scores (SAT or ACT), and three letters of recommendation. All application materials must be received by the deadline of February 1.

Contact: AGI Minority Geoscience Scholarships
American Geological Institute
4220 King Street
Alexandria, VA 22302-1507
(703) 379-2480; FAX (703) 379-7563

❖ ASM Undergraduate Scholarship Program

Sponsor: ASM Foundation for Education and Research

Type of Award: Scholarships for students entering their second year of college and majoring in metallurgy, materials science and engineering

Qualifications: Applicants must be citizens of the United States, Canada, or Mexico and be enrolled in a college or university in one of these countries. They must intend or have declared a major in metallurgy/materials sciences and be entering the sophomore, junior, or senior year of study.

Award Specifics: The ASM Foundation awards nearly 40 scholarships intended to encourage and support capable students interested in pursuing degrees in the field of materials science. One award for juniors or seniors provides full tuition. Three ASM Outstanding Scholars Awards provide stipends of $2,000 each. Thirty-four additional awards are also made to ASM Scholars in the amount of $500.

How to Apply: Students apply for the ASM Scholarships by submitting an application package that includes the official application form, an individual statement describing career plans, special projects and work experience, an up-to-date transcript of college academic work, and three letters of recommendation from teachers and/or employers. The scholarship committee bases its selections on the applicant's academic record, achievements, motivation, potential, citizenship, and interest in metallurgy/materials. All of the awards with the exception of the N.J. Grant award (full-tuition award) are merit awards. The N.J. Grant award selection is partially based on financial need. Applications become available in January.

Contact: ASM Undergraduate Scholarship Program
ASM Foundation for Education and Research
Materials Park, OH 44073-0002
(216) 338-5151 ext. 506

❖ A.T. Anderson Memorial Scholarship Program

Sponsor: American Indian Science and Engineering Society (AISES)

Type of Award: $1,000 scholarships

Qualifications: Applicants must be student members of AISES. Recipients must be American Indians with at least one-fourth degree of Indian blood or proof of tribal membership.

Award Specifics: Each year, numerous scholarships are awarded to full-time students enrolled in a post-secondary program that leads to a four-year degree. Recipients must be majoring in science, mathematics, engineering, or in a related field of study.

How to Apply: Student members of AISES apply by requesting an application from the Scholarship Committee. Application deadline: August 1.

Contact: A.T. Anderson Memorial Scholarship Program
American Indian Science and Engineering Society (AISES)
AISES Scholarship Committee
1085 14th Street, Suite 1506
Boulder, CO 80302
(303) 492-8658

❖ AT&T Engineering Scholarship Program

Sponsor: AT&T Bell Laboratories

Type of Award: Full, four-year scholarships

Qualifications: Applicants are limited to African Americans, Hispanics, American Indians, and women majoring in electrical, mechanical, computer, or systems engineering.

Award Specifics: In order to encourage members of traditionally underrepresented groups to embark on a career in engineering, Bell Laboratories annually offers 15 full scholarships for qualified engineering students. The scholarships provide full tuition, room and board, books and fees, and travel expenses. A summer housing allowance is also included.

How to Apply: Applicants contact the Engineering Scholarship Program Administrator at Bell Labs for an application package. Recipients must maintain a 3.0 GPA to continue in the program. Application deadline: January 15.

Contact: AT&T Engineering Scholarship Program
AT&T Bell Laboratories
Room #1E213
Crawfords Corner Road
Holmdel, NJ 07733
(201) 949-4300

❖ Bausch & Lomb Honorary Science Award and Science Scholarship Program

Sponsor: Bausch & Lomb Inc.

Type of Award: Bausch & Lomb has honored outstanding high school science students with the Honorary Science Award Medal each year since 1933. From the ranks of the medalists, students become eligible to compete for the Bausch & Lomb Scholarships for use at the University of Rochester.

Qualifications: The medal is awarded to the most outstanding science student of the current junior class at participating U.S. high schools. The student is selected by a nominating committee at his or her high school. Winners of the Science Award Medal are eligible to compete for the scholarship.

Award Specifics: Each year, Bausch & Lomb awards merit scholarships for use at the University of Rochester to outstanding science students. The scholarships provide a minimum award of $5,000 per year and may be much higher, depending upon the student's financial need.

How to Apply: Medal winners who wish to enter the scholarship competition simply complete and return a University of Rochester application form. Medal winners have their application fee waived. Completed applications must be on file by January 31. Winners are selected on the basis of academic achievements, along with other criteria such as character, participation in extracurricular activities, and evidence of interest in science.

Contact: Science Award Committee
Bausch & Lomb Honorary Science Award and Science Scholarship Program
Bausch & Lomb Inc.
One Lincoln First Square
Rochester, NY 14604
(716) 338-5174 or 338-5918

❖ DAR Scholarships

Sponsor: National Society Daughters of the American Revolution (NSDAR)

Type of Award: Scholarships ranging in value from $500 to $2,000

Qualifications: Applicants must be U.S. citizens and attend an accredited U.S. college or university. Each applicant must obtain a letter of sponsorship from a local chapter of the Daughters of the American Revolution (DAR). A few of the awards require relationship to a member of the DAR.

Award Specifics: A number of undergraduate scholarships are awarded on the basis of academic excellence, commitment to the field of study, and need. Science-related scholarships include the Holt and Cogswell Nursing Scholarships ($500 to students currently enrolled in an accredited school of nursing) and the Occupational Therapy Scholarships ($500 to $1,000 to students enrolled in an accredited school of occupational or physical therapy). The undesignated Dunn Scholarships provide renewable $1,000 awards to outstanding daughters of current members.

How to Apply: An application packet can be requested by writing to the contact below. A complete application includes the application form, a letter from a sponsoring local chapter, a financial-need form, a transcript of high school (or college) grades, letters of recommendation from teachers, supporting documents attesting to citizenship and college acceptance, a list of accomplishments, and an essay describing career objectives and reasons for college and career choices. Application packets are due to the National Chairman by February 15; awards are made in late April. (Several scholarship programs have an additional application deadline.)

Contact: DAR Scholarships
National Society Daughters of the American Revolution (NSDAR)
Office of the Committees
1776 D Street, NW
Washington, DC 20006-5392

❖ Dow Chemical Premier Scholarship Program

Sponsor: Dow Chemical U.S.A.

Type of Award: Four-year tuition scholarships of $3,000 per year

Qualifications: Eligible are minority students majoring in chemistry, chemical engineering, mechanical engineering, electrical engineering, or other scientific or technical field with applications in Dow Chemical.

Award Specifics: Each year, 45 scholarships provide the recipients with $3,000 per year for tuition and college-related expenses. In addition, students are offered summer internships with Dow Chemical and agree to spend at least two summers working for Dow. Recipients must maintain an average of at least a 2.7 GPA to retain the scholarship.

How to Apply: An application packet can be obtained by writing to Dow at the address listed. Application deadline: April 30.

Contact: Dow Chemical Premier Scholarship Program
Dow Chemical U.S.A.
2020 Willard H. Dow Center
Midland, MI 48674
(517) 636-3451

❖ Electron Microscopy Society of America Undergraduate Scholarship

Sponsor: Electron Microscopy Society of America (EMSA)

Type of Award: Scholarship for undergraduate research

Qualifications: The awards are limited to U.S. citizens or resident aliens who are fulltime undergraduate students pursuing careers in electron microscopy. When possible, at least one of the four scholarships that may be awarded annually will be given to an underrepresented minority applicant. The research for which the scholarships are awarded must be carried out in U.S. laboratories.

Award Specifics: The Electron Microscopy Society of America awards undergraduate research scholarships worth up to $3,000 each to further the educational and research potential of college students interested in careers in electron microscopy. The funds must be used within one year of award date. Preference is given to proposals that use facilities other than those at the student's university.

How to Apply: Completed applications include the application form and a research proposal limited to three pages. The applicant must also provide a budget proposal describing how the award will be used, a letter from the laboratory supervisor supporting the research to be conducted at that facility, a curriculum vitae (including career goals), and two letters of reference. Application deadline: November 15. Awards are made by March 1.

Contact: Dr. M.G. Burke
Electron Microscopy Society of America Undergraduate Scholarship
Electron Microscopy Society of America (EMSA)
Westinghouse Science & Technology Center
1310 Beulah Road
Pittsburgh, PA 15235

❖ Grants-in-Aid of Research

Sponsor: Sigma Xi, The Scientific Research Society

Type of Award: Research awards made to support scientific investigations in any field

Qualifications: Eligible for these grants are undergraduate and graduate students in degree programs who seek funding for a specific science research project. Both U.S. citizens and foreign students are eligible for these grants.

Award Specifics: Small research grants (up to a maximum of $1,000) are available. While it is not necessary to precisely match one of the fields listed below, grants are generally made in the following areas: physical science and engineering (including chemistry, computer science/math, hydrology, paleontology, geochemistry, physics, tectonics) and the behavioral and life sciences (including anthropology, botany, cell biology/biochemistry, ecology, physiology, psychology, zoology).

How to Apply: Applicants send completed applications with supporting materials for evaluation by the Committee on Grants-in-Aid of Research. A complete description of the proposed study must be submitted along with recommendations by two specialists in the field in support of the project. One recommender must be the faculty advisor for the project. The Committee meets three times a year. Decisions are made within eight weeks of the three application deadlines: February 1, May 1, and November 1.

Contact: Grants-in-Aid of Research
Sigma Xi, The Scientific Research Society

99 Alexander Drive
PO Box 13975
Research Triangle Park, NC 27709
(919) 549-4691; FAX (919) 549-0090

❖ IHS Scholarships for Native Americans

Sponsor: The Indian Health Service (IHS)

Type of Award: Preparatory and preprofessional scholarships that provide a monthly stipend to cover tuition, books, fees, some incidentals, equipment, and tutorial services

Qualifications: Scholarships are limited to American Indian and Alaska Natives. Preference is given to those applicants who possess official documentation of tribal membership or proof that they are the natural children or grandchildren of a tribal member. The preprofessional scholarship is limited to students in a premedicine track.

Award Specifics: The scholarships can be used at any school. The Preparatory Scholarship funds undergraduate study for up to two years. The Preprofessional Scholarship funds students in a premedicine track for up to four years of study. The number of scholarships awarded depends upon availability of funds.

How to Apply: Write to the contact listed for more information. Application deadline: usually mid-April.

Contact: Wes Piccotti
              IHS Scholarships for Native Americans
              The Indian Health Service
              Division of Health Professions, Recruitment and Training
              12300 Twinbrook Parkway, Suite 100
              Rockville, MD 20852
              (301) 443-6197

❖ The Juliette A. Southard Scholarship Trust Fund

Sponsor: American Dental Assistants Association (ADAA)

Type of Award: Scholarships for dental-assisting students

Qualifications: U.S. citizens enrolled in an accredited dental-assisting program are eligible. Candidates are considered on the basis of academic achievement, ability, personal qualities, and interest in dentistry.

Award Specifics: The Scholarship Trust Fund awards scholarships in varying amounts to students interested in furthering their education in the field of dental assisting. If a recipient withdraws from school before completing the course of study, the scholarship is regarded as a non-interest-bearing loan and must be repaid to the Trust.

How to Apply: Two letters of reference (one from a dental professional who is a member of the ADAA or ADA and one of the applicant's own choosing), transcripts of the applicant's high school and any college records, and other supporting documents must be received by the ADAA by the application deadline: September 1.

Contact: The Juliette A. Southard Scholarship Trust Fund
American Dental Assistants Association (ADAA)
919 North Michigan Avenue
Chicago, IL 60611
(312) 664-3327

❖ LULAC National Scholarship Fund

Sponsor: LULAC National Educational Service Centers

Type of Award: Need-based and merit-based scholarships ranging in value from $200 to $2,000

Qualifications: LULAC (League of United Latin American Citizens) scholarships are open to Hispanic and other minority students. Some of the awards are made to students pursuing any field of study; other awards are designated for specific areas of study such as science and engineering.

Award Specifics: LULAC awards approximately 1,000 scholarships totaling about one-half million dollars each year to deserving Hispanic and other minority students. Money raised locally by LULAC Councils is matched by corporate grants and is distributed in each community through the LULAC National Educational Service Centers.

How to Apply: Interested students should contact the National Educational Service Center in Washington, DC, or check local listings for a center in their area to obtain further information. Application deadline: May 15.

Contact: LULAC National Scholarship Fund
LULAC National Educational Service Centers
400 First Street, NW, Suite 716
Washington, DC 20001
(202) 347-1652

❖ NACME Incentive Grants Program

Sponsor: National Action Council for Minorities in Engineering, Inc. (NACME)

Type of Award: Renewable awards ranging from $500 to $3,000

Qualifications: The program is limited to African Americans, Mexican Americans, Puerto Ricans, and American Indians enrolled fulltime in an undergraduate engineering program at one of the 72 participating colleges and universities. Recipients must be U.S. citizens or permanent residents and must maintain a GPA of at least 2.5 to retain the award.

Award Specifics: The Incentive Grants Program is the largest privately supported scholarship fund for minorities in the field of engineering. Since the program began in 1975, more than 10 percent of all minority students who have earned engineering degrees in the United States have been NACME scholars. Block grants are made to participating colleges and universities, which then award the funds to individual eligible students.

How to Apply: Since this fund is distributed by the participating schools, qualified applicants can contact their college or university to determine if the institution participates in the program. High school students can contact NACME for information about the participating schools.

Contact: NACME Incentive Grants Program
National Action Council for Minorities in Engineering, Inc. (NACME)
3 West 35th Street
New York, NY 10001-2281
(212) 279-2626

❖ The National Campers and Hikers Association (NCHA) Scholarships

Sponsor: The National Campers and Hikers Association, Inc.

Type of Award: Annual renewable awards ranging from $500 to $2,000 per year for study in a two- or four-year undergraduate program

Qualifications: Award recipients must have been members or dependents of members of NCHA for at least one year before applying and must maintain membership during the time of the award. They must be enrolled in either full- or part-time study. High school applicants should be in the top 40 percent of their graduating class; college applicants should have a B average. Special consideration is given to students majoring in conservation, ecology, or fields related to outdoor activities.

Award Specifics: College scholarships are awarded to members of NCHA or their dependents for undergraduate study in an accredited institution of higher learning. The annual scholarships carry stipends of $500 to $2,000 per year. General considerations include the applicant's maturity, leadership activities, and goals and activities as they relate to the general goals of the NCHA. Financial need is considered but is not a final criterion in selecting winners.

How to Apply: Applicants for either an initial award or a renewal award must submit an application package by the deadline date. The completed package includes an application form, an updated financial report, recommendations from a teacher or school administrator and from an unrelated NCHA member, an official high school transcript for initial award or a college transcript if reapplying, a recent photo, and an explanation of the past year's activities. The committee is interested in work and academic experiences, extracurricular activities, and any other activities worthy of note. Application deadline: April 15.

Contact: Scholarship Director
The National Campers and Hikers Association (NCHA) Scholarships
The National Campers and Hikers Association, Inc.
4804 Transit Road, Building 2
Depew, NY 14043-4704

❖ National Council of State Garden Clubs (NCSGC) Scholarships

Sponsor: National Council of State Garden Clubs, Inc.

Type of Award: $4,000 scholarships for undergraduate and graduate study in the fields of horticulture, floriculture, landscape design, city planning, land management, and allied subjects

Qualifications: Of the 30 scholarships available, all but two are awarded to college juniors, seniors, and graduate students. One award is a four-year college scholarship; another award is for high school gardeners. Applicants must be pursuing a course of study in the fields listed above.

Award Specifics: All applications are first submitted to the state organizations for judging in the early fall. Each state nominates one applicant for the national competition, submitting the application by December 1. Final judging takes place in January.

How to Apply: Applicants who wish to study and prepare themselves for careers in one of the fields listed above should write to the National Council for the name of the state chairperson, to whom the application is submitted directly for consideration by the deadline date indicated on the application.

Contact: National Council of State Garden Clubs (NCSGC) Scholarships
National Council of State Garden Clubs, Inc.
4401 Magnolia Avenue
St. Louis, MO 63110
(314) 776-7574

❖ National Federation of the Blind Scholarship Program

Sponsor: National Federation of the Blind

Type of Award: Some scholarships are designated specifically for students planning to study science, engineering, medicine, or related fields. Others can be used for postsecondary study in any field.

Qualifications: All applicants must be legally blind and pursuing or planning to pursue fulltime postsecondary study.

Award Specifics: Scholarships are awarded annually. Applicants must resubmit applications each year to be considered for renewal of awards. Scholarships range in value from $2,000 to $10,000. All scholarships are awarded on the basis of academic excellence, service to the community, and financial need.

How to Apply: Students complete the application materials and include with them a letter answering questions asked on the application, two letters of recommendation, a current transcript, and a letter from a state officer of the National Federation of the Blind. Each applicant will be considered for all scholarships for which he or she qualifies. Application deadline: March 31. Scholarship winners are selected by June 1; awards are made at the National Federation of the Blind convention in July. In addition to the scholarship grant, winners receive a trip to the convention at the Foundation's expense.

Contact: Miss Peggy Pinder
National Federation of the Blind Scholarship Program
National Federation of the Blind
Grinnell State Bank Building, 2nd Floor
814 Fourth Avenue
Grinnell, IA 50112
(515) 236-3366

❖ National FFA College and Vocational/Technical School Scholarship Program

Sponsor: National FFA (Future Farmers of America) Foundation

Type of Award: Scholarships for postsecondary study for students who are members of the FFA

Qualifications: Scholarships are available to FFA members who are high school seniors or who are high school graduates preparing to enter postsecondary study and to college students who are or have been members of FFA. Most of the scholarships are designated for students pursuing study in some area of agriculture or agribusiness.

Award Specifics: The National FFA Scholarship Program offers educational awards to member students. The individual scholarship programs are supported by a variety of organizations. Some of the scholarships are open to all students; others have been designated for students from specific states and/or pursuing specific areas of study. Awards are paid directly to the student winners and range in value from $500 to $10,000. Some of the scholarships are partially based on family need.

How to Apply: Students apply for all of the scholarships for which they meet the individual requirements by completing the National application and circling the numbers of the scholarship awards for which they wish to be considered. The financial analysis section of the application is completed only if this is a requirement of any of the scholarship programs circled. The entire application must be mailed to the National FFA Organization by the application deadline: February 15.

Contact: National FFA College and Vocational/Technical School Scholarship Program
National FFA Foundation
PO Box 15160
5632 Mt. Vernon Memorial Highway
Alexandria, VA 22309-0160
(703) 360-3600

❖ National Science Scholars Program (NSSP)

Sponsor: U.S. Department of Education

Type of Award: Scholarships for up to four years of undergraduate study

Qualifications: The program is open to U.S. citizens, nationals, and permanent residents graduating from a public or private secondary school or obtaining a GED during the school year prior to the NSSP award. Applicants must have demonstrated outstanding academic achievement in the physical, life, or computer sciences, mathematics, or engineering. Only students intending to pursue a fulltime college program with a major in physical or life sciences, computers, math, or engineering are eligible.

Award Specifics: Initial scholarships of up to $5,000 for the first year of undergraduate study are awarded to high school students who are selected by the individual state nominating committees from all eligible students who submit applications to be National Science Scholars. Subsequent awards are made if the scholar maintains eligibility. Scholars also receive priority for federally financed summer employment in research and development centers and agencies.

How to Apply: Each state that desires to participate in this program appoints a state nominating committee to evaluate student applications. Applicants are evaluated on evidence of exceptional academic achievement and on evidence of nonacademic accomplishment in extracurricular activities and in the physical, life, or computer sciences, mathematics, or engineering. Students must submit letters of recommendation; an essay that reflects the applicant's desire to pursue a career in the sciences, mathematics, or engineering; and an evaluation of how well the applicant demonstrates the ability to meet the goals of the NSSP. At least four nominees, half of whom must be female, are selected by the nominating committee for each congressional district in the state. The President selects two scholars from the nominees for each congressional district. More information on the process as well as application materials are available from the chief state school officer in the participating state's department of education. High school guidance counselors may also have applications available.

Contact: National Science Scholars Program (NSSP)
U.S. Department of Education
Washington, DC 20202-5447

❖ National Society of Black Engineers Scholars Program

Sponsor: National Society of Black Engineers (NSBE)

Type of Award: Annual graduate and undergraduate scholarships: most awards are for $1,500; one award carries a stipend of $2,500.

Qualifications: The program is open to members of the NSBE. Applicants must be endorsed by the local chapter's advisor, the minority engineering program director, or the dean of engineering.

Award Specifics: Each year, approximately 40 undergraduate and graduate scholarships are awarded. The scholarship recipients are chosen on the basis of academic achievement as well as service to the NSBE. Also considered are the applicant's professional involvement and campus and community activities.

How to Apply: Interested students should obtain an application packet from the address listed and request endorsement by the NSBE advisor or other qualified recommender. Application deadline: January 1.

Contact: National Society of Black Engineers Scholars Program
National Society of Black Engineers (NSBE)
344 Commerce Street
Alexandria, VA 22314

❖ NSPE Education Foundation Scholarships

Sponsor: National Society of Professional Engineers (NSPE) Education Foundation

Type of Award: Private-sector-sponsored scholarships: undesignated awards require only that the applicant enroll in an engineering program accredited by the Accreditation Board for Engineering and Technology (ABET) at the university of the applicant's choice; designated scholarships required specific fields of study, geographic guidelines, or universities.

Qualifications: Applicants must be high school seniors, citizens of the United States, with a GPA of at least a 3.0 on a 4.0 scale. Applicants must also achieve a set minimal score on either the SAT, ACT, the WPC, or the PAA to be considered in the competition. Applicants must intend to earn a degree in engineering and to enter the practice of engineering after graduation.

Award Specifics: The NSPE Education Foundation administers a number of designated and undesignated scholarships designed to enable talented graduating high school seniors to pursue degrees in engineering. Some scholarships are for one year only; others are renewable annually. Five of the scholarships are designated for females, two for minority students, and 18 as regional awards (three per region).

How to Apply: Initial judging takes place on the local chapter level; applicants selected on the basis of high school record continue to the state and national consideration levels. Judging is based on a possible 100 points. Up to 45 points are awarded for activities and honors, up to 20 points for grade point average, up to 15 points for essay, and up to 20 points of supplemental credit for math, science, and technical classes as well as honors and advanced placement courses selected. Completed applications are sent to the State Societies of the National Society of Professional Engineers. Application deadline: beginning of December (as noted on application).

Contact: NSPE Education Foundation Scholarships
National Society of Professional Engineers Education Foundation
1420 King Street
Alexandria, VA 22314
(703) 684-2858; FAX (703) 836-4875

❖ Regents Professional Opportunity Scholarship Program

Sponsor: The New York State Education Department

Type of Award: Scholarships valued between $1,000 and $5,000 per year for up to four years of study

Qualifications: Candidates must be U.S. citizens, permanent residents, or selected refugees and must have been legal residents of New York State for at least one year prior to date of award. Applicants must be beginning or be enrolled fulltime in an approved program leading to a degree in a profession licensed by the Board of Regents. Priority is given to economically disadvantaged and/or underrepresented minority students and to graduates of EOP, HEOP, SEEK, or College Discovery programs.

Award Specifics: The New York State Commissioner of Education annually awards 220 scholarships for study in professional areas licensed by the Board of Regents: architecture, dental hygiene, engineering, nursing, occupational therapy, pharmacy, physical therapy, and psychology, among other fields. Awards ranging up to $5,000 per year are designed to increase the number of minority and disadvantaged students in these professions. Recipients agree to practice through full-time employment in their chosen profession in New York State for 12 months for each annual award received.

How to Apply: Application materials become available in October of each year. Students should write to the contact listed to request application forms, deadline dates, and further information.

Contact: Regents Professional Opportunity Scholarship Program
The New York State Education Department
Bureau of Postsecondary Grants Administration
Cultural Education Center, Room 5B68 Empire State Plaza
Albany, NY 12230
(518) 474-5705

❖ Society of Exploration Geophysicists (SEG) Foundation Scholarships

Sponsor: The SEG Foundation

Type of Award: Scholarships ranging in value from $750 to $1,000

Qualifications: The program is open to students majoring in any field that would be applicable to a career in geophysics.

Award Specifics: The scholarships are awarded each year to students pursuing degrees that will prepare them for careers in geophysics. These awards are designed to encourage students to consider careers in geophysics. The awards are available for entering college freshmen, undergraduates, and graduate students.

How to Apply: Eligible students should write to the society's scholarship committee to request an application. Application deadline: March 1.

Contact: Society of Exploration Geophysicists (SEG) Foundation Scholarships
The SEG Foundation
PO Box 702740
Tulsa, OK 74170

❖ Society of Hispanic Professional Engineers (SHPE) Educational Grants Program

Sponsor: The Society of Hispanic Professional Engineers Foundation

Type of Award: Numerous educational awards ranging in value from $300 to $1,500

Qualifications: Recipients must be fulltime minority students who are pursuing a degree in science or engineering and who demonstrate financial need.

Award Specifics: In order to encourage the entrance of minority students into the engineering and scientific professions, the Society of Hispanic Professional Engineers awards educational grants. Although all minority students are eligible, preference is given to SHPE members. Selection is based on academic achievement and on demonstrated school and community activities.

How to Apply: Interested students should contact SHPE for an application package. Application deadline: April 1.

Contact: Society of Hispanic Professional Engineers (SHPE) Educational Grants
The Society of Hispanic Professional Engineers Foundation

Suite 225
5400 East Olympic Boulevard
Los Angeles, CA 90022
(213) 888-2080

❖ Society of Women Engineers Scholarship Program: Westinghouse Bertha Lamme Scholarships and General Electric Foundation Scholarships

Sponsor: The Society of Women Engineers (SWE): Freshmen Scholarship Committee supported by grants from the Westinghouse Educational Foundation and the General Electric Foundation

Type of Award: $1,000 scholarships awarded annually to entering freshman women

Qualifications: Applicants must be women students entering their freshman year and majoring in engineering in a college or university with an accredited engineering program. Recipients must be U.S. citizens or permanent residents.

Award Specifics: Six scholarships are awarded each year to attract women to the field of engineering. Three $1,000 Bertha Lamme Scholarships are awarded in memory of the first woman engineer employed by Westinghouse. Three $1,000 General Electric Foundation Scholarships are awarded on the basis of academic merit to young women pursuing a course of study leading to a bachelor's degree in engineering. The G.E. Scholarships are renewable for three more years with continued academic achievement. In addition, the G.E. Foundation provides a grant of $500 to each recipient so she can attend the National Convention/Student Conference.

How to Apply: Applicants must submit a completed application form, a copy of their high school transcript, a copy of their acceptance into an undergraduate engineering program at an accredited institution, and two letters of reference. In addition, each applicant must submit a one-page letter telling why she wants to be an engineer and why she wants/needs a scholarship. The applicant may also apply for one of the other freshman scholarships offered by the SWE at the same time. Applications must be postmarked by May 15. Recipients are notified by September 15.

Contact: Society of Women Engineers Scholarship Program
The Society of Women Engineers (SWE): Freshmen Scholarship Committee
United Engineering Center, Room 305
345 East 47th Street
New York, NY 10017

❖ Steel Cycles Scholarship Program

Sponsor: Steel Can Recycling Institute (SCRI).

Type of Award: $1,000 scholarship awarded to 70 students from 14 states

Qualifications: Each high school in selected states may nominate one high school senior to compete for this scholarship. Fourteen states are invited each year to take part in this competition.

Award Specifics: Each of the 14 states selected for participation in this project is allocated up to five $1,000 scholarships. The awards are made on the basis of an essay written by the applicant. Creativity and the applicability of the ideas presented in the essay are the criteria used in evaluating the essays.

How to Apply: High schools in selected states are asked to nominate one senior for the award. This individual completes the application and writes an essay dealing with an issue related to recycling. The complete application must be submitted to the program administrators by the deadline date in mid-April.

Contact: Steel Cycles Scholarships Program
Steel Can Recycling Institute (SCRI)
680 Andersen Drive
Pittsburgh, PA 15220
(412) 922-2772

❖ Tandy Technology Scholars Program

Sponsor: Tandy Corporation/Texas Christian University

Type of Award: $1,000 cash scholarship for academic excellence in the field of science, mathematics, or computer science

Qualifications: High school seniors who demonstrate excellence in the fields of science, mathematics, or computer science. Schools participating in the Tandy Technology program may nominate one student for this cash award and may also recognize students in the top two percent of the graduating class for their achievements.

Award Specifics: One hundred students from across the United States are selected as National Finalists. Each selected student receives a cash scholarship award in the amount of $1,000. Accredited participating U.S. high schools may nominate the one student from the current graduating class who shows the highest achievement in one of the fields listed. The student and school complete the application and submit all forms by the deadline date noted (in mid-October).

How to Apply: Schools must be registered in the Tandy Technology program to nominate students. Once registered, the school determines which student should be nominated for this honor, completes their portion of the application, and notifies the student of the selection. The student completes his/her part of application and returns it to the school for submission. The National Finalists are selected by a panel of educators and approved by the National Advisory Council.

Contact: Tandy Technology Scholars Program
Tandy Corporation/Texas Christian University
PO Box 32897
TCU Station
Fort Worth, TX 76129
(817) 924-4087; FAX (817) 927-1942

Resources for Women and Minorities

Historically, the fields of science and engineering have been dominated by white, middle-class males. This pool, however, is no longer sufficient to provide the number of graduate scientists and engineers that are needed if the United States is to maintain (or possibly regain) its place at the forefront of science and technology. The National Science Foundation has predicted that the United States will experience a shortage of 400,000 scientists and 275,000 engineers by the year 2006, unless young women and members of historically underrepresented minority groups, including Black Americans, Native Americans, and Hispanics, are encouraged to attend college and to pursue careers in math, science, and engineering. [Holden (June 30, 1989) *SCIENCE*, 244 p. 1536]

Because the federal government has recognized the importance of increasing representation of all populations in science and engineering, many programs are now being funded by the government as well as by private industry to increase participation of these minority members in the scientific professions. Numerous programs described throughout this book are funded in whole or in part by governmental agencies, such as the National Science Foundation, or by private groups, such as the Howard Hughes Foundation.

The organizations in the following list provide services to students from populations underrepresented in the sciences and engineering. The National Association of Precollege Directors (NAPD) is a consortium of regional organizations whose goal is to increase the number of minority students who pursue college study leading to careers in science and engineering. The member organizations offer programs that include academic enrichment through school year classes and summer programs, student internships and research projects, academic advisement and college counseling, and contacts with practicing scientists and engineers. The names of programs in any region can be obtained by contacting NAPD, as well as by writing to other groups in the following list for more information.

National Association of Precollege Directors (NAPD)
Gil Lopez, Chairperson of NAPD
c/o CMSP
51 Astor Place
New York, NY 10003
(212) 228-0950

American Indian Science & Engineering Society (AISES)
Catherine Abeita, Precollege Director AISES
1085 14th Street, Suite 1506
Boulder, CO 80302
(303) 492-8658

California—Math, Engineering & Science Achievement (CA—MESA)
Fred Easter, Director
University of California
Lawrence Hall of Science
Berkeley, CA 94720
(415) 642-7858

National Action Council for Minorities in Engineering (NACME)
George Campbell, Jr., President
3 West 35th Street
New York, NY 10001-2281
(212) 279-2626

National Society of Black Engineers (NSBE)
Florida Morehead, Director
344 Commerce Street
Alexandria, VA 22314
(703) 549-2207; FAX (703) 683-5312

Southeastern Consortium for Minorities in Engineering (SECME) (Students
from participating schools in Alabama, Florida, Georgia, Kentucky, North
Carolina, South Carolina, Tennessee, and Virginia)
R. Guy Vickers, Director
Georgia Institute of Technology
225 North Avenue, NW
Atlanta, GA 30332-0270
(404) 894-3314

U.S. Department of Energy
John Ortman, Education Specialist
1000 Independence Avenue, SW
Washington, DC 20585
(202) 586-1634

**U.S. Geological Survey's Minority Participation in the Earth Sciences
Program (MPES)** (earth science programs in Colorado, California, Oregon,
Washington, Idaho, Alaska, Virginia, Arizona, and Hawaii)
Jane Wallace
2646 Main Interior Building
1849 C Street, NW
Washington, DC 20240
(202) 208-3888

The following organizations provide programs and services for the target populations described. Student members of these populations can contact appropriate
groups to inquire about scholarships, study programs, opportunities for internships,
and student memberships.

ASPIRA
1112 16th Street, NW #340
Washington, DC 20036
(202) 835-3600; FAX (202) 223-1253
Targets Hispanic youth. Young people are encouraged to continue their postsecondary education. ASPIRA offers scholarships and career information.

Association for Women in Science
1522 K Street, NW Suite 820
Washington, DC 20005
(202) 408-0742; FAX (202) 408-8321
Provides career information and publications about women in the sciences.

Association of American Indian Physicians (AAIP)
Terry Hunter, Director
10015 South Pennsylvania, Building D
Oklahoma City, OK 37159
(405) 692-1202
Recruits and provides support for Native American students interested in careers in the health sciences.

Association of Black Engineers and Applied Scientists (ABEAS)
Kelvin Martin
President, ABEAS
5050 Anthony Wayne Drive, Room 1212.1
Wayne State University
Detroit, MI 48202
(313) 577-3794
Promotes minority student achievement and encourages Black students to pursue careers in science and engineering.

Association of Puerto Ricans in Science and Engineering (APRISE)
Eugenio Barrios
1333 H Street, NW Room 1103
Washington, DC 20005
(202) 326-6670

The Foundation on Employment & Disability, Inc. (TFED)
Dale Fedderson
Program Manager
3820 Del Amo Boulevard, Suite 201
Torrance, CA 90503
(310) 214-3430; TDD (310) 214-1413; FAX (310) 214-4153
Develops and operates educational programs that promote employment opportunities for people with disabilities. One program, "Scientists on Call," brings scientists with disabilities into classrooms to teach hands-on science lessons to students. Other programs include summer-session workshops and college and career information.

LULAC
Lulac National Educational Service Centers
400 First Street, NW, Suite 716
Washington, DC 20001
(202) 347-1652
Provides scholarships and educational counseling to Hispanic students seeking opportunities for postsecondary education.

Math/Science Network
2727 College Avenue
Berkeley, CA 94705
(415) 841-6284
Offers resources to encourage young women to pursue careers in science, math, and technology.

Minority Access to Research Careers (MARC)
National Institutes of Health
9000 Rockville Pike
Bethesda, MD 20892
(301) 496-5231

Minority Women in Science (MWIS)
AAAS Directorate for Education and Human Resources Programs
1333 H Street
Washington, DC 20005
(202) 326-6670
Seeks to improve the science and mathematics education of minority students and encourage participation of women in scientific and technical careers. MWIS is open to men and women of any race, but membership consists primarily of minority women scientists.

National Association of Black Geologists and Geophysicists (NABGG)
Ms. Millicent McCaskill, Program Chairperson
PO Box 720157
Houston, TX 77272
(713) 778-7128
Career guidance for minority students.

Society for the Advancement of Chicanos and Native Americans in Science (SACNAS)
George Castro, President SACNAS
IBM Almaden Research Center
650 Harry Road
San Jose, CA 95120-6099
(408) 927-2400; FAX (408) 927-2510

Society of Exploration Geophysicists (SEG): Committee for Women in Geophysics
PO Box 702740
Tulsa, OK 74170-2740
Seeks to encourage young women to pursue careers in geophysics.

Society of Hispanic Professional Engineers (SHPE)
5400 East Olympic Boulevard, Suite 225
Los Angeles, CA 90022
(213) 888-2080
Provides scholarships to Hispanic students majoring in engineering and introduces secondary students to opportunities in science and technology.

Society of Mexican-American Engineers and Scientists (MAES)
Francisco Guevara, President
23 Los Arboles Drive
Los Alamos, NM 87544
(505) 662-6118

National Agencies and Programs

American Association for the Advancement of Science (AAAS)
AAAS Directorate for Education and Human Resources Programs
1333 H Street, NW
Washington, DC 20005
(202) 326-6670; FAX (202) 371-9849

Dwight D. Eisenhower Mathematics and Science Education Program
U.S. Department of Education
School Effectiveness Division
400 Maryland Avenue, SW Room 2040
Washington, DC 20202-6140

ERIC Clearinghouse for Science, Mathematics, and Environmental Education
Ohio State University
1200 Chambers Road
Columbus, OH 43212-1792
(614) 292-6717

National Aeronautics and Space Administration (NASA)
Elementary and Secondary Programs
NASA Headquarters, Code XEE
Washington, DC 20546
(202) 453-8396

National Science Foundation (NSF)
Directorate for Education and Human Resources
1800 G Street, NW
Washington, DC 20550

National Science Resources Center
Smithsonian Institution
Arts and Industries Building
900 Jefferson Drive, SW
Washington, DC 20560
(202) 357-2555

Science Service, Inc.
1719 N Street, NW
Washington, DC 20036
(202) 785-2255

U.S. Department of Energy (DOE)
Education Office
1000 Independence Avenue, SW
Washington, DC 20585
(202) 586-1634

DOE National Laboratories:

Argonne National Laboratory
Educational Programs Division
9700 South Cass Avenue
Argonne, IL 60439

Brookhaven National Laboratory
Educational Programs Office
Upton, NY 11973
(516) 282-3054

Fermi National Accelerator Laboratory
Education Program Office
MS777, Box 500
Batavia, IL 60510
(708) 840-3092

Lawrence Berkeley Laboratory
Science Education Office
Berkeley, CA 94720
(510) 486-5511

Lawrence Livermore National Laboratory
Science Education Center
PO Box 808
Livermore, CA 94551
(510) 373-0778

Los Alamos National Laboratory
Community Relations
P355
Los Alamos, NM 87545
(505) 667-1230

Oak Ridge National Laboratory
Educational Programs
PO Box 2008
Oak Ridge, TN 37831
(615) 574-5919

Pacific Northwest Laboratory
Office of Pre-University Education
PO Box 999
Richland, WA 99352
(509) 375-2800

Solar Energy Research Institute
1617 Colt Boulevard
Golden, CO 80401
(303) 231-1455

Young Scholars Program (YSP)
National Science Foundation
1800 G Street, NW
Washington, DC 20550
(202) 357-7536

General Index

Academically Interested Minorities (AIM), 140
Access to Careers in the Sciences (ACES) Camps, 184
Advanced Chemistry Applications Program, 104
Advanced Chemistry Education Seminar (ACES), 99
Adventures in Veterinary Medicine, 73
Aerospace programs, 6–13. *See also* Index to Summer Programs by Subject, 285.
AGI Minority Geoscience Scholarships, 248
AISES Science Camp, 155
Alaskan Quest Programs, 57
American Association for the Advancement of Science (AAAS), 269
America's Adventure Camping Program Inc., 110
American Dental Assistants Association Scholarship, 253
American Indian Science and Engineering Society (AISES), 263
Apprenticeships in Science and Engineering (ASE) Program, 168
Aquatic Studies Camp, 66
Archaeology and the Natural Sciences, 14
Archaeology programs, 13–15. *See also* Index to Summer Programs by Subject, 285.
Argonne National Laboratory, 270
ASM Undergraduate Scholarship Program, 248
ASPIRA, 265
Association for Women in Science, 265
Association of American Indian Physicians (AAIP), 265
Association of Black Engineers and Applied Scientists (ABEAS), 265
Association of Puerto Ricans in Science and Engineering (APRISE), 265
Astronomy Camp of Steward Observatory, The, 15, 207
Astronomy programs, 15–17. *See also* Index to Summer Programs by Subject, 285.
A.T. Anderson Memorial Scholarship Program, 249
AT&T Engineering Scholarship Program, 249
Aviation Challenge, 6

Bausch & Lomb Honorary Science Award and Science Scholarship Program, 250
Bennett College Saturday Academy, 216
Biological Science programs, 17–30. *See also*

Index to Summer Programs by Subject, 285.
Biology Career Workshop, 25
Brandeis Summer Odyssey, 136
Brandeis Summer Odyssey Science Research Internships, 136
Breckenridge Outdoor Education Center (BOEC) Internships, 58
Bronx High School of Science, The, 214
Brookhaven National Laboratory, 270

California—Math, Engineering and Science Achievement (CA-MESA), 264
Caltech Young Engineering and Science Scholars (YESS), 108
Camp Planet Earth, 66
Camp Watonka, 173
Career Awareness Experiences in Science and Mathematics (CAESM), 120
Careers in Aerospace Summer Camp, 8
Careers in Applied Science and Technology (CAST), 175
Caretta Research Project, 20
Catalina Island Marine Institute: Sea Camp, 82
Center for American Archaeology Field School, 13
Challenges for Youth—Talented and Gifted (CY-TAG), 123
Chemical Engineering Summer Workshop, 50
Chemistry programs. *See also* Index to Summer Programs by Subject, 285.
Chewonki Co-ed Wilderness Expeditions, 128
Chewonki Foundation Wilderness Trips, The, 211
Circumnavigation, 86
Coast Trek, 90
Committee for Advanced Science Training (CAST) Research Program, 107
Cornell Environmental Sciences Interns Program, 63
Crow Canyon Field School, 13

Dan Fox Youth Scholars Institute, The, 171
D-Arrow: A Wilderness Trip Camp, 128
DAR Scholarships, 250
Dimensions in Nursing, 81
Disadvantaged or Disabled Students. *See* Index of Programs for Special Populations, 291.
Discovery, 148

Discovery Hall Program: High School Summer Program in Marine Science, 81

Distance Learning, 203

DOE High School Honors Program in Ecology, 67

DOE High School Honors Program in Environmental Science, 65

DOE High School Honors Program in Materials Science, 97

DOE High School Honors Research Program at the National Synchrotron Light Source, 101

DOE High School Honors Research Program in Particle Physics, 96

DOE High School Life Sciences Honors Program, 20

DOE High School Supercomputer Honors Program, 108

DOE National Laboratories, U.S., 270

Douglass Science Institute for High School Women in Math, Science, and Engineering, 149

Dow Chemical Premier Scholarship Program, 251

Duke Action: A Science Camp for Young Women, 64

Dupont Challenge Science Essay Awards Program, The, 225

Duracell NSTA Scholarship Competition, 225

Dwight D. Eisenhower Mathematics and Science Education Program, 269

Early Experience Program: The Making of an Engineer, 34

Early Identification Program, 52

Earthwatch Expeditions, 196

Electrical Engineering Program for High School Students, 55

Electron Microscopy Society of America Undergraduate Scholarships, 251

Engineering 2000, 34

Engineering Ahead!, 38

Engineering Career Orientation (ECO), 43

Engineering Experience for Minorities: TEEM, The, 46

Engineering programs, 31–57. See also Index to Summer Programs by Subject, 286.

Engineering Summer Institute, 40

Engineering Summer Program, 56

Engineering Summer Residency Program (ESRP), 33

Enrichment Programs at the Allegheny Square Annex, 218

Environmental Education Programs, 221

Environmental Science programs, 57–71. See also Index to Summer Programs by Subject, 286.

Environmental Studies Programs, 70

Epoch Pilot: Private Pilot Training for High School Students, 10

ERIC Clearinghouse for Science, Mathematics, and Environmental Education, 269

Exploration in Biology and the Health Professions, 74

Exploration in Engineering, 47

Exploration in Psychology, 75

Exploration in Veterinary Medicine, 76

Explorations!, 124

ExploraVision Awards, 226

Exploring Career Options in Engineering and Science (ECOES), 147

Exploring Engineering & Science, 37

Exploring the Geosciences: Earth, Atmosphere, and Environment, 167

Exxon Energy Cube, The, 220

Fermi National Accelerator Laboratory, 270

Fernbank Science Center, 204

Field Studies in Multidisciplinary Biology, 28

Florida Accelerated Initiatives Seminar (FAIS), 114

Foundation for Field Research: Research Expeditions, 194

Foundation for Scholastic Advancement Science Invitational Competition, 227

Foundation on Employment and Disability, The (TFED), 265

Fundamentals of Engineering, 45

Future Astronaut Training Program, 9

Future Leaders in Science Summer Workshop, 163

Futures in Science, 168

Futures in Science and Technology, 120

General Electric Foundation Scholarships, 261

Genetics programs. See Index to Summer Program by Subject, 286.

GERI Summer Residential Programs, 122

Geology programs. See Index to Summer Programs by Subject, 286.

Gifted and Talented Students. See Index to Programs for Special Populations, 291.

Governor's School on the Environment, The, 62

Governor's Summer Institute in Biology and Psychology, 27

Grants-in-Aid of Research, 252

Green River Preserve, The, 159

Hancock Natural Science Field Study and Research Program, 169
Hands-On Archaeological Experience, A, 206
Health Science programs, 71–81. See also Index to Summer Programs by Subject, 286.
HHMI High School Science Scholars Program, 179
High School Engineering Institute, 44
High School Field Ecology and Field Natural History, 68
High School Honors Science Program: Research Internship, 139
High School Summer Science Research Fellowship Program, 186
High School Summer Science Research Program, 144
High School SUMMIT, 126
Horizons Unlimited: The Science Program, 105
Howard Hughes Trainee Program, 26
Hughes High School Research Scholars, 25
Hughes Summer Science Camp, 166

Idaho Science Camp, 117
IHS Scholarships for Native Americans, 253
Illinois Aerospace Institute, 8
Intensive Summer Science Program (ISSP), 160
Interdisciplinary Program in Biological Science, 17
Intern '94, 112
International Aerospace Camp, 11
International Bridge Building Contest, 228
International Mathematics and Science Summer Institute, 197
International Physics Olympiad, 240
International Science and Engineering Fair (ISEF), 228
International Summer Institute, The, 153
International Summer Science Institute, 197
Internships. See Index to Research Participation Programs, 289.
Introduction to Analog and Digital Electronics, An, 97
Introduction to Engineering and Computers Workshop, 51
Introduction to Engineering and Science Summer Institute, 145
Investigations in the Sciences, 163
Invitation to Marine Discovery Camp, 89
Itasca Field Biology and Enrichment Program, 24

Jackling Mineral Industries Summer Careers Institute, 146

JETS Summer Program in Engineering, 36
Juliette A. Southard Scholarship Trust Fund, The (ADAA), 253
Junior Engineering Technical Society Summer Workshop: JETS, 36
Junior High Field Ecology, 69
Junior Science and Humanities Symposium, 229

Keewaydin Wilderness Canoe Trips, 186

Lawrence Berkeley Laboratory, 270
Lawrence Hall of Science: Summer Science Camps, 106
Lawrence Livermore National Laboratory, 270
League of United Latin American Citizens (LULAC), 266
Los Alamos National Laboratory, 270
LULAC National Scholarship Fund, 254
LUMCON/NSF Marine Science Young Scholars Program, 88

Maine Coast Semester, The, 212
Marine Labs, 213
Marine Science Camps, 94
Marine Science for Junior Scholars, 92
Marine Science Pre-College Summer Program, 93
Marine Science programs, 81–95. See also Index to Summer Programs by Subject, 287.
Math & Marine Science Program, 90
Math and Science for Minority Students (MS²), 130
Math and Science Spectacles, 116
Math/Science Network, 266
Medical Technology Summer Institute, 73
Michigan Arts and Sciences Summer Program, 138
Minority Access to Research Careers (MARC), 266
Minority Engineering Summer Research Program, 52
Minority Enrichment Seminar in Engineering Training (MESET), 54
Minority High School Student Research Apprenticeship Program, 182
Minority High School Students Research Apprentice Program, 30
Minority Introduction to Engineering (MITE), 31
Minority Introduction to Engineering (MITE) Programs, 31
Minority Scholars in Computer Science and Engineering, 42
Minority Students programs. See Index to Programs for Special Populations, 291.

Minority Women in Science (MWIS), 266
MIT MITES—Minority Introduction to Engineering & Science, 133
Modeling Acid Deposition: An Introduction to Scientific Methods, 190
Model Rocket Contests, 230
Molecular Biology Enrichment for Youth, 21

NACME Incentive Grants Program, 254
National Action Council for Minorities in Engineering (NACME), 264
National Aeronautics and Space Administration (NASA), 269
National Air & Space Museum Science Demonstration Program, 209
National Association of Black Geologists and Geophysicists (NABGG), 266
National Association of Precollege Directors (NAPD), 263
National Campers and Hikers Association (NCHA) Scholarships, The, 255
National Council of State Garden Clubs (NCSGC) Scholarships, 255
National Engineering Aptitude Search, The (NEAS), 231
National Federation of the Blind Scholarship Program, 256
National FFA Agriscience Student Recognition Program, 231
National FFA College and Vocational/Technical School Scholarship Program, 257
National High School Institute—Science and Engineering, 119
National Junior Horticultural Association (NJHA) Projects and Contests, 232
National Science Foundation (NSF), 269
National Science Olympiad, 233
National Science Resources Center, 269
National Science Scholars Program (NSSP), 257
National Society of Black Engineers (NSBE), 264
National Society of Black Engineers Scholars Program, 258
National Society of Professional Engineers (NSPE) Scholarships, 258
National Youth Science Camp (NYSC), 188
Natural Resources Career Workshop for High School Students, 68
New York Academy of Sciences Educational Programs, 215
New York State Regents Professional Opportunity Scholarship Program, 259
New York State Summer Institute for Science and Mathematics (Buffalo), 151

New York State Summer Institute for Science and Mathematics (Syracuse), 152
New York State Summer Institute for Science and Mathematics–Environmental Sciences, 62
New York State Summer Institute for Science and Mathematics—Student Research Program in Science, 152
Northeast Science Enrichment Program, 130
Northwest Natural Science Camp, 170
Nuclear Science and Technology, 102

Oak Ridge National Laboratory, 270
Oceanology at Occidental College, 84
Odyssey of the Mind Program, The, 233
Oglebay Institute Junior Nature Camp, 189
Oklahoma Aerospace Academy, 11
OMSI Spring Break Safari, Whale Camp, and Naturalist Camp, 218
OPTIONS in Science, 221
Oregon Graduate Institute Saturday Academy, 217

Pacific Marine Science Camp, 170
Pacific Northwest Laboratory Programs, 221, 271
Penn Summer Science Academy, 174
Pennsylvania Governor's School for the Agricultural Sciences, 29
Pennsylvania Governor's School for the Health Care Professions, 77
Pennsylvania Governor's School for the Sciences, 175
Physical and Mathematical Sciences Academic Camps, 161
Physical Science programs, 95–104
Physical Sciences Institute, 98
Physics programs. See Index to Summer Programs by Subject, 287.
Precollege Academic Experience in Mathematics and Science (PAEMS), 126
Pre-College Engineering Program (PREP), 35
Precollege Summer Scholars Program, 83
PREFACE, 38
Preface Program, 48
Program in Mathematics for Young Scientists— PROMYS, 131
Project Earth–Young Scholars, 59
Project SEE, 143
Project YES (Young Exceptional Scholars), 18
Psychology programs. See Index to Summer Programs by Subject, 287.

Radcliffe Summer Program in Science, 134

Recruitment into Engineering of High Ability Minority Students (REHAMS), 39

Regents Professional Opportunity Scholarship Program, 259

Rensselaer Preface Program, 48

Research and Engineering Apprentice Program (REAP), 192

Research Apprentice Program in Veterinary Medicine for Minority High School Students, 76

Research in Science at Erskine (RISE): Scientific Application of Technology, 178

Research Participation Program in Science, The, 27

Research Science Institute, 133

Ross Young Scholars Program, 162

Sargent Camp Internship in Environmental Education, 214

Saturday Academy, The (Bennett College), 216

Saturday Academy (Oregon), 217

Saturday Scholars Program (Rensselaer), 216

Science and Engineering Honors Program, 132

Science and Engineering Research Academy (SERA), 176

Science and Summer at Trinity, 185

Science and Technology Camp, 127

Science-By-Mail, 212

Science Careers Opportunity Enhancement (SCOPE), 79

Science Demonstration Program, 209

Science Olympiad, 234

Science Scholarships, 245

Science Schools, 204

Science Service, Inc., 269

Science Transition Program, 111

Science Quest, 172

Science World, 190

Scientific Application of Technology, 178

Scientific Discovery Program—Young Scholars/ PREP Program, 144

Sci-Tech: Technion's International Science and Technology Research, 198

SCOPES, 155

Seacamp (Florida), 87

Seacamp (San Diego), 86

Sea Camp (Texas), 92

Secondary Student Training Program (SSTP): Research Participation Program, 125

Seiko Youth Challenge, 234

Simons Summer Research Fellowship Program, The, 157

Smith Summer Science Program, 135

Society for the Advancement of Chicanos and Native Americans in Science (SACNAS), 266

Society of Exploration Geophysicists: Committee for Women in Geophysics, 267

Society of Exploration Geophysicists (SEG) Foundation Scholarships, 260

Society of Hispanic Professional Engineers (SHPE) Educational Grants Program, 260

Society of Mexican-American Engineers and Scientists (MAES), 267

Society of Women Engineers Scholarship Program, 261

Solar Energy Research Institute, 271

Southeastern Consortium for Minorities in Engineering (SECME), 264

Space Science Activities Workshop, 9

Spring Field Biology Camp, 219

SST (Scientific Tools and Techniques) Independent Study Program, 209

Steel Cycles Scholarship Program, 261

STRIVE for College and Careers in Science, Mathematics, and Engineering, 137

Student Conservation Association High School Work Groups (HSWG), 61

Student Energy Research Competition (SERC), 235

Student Introduction to Engineering (SITE), 49

Student Science Training Program (SSTP), 114

Student Science Training Program (SSTP) in Calculus-Physics, 95

Student Science Training (SST) Programs in Stellar Astronomy and Nuclear Radiation Applications, 122

Summer Academy in Technology and Science, 150

Summer "AD"Ventures in Math, Science, and Technology I & II, 117

Summer College Engineering Program, 47

Summer Engineering Academy (SEA): Summer Apprentice Program (SAP), 43

Summer Enrichment Program for Gifted and Talented Youth, The, 158

Summer Exploration of the Environment in Dubuque (SEED), 59

Summer Field Studies in Marine Biology, 91

Summer Glaciological and Arctic Studies Expeditionary Institute, 57

Summer Institute for the Gifted at Bryn Mawr College, The, 150

Summer Marine Biology Program, 85

Summer Minority Student Science Training Program, 104

Summer Pre-Engineering Program, 54
Summer Program in Marine Science, 94
Summer Research and Apprenticeship Program in Science and Mathematics, 156
Summer Research Program for High School Students, 78
Summer Research Training Program, 154
Summer Resident Scholars Program, 181
Summer Scholars: Premedical Studies, 80
Summer Scholars Program, 187
Summer Scholars Program—Biotechnology and Human Reproduction, 23
Summer Scholars Program in Marine Science, 87
Summer Scholars Program in Medicine and Public Health, 72
Summerscience, 189
Summer Science and Engineering Enrichment Program, 177
Summer Science Camps, 141
Summer Science Institute: Gene Cloning, 23
Summer Science Program, 157
Summer Science Program for Gifted and Talented Students, 180
Summer Scientific Seminar, 110
Summer Sea Session, 89
Summer Space Academy, 12
Summer Student Grants at the National Institutes of Health, 129
Summer Study in Engineering Program for High School Women, 41
Summer Study in Engineering: Young Scholars Program, 41
Summer Ventures in Science and Math (SVSM), 159
Summer Youth Program, 141
Sun Flight, 7
SuperQuest Computer Competition, 236

TAG (Talented and Gifted) Science Program, 183
Talcott Mountain Academy of Science, Mathematics, and Technology, 207
Talcott Mountain Science Center Programs, 208
Tandy Technology Scholars Program, 262
Technology, Education, Kids: TEK Camp, 100
Technology Student Association Competitive Events, 237
Tennessee Governor's School for the Sciences, 180
Technology Connection, The, 113
Thacher School Summer Science Program, 16
Thomas Edison/Max McGraw Scholarship Program, 237

Trailside Discovery's Alaskan Quest Programs, 57
Training for Research: The Summer Student Program, 22
Tuskegee University MITE, 31

U.S. Department of Energy (DOE), 264, 270
U.S. DOE National Laboratories, 270
U.S. FIRST Competition, 238
U.S. Geological Survey: Minority Participation in the Earth Sciences Program, 264
U.S. National Chemistry Olympiad (USNCO), 239
United States Physics Team for the International Physics Olympiad, 240
U.S. Space Academy, 6, 205
University of Connecticut—NSF Young Scholars Program, 112
University of Dayton Women in Engineering, 50
University Research Expeditions (UREP), 195
Upward Bound, 138

Veterinary Enrichment Program, 79
Volunteer Involvement, 205
Volunteer for Science, 193, 220

W. Alton Jones Camp: Teen Expeditions, 177
Westinghouse Bertha Lamme Scholarships, 402
Westinghouse Science Talent Search, 241
White Mountain Archaeological Center, 206
Wilderness programs. See Index to Summer Programs by Subject, 287.
Wilderness Adventures, 210
Wilderness Southeast Camps: Mountain Trek, Mountain Adventure, Coastal Experience, and Tropical Venture, 194
Wilderness Ventures Inc., 193
WISE Academic Camp, 165
WISE: Women Investigating Sciences and Environments, 147
Women in Engineering Program, 45
Women in Engineering Program (WIE), 50
Women in Science and Engineering Program (WISE), 118
Women in Science and Mathematics Workshop, 161
Women in the Sciences, 164
Women's programs. See Index to Programs for Special Populations, 292.

Yale Summer Psychology Program (YSPP), 71
YMCA Camp Kern: Camp Challenge, The Voyagers, Archaeology Camp, and Science Camp, 165

YMCA Camp Menogyn: Wilderness Adventures, 142

YMCA Camp Oakes: Basic Wilderness, 106

Young America Horticultural Contests, 241

Young Inventors' Contest, 242

Young Scholars in Yellowstone National Park, 70

Young Scholars Ocean Science Institute, 83

Young Scholars Program (YSP), 271

Young Scholars Program (Florida), 115

Young Scholars Program (Saint Vincent College), 173

Young Scholars Program (Texas A&M), 53

Young Scholars Program: An Introduction to Analog and Digital Electronics, 97

Young Scholars Program at Haystack Observatory, 17

Young Scholars Program: Engineering Summer Program, 56

Young Scholars Program: Exploration of Careers in Science, 121

Young Scholars Program in Coastal Erosion and Preservation, 60

Young Scholars Program in Life Sciences & Biochemistry, Chemistry & Physics with Research Participation, 183

Young Scholars Program in Paleontology/ Geology, 15

Young Scholars Program in Physics, 103

Young Scholars Program: Introduction to Engineering and Computers Workshop, 51

Young Scholars Program: Investigations in Trajectories, 99

Young Scholars Research Participation Programs in Aquatic Ecology and High Desert Ecology, 64

Young Scholars Research Program in Chemistry, 101

Young Scholars Summer Session (YSSS), 109

Young Scientist Program: A Research Experience in Biology, 19

Young Scientists Program, 171

Youthsummer, 191

State and Regional Index

Alabama

Aviation Challenge, 6
Discovery Hall Program: High School Summer Program in Marine Science, 81
Minority Introduction to Engineering (MITE), 31
Summer Minority Student Science Training Program, 104
U.S. Space Academy, 6, 205

Alaska

Summer Glaciological and Arctic Studies Expeditionary Institute, 57
Trailside Discovery's Alaskan Quest Programs, 57

Arizona

Astronomy Camp of Steward Observatory, The, 15, 207
Hands-On Archaeological Experience, A, 206
Horizons Unlimited: The Science Program, 105

California

Caltech Young Engineering and Science Scholars (YESS), 108
Catalina Island Marine Institute: Sea Camp, 82
Committee for Advanced Science Training (CAST) Research Program, 107
DOE High School Life Sciences Honors Program, 20
DOE High School Supercomputer Honors Program, 108
Engineering Summer Residency Program, 33
Interdisciplinary Program in Biological Science, 17
Lawrence Hall of Science: Summer Science Camps, 106
Oceanology at Occidental College, 84
Precollege Summer Scholars Program, 83
Project YES (Young Exceptional Scholars), 18
Seacamp San Diego, 86
Summer Marine Biology Program, 85
Thacher School Summer Science Program, 16
YMCA Camp Oakes: Basic Wilderness Camp, 106
Young Scholars Ocean Science Institute, 83

Colorado

America's Adventure Camping Program Inc., 110
Breckenridge Outdoor Education Center (BOEC) Internships, 58
Crow Canyon Archaeological Center Field School, 13

Early Experience Program: The Making of an Engineer, 34
Summer Scientific Seminar, 110
Young Scholars Summer Session, 109
Young Scientist Program: A Research Experience in Biology, 19

Connecticut

Circumnavigation, 86
Science Transition Program, 111
Talcott Mountain Academy of Science, Mathematics, and Technology, 207
Talcott Mountain Science Center Programs, 208
University of Connecticut—NSF Young Scholars Program, 112
Yale Summer Psychology Program (YSPP), 71

District of Columbia

Engineering 2000, 34
Intern '94, 112
Science Demonstration Program, 209

Florida

Florida Accelerated Initiatives Seminar (FAIS), 114
Project Earth–Young Scholars, 59
Seacamp, 87
Student Science Training Program (SSTP), 114
Summer Scholar Program in Marine Science, 87
Summer Scholars Program in Medicine and Public Health, 72
Sun Flight, 7
Technology Connection, The, 113
Young Scholars Program, 115

Georgia

Caretta Research Project, 20
Math and Science Spectacles, 116
Minority Introduction to Engineering, 31
Pre-College Engineering Program (PREP), 35
SST (Scientific Tools and Techniques) Independent Study Program, 209
Wilderness Southeast Camps, 194
Wilderness Southeast Spring Break Adventures, 210

Hawaii

Student Science Training Program (SSTP) in Calculus-Physics, 95

Idaho

Idaho Science Camp, 117

Junior Engineering Technical Society Summer Workshop: JETS, 36

Illinois
Career Awareness Experiences in Science and Mathematics (CAESM), 120
Careers in Aerospace Summer Camp, 8
Center for American Archaeology Field School, 13
DOE High School Honors Program in Materials Science, 97
DOE High School Honors Research Program in Particle Physics, 96
Futures in Science and Technology, 120
Illinois Aerospace Institute, 8
JETS Summer Program in Engineering, 36
Minority Introduction to Engineering, 31
National High School Institute—Engineering and Science, 119
Summer "AD"Ventures in Math, Science & Technology, 117
Women in Science and Engineering Program (WISE), 118
Young Scholars Program: Archaeology and Natural Science, 14

Indiana
Exploring Engineering & Science, 37
GERI Summer Residential Programs, 122
Minority Introduction to Engineering, 31
PREFACE, 38
Student Science Training (SST) Programs in Stellar Astronomy and Nuclear Radiation Application, 122
Young Scholars Program: Exploration of Careers in Science, 121
Young Scholars Program: An Introduction to Analog and Digital Electronics, 97

Iowa
Challenges for Youth—Talented and Gifted (CY-TAG), 123
Explorations!, 124
Molecular Biology Enrichment for Youth, 21
Secondary Student Training Program (SSTP): Research Participation Program, 125
Space Science Activities Workshop, 9
Summer Exploration of the Environment in Dubuque (SEED), 59

Kansas
Future Astronaut Training Program, 9
High School SUMMIT, 126

Kentucky
Engineering Ahead!, 38

Precollege Academic Experience in Mathematics and Science (PAEMS), 126
Science and Technology Camp, 127

Louisiana
Engineering Summer Institute, 40
LUMCON/NSF Marine Science Young Scholars Program, 88
Recruitment into Engineering of High Ability Minority Students (REHAMS), 39
Young Scholars Program in Coastal Erosion and Preservation, 60

Maine
Chewonki Co-ed Wilderness Expeditions, 128
Chewonki Foundation Wilderness Trips, The, 211
D-Arrow: A Wilderness Trip Camp, 128
Maine Coast Semester, The, 212
Summer Sea Session, 89
Training for Research: The Summer Student Program, 22

Maryland
Minority Scholars in Computer Science and Engineering, 42
Summer Science Institute: Gene Cloning, 23
Summer Student Grants at the National Institutes of Health, 129
Summer Study in Engineering Program for High School Women, 41
Summer Study in Engineering: Young Scholars Program, 41

Massachusetts
Adventures in Veterinary Medicine, 73
Brandeis Summer Odyssey, 136
Brandeis Summer Odyssey Science Research Internships, 136
Engineering Career Orientation (ECO), 43
Math and Science for Minority Students (MS²), 130
MIT MITES—Minority Introduction to Engineering & Science, 133
Northeast Science Enrichment Program, 130
Program in Mathematics for Young Scientists—PROMYS, 131
Radcliffe Summer Program in Science, 134
Research Science Institute, 133
Science and Engineering Honors Program, 132
Science-By-Mail, 212
Smith Summer Science Program, 135
STRIVE for College and Careers and Science, Math, and Engineering, 137
Young Scholars Program at Haystack Observatory, 17

Michigan
Academically Interested Minorities, 140
High School Engineering Institute, 44
High School Honors Science Program: Research Internship, 139
Medical Technology Summer Institute, 73
Michigan Arts and Sciences Summer Program, 138
Summer Engineering Academy (SEA): Summer Apprenticeship Program (SAP), 43
Summer Science Camps, 141
Summer Youth Program, 141
Upward Bound, 138
Women in Engineering Program, 45

Minnesota
High School Summer Science Research Program, 144
Itasca Field Biology and Enrichment Program, 24
Project SEE (Summer Education Experience), 143
Scientific Discovery Program—Young Scholars/PREP Program, 144
Summer Scholars Program—Biotechnology and Human Reproduction, 23
YMCA Camp Menogyn: Wilderness Adventures, 142

Mississippi
Invitation to Marine Discovery Camp, 89
Physical Sciences Institute, 98
Young Scholars Program: Investigations in Trajectories, 99

Missouri
Advanced Chemistry Education Seminar (ACES), 99
Fundamentals of Engineering, 45
Introduction to Engineering and Science Summer Institute, 145
Jackling Mineral Industries Summer Careers Institute, 146

Nebraska
Biology Career Workshop, 25
Technology, Education, Kids: TEK Camp, 100
WISE: Women Investigating Sciences and Environments, 147

Nevada
Howard Hughes Trainee Program, 26
Hughes High School Research Scholars, 25

New Hampshire
Marine Labs, 213
Math & Marine Science Program, 90
Sargent Camp Internship in Environmental Education, 214

Student Conservation Association High School Work Groups (HSWG), 61

New Jersey
Discovery, 148
Douglass Science Institute for High School Women in Math, Science, and Engineering, 149
Engineering Experience for Minorities: TEEM, The, 46
Exploring Career Options in Engineering and Science (ECOES), 147
Governor's School on the Environment, The, 62
Summer Academy in Technology and Science, 150
Summer Institute for the Gifted at Bryn Mawr College, The, 150

New York
AISES Science Camp, 155
Bronx High School of Science, The, 214
Cornell Environmental Sciences Interns Program, 63
DOE High School Honors Research Program at the National Synchrotron Light Source, 101
Exploration in Biology and the Health Professions, 74
Exploration in Engineering, 47
Exploration in Psychology, 75
Exploration in Veterinary Medicine, 76
International Mathematics and Science Summer Institute, 197
International Summer Institute, The, 153
New York Academy of Sciences Educational Programs, 215
New York State Summer Institute for Science and Mathematics (Buffalo), 151
New York State Summer Institute for Science and Mathematics (Syracuse), 152
New York State Summer Institute for Science and Mathematics–Environmental Sciences, 62
New York State Summer Institute for Science and Mathematics—Summer Research Program in Science, 152
Preface Program, 48
Research Apprentice Program in Veterinary Medicine for Minority High School Students, 76
Research Participation Program in Science, The. 27
Saturday Scholars Program, 216
SCOPES, 155
Simons Summer Research Fellowship Program, The, 157
Summer College Engineering Program, 47
Summer Research and Apprenticeship Program in Science and Mathematics, 156
Summer Research Training Program, 154

Young Scholars Research Program in Chemistry, 101

North Carolina
Coast Trek, 90
Duke Action: A Science Camp for Young Women, 64
Green River Preserve, The, 159
Intensive Summer Science Program (ISSP), 160
Nuclear Science and Technology, 102
Physical and Mathematical Sciences Academic Camps, 161
Saturday Academy, The (Bennett College), 216
Student Introduction to Engineering (SITE), 49
Summer Enrichment Program for Gifted and Talented Youth, The, 158
Summer Science Program, 157
Summer Ventures in Science and Math (SVSM), 159

North Dakota
Epoch Pilot: Private Pilot Training for High School Students, 10
International Aerospace Camp, 11

Ohio
Chemical Engineering Summer Workshop, 50
Future Leaders in Science Summer Workshop, 163
Governor's Summer Institute in Biology and Psychology, 27
Hughes Summer Science Camp, 166
Investigations in the Sciences, 163
Ross Young Scholars Program, 162
WISE Academic Camp, 165
Women in Engineering Program (WIE), 50
Women in Science and Mathematics Workshop, 161
Women in the Sciences, 164
YMCA Camp Kern: Camp Challenge, The Voyagers, Archaeology Camp, and Science Camp, 165

Oklahoma
Exploring the Geosciences: Earth, Atmosphere, and Environment, 167
Field Studies in Multidisciplinary Biology, 28
Futures in Science, 168
Oklahoma Aerospace Academy, 11

Oregon
Apprenticeships in Science and Engineering (ASE) Program, 168
Hancock Natural Science Field Study and Research Program, 169
Northwest Natural Science Camp, 170
OMSI Spring Break Safari, Whale Camp, and Naturalist Camp, 218

OPTIONS in Science, 221
Pacific Marine Science Camp, 170
Saturday Academy, 217
Sharing Science with Schools, 221
Young Scholars Research Participation Programs in Aquatic Ecology and High Desert Ecology, 64
Young Scholars Research Program in Paleontology/Geology, 15

Pennsylvania
Camp Watonka, 173
Careers in Applied Science and Technology (CAST), 175
Dan Fox Youth Scholars Institute, The, 171
Enrichment Programs at the Allegheny Square Annex, 218
Penn Summer Science Academy, 174
Pennsylvania Governor's School for the Agricultural Sciences, 29
Pennsylvania Governor's School for the Health Care Professions, 77
Pennsylvania Governor's School for the Sciences, 175
Science & Engineering Research Academy (SERA), 176
Science Quest, 172
Summer Space Academy, 12
Young Scholars Program (Saint Vincent College), 173
Young Scientists Program, 171

Rhode Island
Summer Field Studies in Marine Biology, 91
W. Alton Jones Camp: Teen Expeditions, 177

South Carolina
Marine Science for Junior Scholars, 92
Scientific Application of Technology, 178
Summer Science and Engineering Enrichment Program, 177
Young Scholars Program in Physics, 103

South Dakota
Spring Field Biology Camp, 219

Tennessee
DOE High School Honors Program in Environmental Science, 65
Early Identification Program, 52
HHMI High School Science Scholars Program, 179
Introduction to Engineering and Computers Workshop, 51
Minority Engineering Summer Research Program, 52
Minority High School Student Research Apprenticeship Program, 182

Summer Resident Scholars Program, 181
Summer Science Program for Gifted and
    Talented Students, 180
Tennessee Governor's School for the Sciences, 180

Texas

Access to Careers in the Sciences (ACES)
    Camps, 184
Advanced Chemistry Applications Program, 104
Aquatic Studies Camp, 66
Camp Planet Earth, 66
High School Summer Science Research
    Fellowship Program, 186
Minority Enrichment Seminar in Engineering
    Training (MESET), 54
Minority High School Students Research
    Apprentice Program, 30
Prairie View MITE, 33
Science and Summer at Trinity, 185
Science Careers Opportunity Enhancement
    Program, 79
Sea Camp, 92
Summer Pre-Engineering Program, 54
Summer Research Program for High School
    Students, 78
TAG (Talented and Gifted) Science Program, 183
Veterinary Enrichment Program, 79
Young Scholars Program (Texas A&M), 53
Young Scholars Program in Life Sciences &
    Biochemistry, Chemistry & Physics with
    Research Participation, 183

Vermont

Keewaydin Wilderness Canoe Trips, 186

Virginia

Marine Science Pre-College Summer Program, 93
Minority Introduction to Engineering, 32
Summer Program in Marine Science, 94
Summer Scholars: Premedical Studies, 80

Washington

DOE High School Honors Program in Ecology, 67
Marine Science Camps, 94
OPTIONS in Science, 221
Sharing Science with Schools (Pacific Northwest
    Laboratory), 221
Summer Scholars Program, 187

West Virginia

National Youth Science Camp (NYSC), 188
Oglebay Institute Junior Nature Camp, 189

Wisconsin

Dimensions in Nursing, 81
Electrical Engineering Program for High School
    Students, 55
Environmental Education Programs, 221
Modeling Acid Deposition: An Introduction to
    Scientific Methods, 190
Natural Resources Career Workshop for High
    School Students, 68
Science World, 190
Summerscience, 189
Youthsummer, 191

Wyoming

Engineering Summer Program, 56
High School Field Ecology and Field Natural
    History, 68
Junior High Field Ecology, 69
Young Scholars in Yellowstone National Park, 70

Programs Abroad

Earthwatch Expeditions, 196
Environmental Studies Program, 70
Foundation for Field Research Expeditions, 194
International Mathematics and Science Summer
    Institute, 197
International Summer Science Institute, 197
School for Field Studies Environmental Studies
    Program, 70
Sci-Tech: Technion's International Science and
    Technology Research Program, 198
University Research Expeditions (UREP), 195

Regional or National Programs

Chewonki Foundation Wilderness Trips, The, 211
Research and Engineering Apprenticeship
    Program (REAP), 192
Volunteer for Science, 193, 220
Wilderness Adventures, 210
Wilderness Southeast Camps: Mountain Trek,
    Mountain Adventure, Coastal Experience,
    and Tropical Venture, 194
Wilderness Ventures Inc., 193

Index to Summer Programs by Subject

Aerospace
Aviation and Aerospace programs, 6–13
Florida Accelerated Initiatives Seminar (Space Sciences), 114
International Summer Institute, The, 153
Young Scholars Program: Investigations in Trajectories, 99
Youthsummer, 191

Archaeology
Archaeology and Paleontology programs, 13–15
Earthwatch Expeditions: EarthCorps Volunteers, 196
Foundation for Field Research: Research Expeditions, 194
Summer Exploration of the Environment in Dubuque (SEED), 59
University Research Expeditions, 195
YMCA Camp Kern: Archaeology Camp, 165

Astronomy
Astronomy programs, 15–17
Caltech Young Engineering and Science Scholars, 108
Explorations!, 124
Investigations in the Sciences, 163
Northwest Natural Science Camp (Astronomy Camp), 170
Physical Sciences Institute, 98
Science and Engineering Honors Program, 132
Student Science Training Program (Stellar Astronomy), 122
Young Scholars Program: Exploration of Careers in Science, 121
Young Scholars Summer Session, 109

Biological Science
Biological Science programs, 17–30
Brandeis Summer Odyssey, 136
Brandeis Summer Odyssey Science Research Internships, 136
Caltech Young Engineering and Science Scholars, 108
Exploration in Biology and the Health Professions, 74
Florida Accelerated Initiatives Seminar (Biotechnology), 114
Futures in Science, 168
HHMI High School Science Scholars Program, 179
International Summer Institute, The, 153

Investigations in the Sciences, 163
New York State Summer Institute for Science and Mathematics, 151
Penn Summer Science Academy (Molecular Biology), 174
Precollege Academic Experience in Mathematics and Science, 126
Research Science Institute, 133
Science and Engineering Honors Program, 132
Summer Research Training Program, 154
Summer Science Camps (Molecular Biology Camp), 141
Young Scholars Program in Life Sciences & Biochemistry, 183
Young Scholars Summer Session (YSSS), 109
Young Scientists Program, 171

Chemistry
Academically Interested Minorities (AIM), 140
Advanced Chemistry Applications Program, 104
Advanced Chemistry Education Seminar (ACES), 99
Brandeis Summer Odyssey Science Research Internships, 136
Challenges for Youth—Talented and Gifted (CY-TAG), 123
Exploring Career Options in Engineering and Science (ECOES), 147
Futures in Science, 168
HHMI High School Science Scholars Program, 179
International Summer Institute, The, 153
Investigations in the Sciences, 163
Molecular Biology Enrichment for Youth, 21
Physical and Mathematical Sciences Academic Camps, 161
Precollege Academic Experience in Mathematics and Science, 126
Science and Engineering Honors Program, 132
Summer Academy in Technology and Science, 150
Summer Science Camps (Chemistry and Physics Camp), 141
Summer Science Program, 157
Young Scholars Program in Chemistry and Physics, 183
Young Scholars Research Program in Chemistry, 101
Young Scientists Program, 171

Engineering

Engineering programs, 31–57
Academically Interested Minorities (AIM), 140
Douglass Science Institute for High School Women in Math, Science, and Engineering, 149
Exploring Career Options in Engineering and Science (ECOES), 147
Futures in Science and Technology, 120
Introduction to Engineering and Science Summer Institute, 145
Jackling Mineral Industries Summer Careers Institute, 146
Michigan Arts and Sciences Summer Program, 138
MIT MITES—Minority Introduction to Engineering & Science, 133
National High School Institute—Engineering and Science, 119
Research and Engineering Apprentice Program (REAP), 192
Research Science Institute, 133
Science and Engineering Honors Program, 132
Science & Engineering Research Academy (SERA), 176
STRIVE for College and Careers in Science, Mathematics, and Engineering, 137
Summer Science and Engineering Enrichment Program, 177
Technology Connection, The, 113
Women in Science and Engineering Program (WISE), 118
Young Scholars Program: Investigations in Trajectories, 99

Environmental Science

Ecology and Environmental Science programs, 57–71
Coast Trek, 90
Discovery, 148
Earthwatch Expeditions: EarthCorps Volunteers, 196
Exploring the Geosciences: Earth, Atmosphere, and Environment, 167
Foundation for Field Research: Research Expeditions, 194
Hancock Natural Science Field Study and Research Program, 169
International Summer Institute, The, 153
Lawrence Hall of Science: Summer Science Camps, 106
Michigan Arts and Sciences Summer Program, 138
Modeling Acid Deposition: An Introduction to Scientific Methods, 190
New York State Summer Institute for Science and Mathematics, 152

Northwest Natural Science Camp (Naturalist Program), 170
Oglebay Institute Junior Nature Camp, 189
Penn Summer Science Academy, 174
Science and Summer at Trinity, 185
Scientific Discovery Program, 144
University Research Expeditions (UREP), 195
WISE: Women Investigating Sciences and Environments, 147
Young Scientist Program: A Research Experience in Biology, 19

Genetics

International Summer Institute, The, 153
New York State Summer Institute for Science and Mathematics, 152
Research in Science at Erskine (RISE): Scientific Application of Technology, 178
Summer Research Training Program, 154
Summer Resident Scholars Program, 181
Summer Scholars Program in Medicine and Public Health, 72
Summer Science Camps (Molecular Biology Camp), 141
Summer Science Institute: Gene Cloning, 23

Geology

Exploring the Geosciences: Earth, Atmosphere, and Environment, 167
Hancock Natural Science Field Study and Research Program, 169
Investigations in the Sciences, 163
Jackling Mineral Industries Summer Careers Institute, 146
New York State Summer Institute for Science and Mathematics, 151, 152
Northwest Natural Science Camp (Geology and Fossils Program), 170
Summer Glaciological and Arctic Studies Expeditionary Institute, 57
Volunteer for Science (U.S. Geological Survey), 193
Young Scholars Program: Exploration of Careers in Science, 121
Young Scholars Research Participation Program in Paleontology/Geology, 15
Young Scientists Program, 191

Health Science

Health Sciences programs, 71–81
Brandeis Summer Odyssey, 136
Hughes High School Research Scholars, 25
Michigan Arts and Sciences Summer Program, 138
Minority High School Student Research Apprenticeship Program, 182

Minority High School Students Research Apprentice Program, 30
Secondary Student Training Program (SSTP): Research Participation Program, 125
Summer Scholars Program—Biotechnology and Human Reproduction, 23
Summer Student Grants at the National Institutes of Health, 129
Youthsummer, 191

Marine Science
Marine Biology and Marine Science programs, 81–95
Brandeis Summer Odyssey, 136
Florida Accelerated Initiatives Seminar (FAIS), 114
Foundation for Field Research: Research Expeditions, 194
Pacific Marine Science Camp, 170
Physical and Mathematical Sciences Academic Camps, 161

Physics
Brandeis Summer Odyssey Science Research Internships, 136
Caltech Young Engineering and Science Scholars (YESS), 108
Challenges for Youth—Talented and Gifted (CY-TAG), 123
DOE High School Honors Program in Materials Science, 97
DOE High School Honors Research Program at the National Synchrotron Light Source (NSLS), 101
DOE High School Honors Research Program in Particle Physics, 96
DOE High School Supercomputer Honors Program, 108
Exploring Career Options in Engineering and Science (ECOES), 147
Futures in Science, 168
International Mathematics and Science Summer Institute, 197
International Summer Science Institute, 197
New York State Summer Institute for Science and Mathematics, 152
Nuclear Science and Technology, 102
Physical and Mathematical Sciences Academic Camps, 161
Physical Sciences Institute, 98
Research Science Institute, 133
Science and Engineering Honors Program, 132
Science and Technology Camp, 127
Student Science Training Program in Calculus-Physics, 95

Student Science Training Program in Nuclear Radiation Applications, 122
Summer Academy in Technology and Science, 150
Summer Science Camp: Chemistry and Physics Camp, 141
Technology, Education, Kids: TEK Camp, 100
Young Scholars Program: An Introduction to Analog and Digital Electronics, 97
Young Scholars Program: Exploration of Careers in Science, 121
Young Scholars Program in Chemistry & Physics, 183
Young Scholars Program in Physics, 103
Young Scholars Program: Investigations in Trajectories, 99
Young Scientists Program, 171

Psychology
Brandeis Summer Odyssey Science Research Internships, 136
Challenges for Youth—Gifted and Talented (CY-TAG), 123
Exploration in Psychology, 75
Governor's Summer Institute in Biology and Psychology, 27
Investigations in the Sciences, 163
Summer Science Program, 157
Yale Summer Psychology Program (YSPP), 71
Young Scholars Program: Exploration of Careers in Science, 121

Robotics
Early Experience Program: The Making of an Engineer, 34
Engineering 2000, 34
Explorations!, 124
Michigan Arts and Science Summer Program, 138
Sci-Tech: Technion's International Science and Technology Research Program, 198
Summer Resident Scholars Program, 181

Wilderness Programs
America's Adventure Camping Program, Inc., 110
Chewonki Co-ed Wilderness Expeditions, 128
D-Arrow: A Wilderness Trip Camp, 128
Keewaydin Wilderness Canoe Trips, 186
Lawrence Hall of Science: Outdoor Skills and Backpacking Camp, 106
W. Alton Jones Camp: Teen Expeditions, 177
Wilderness Southeast Camps, 194
Wilderness Ventures Inc., 193
YMCA Camp Kern, 165
YMCA Camp Menogyn: Wilderness Adventures, 142
YMCA Camp Oakes: Basic Wilderness Camp, 106

Index to Field Experiences

Astronomy Camp of Steward Observatory, The, 207
Caretta Research Project, 20
Center for American Archaeology: One Week Field School, 13
Crow Canyon Archaeological Center High School Field School, 13
Discovery Hall Program: High School Summer Program in Marine Science, 81
Earthwatch Expeditions: EarthCorps Volunteers, 196
Environmental Education Programs, 221
Foundation for Field Research: Research Expeditions, 194
Hancock Natural Science Field Study and Research Program, 169
Hands-On Archaeological Experience, A, 206
High School Field Ecology and Field Natural History (Teton Science School), 68
Itasca Field Biology and Enrichment Program, 24

Junior High Field Ecology (Teton Science School), 69
Marine Labs, 213
Northwest Natural Science Camp, 170
OMSI Spring Break Programs, 218
Pacific Marine Science Camp, 170
Project Earth—Young Scholars, 59
Spring Field Biology Camp, 219
Summer Glaciological and Arctic Studies Expeditionary Institute, 57
Summer Sea Session (Maine Maritime Academy), 89
University Research Expeditions (UREP), 195
Young Scholars in Yellowstone National Park, 70
Young Scholars Research Participation Program in Paleontology/Geology, 15
Young Scholars Research Participation Programs in Aquatic Ecology and High Desert Ecology, 64

Index to Research Participation (Internship) Programs

Advanced Chemistry Applications Program, 104

Apprenticeships in Science and Engineering (ASE) Program, 168

Brandeis Summer Odyssey Science Research Internships, 136

Breckenridge Outdoor Education Center (BOEC) Internships, 58

Career Awareness Experiences in Sciences and Mathematics (Junior High Students), 120

Committee for Advanced Science Training (CAST) Research Program, 107

Cornell Environmental Sciences Interns Program, 63

Discovery, 148

DOE High School Honors Program in Ecology, 67

DOE High School Honors Program in Environmental Science, 65

DOE High School Honors Program in Materials Science, 97

DOE High School Honors Research Program at the National Synchrotron Light Source (NSLS), 101

DOE High School Honors Research Program in Particle Physics, 96

DOE High School Life Sciences Honors Program, 20

DOE High School Supercomputer Honors Program, 108

Early Experience Program: The Making of an Engineer, 34

Exploring Career Options in Engineering and Science (ECOES), 147

High School Honors Science Program: Research Internship, 139

High School Summer Science Research Fellowship Program, 186

High School Summer Science Research Program, 144

Howard Hughes Trainee Program, 26

Hughes High School Research Scholars, 25

Interdisciplinary Program in Biological Science with an Emphasis on Research, 17

Intern '94, 112

International Summer Science Institute (Israel), 197

LUMCON/NSF Marine Science Young Scholars Program, 88

Minority Engineering Summer Research Program, 52

Minority High School Student Research Apprenticeship Program, 182

Minority High School Students Research Apprentice Program, 30

New York State Summer Institute for Science and Mathematics (Buffalo), 151

New York State Summer Institute for Science and Mathematics (Syracuse), 152

Nuclear Science and Technology, 102

Research and Engineering Apprentice Program (REAP), 192

Research Participation Program in Science, The, 27

Research Science Institute, 133

Sargent Camp Internship in Environmental Education, 214

Science and Engineering Honors Program, 132

Science & Engineering Research Academy (SERA), 176

Scientific Application of Technology, 178

Sci-Tech: Technion's International Science and Technology Research Program, 198

Secondary Student Training Program (SSTP): Research Participation Program, 125

Simons Summer Research Fellowship Program, The, 157

Smith Summer Science Program, 135

STRIVE for College and Careers in Science, Mathematics, and Engineering, 137

Student Conservation Association High School Work Groups (HSWG), 61

Student Science Training Program (SSTP), 114

Student Science Training Program (SSTP) in Stellar Astronomy and Nuclear Radiation Applications, 122

Summer Engineering Academy (SEA): Summer Apprenticeship Program (SAP), 43

Summer Minority Student Science Training Program, 104

Summer Research and Apprenticeship Program in Science and Mathematics, 156

Summer Research Program for High School Students, 78

Summer Research Training Program, 154

Summer Space Academy, 12

Summer Student Grants at the National Institutes of Health, 129

Training for Research: The Summer Student Program, 22

University of Connecticut—Young Scholars
Program, 112
Volunteer for Science (U.S. Geological Survey),
193
Young Scholars Program: Exploration of Careers
in Science, 121

Young Scholars Program in Life Sciences &
Biochemistry, Chemistry & Physics with
Research Participation, 183
Young Scholars Research Program in Chemistry,
101
Young Scientist Program: A Research Experience in Biology, 19

Index to Programs for Special Populations

Disadvantaged or Disabled Students

Although many programs encourage disadvantaged or disabled students to apply, the following are especially designed for these populations.
Camp Planet Earth, 66
Engineering Summer Residency Program (ESRP), 33
Minority High School Students Research Apprentice Program, 30
National Federation of the Blind Scholarship Program, 256
Northeast Science Enrichment Program, 130
Project YES (Young Exceptional Scholars), 18
Research and Engineering Apprentice Program (REAP), 192
Summer Program in Marine Science (for the Hearing-Impaired), 94
Upward Bound, 138
Veterinary Enrichment Program, 79

Gifted and Talented Students

The following programs are limited to students identified as "gifted and/or talented."
Bronx High School of Science, 214
Challenges for Youth—Talented and Gifted (CY-TAG), 123
Coast Trek: A Marine Science and Environmental Studies Program, 90
Explorations!, 124
GERI Summer Residential Programs, 122
Governor's School on the Environment, The, 62
Green River Preserve, The, 159
High School SUMMIT, 126
Research Participation Program in Science, The, 27
Research Science Institute, 133
Summer Enrichment Program for Gifted and Talented Youth at Camp Broadstone, 158
Summer Institute for the Gifted at Bryn Mawr College, The, 150
Summer Scholars Program, 187
Summer Scholars Program—Biotechnology and Human Reproduction: Tinkering with Nature, 23
Summer Science Program, 157
Summer Study in Engineering: Young Scholars Program, 41
TAG (Talented and Gifted) Science Program, 183
WISE Academic Camp, 165

Minority Students

Many other programs encourage applications from minority students.
Academically Interested Minorities (AIM), 140
AGI Minority Geoscience Scholarships, 248
AISES Science Camp, 155
A.T. Anderson Memorial Scholarship Program, 249
AT&T Engineering Scholarship Program, 249
Discovery, 148
Dow Chemical Premier Scholarship Program, 251
Early Identification Program, 52
Engineering Career Orientation (ECO), 43
Engineering Experience for Minorities: TEEM, The, 46
Engineering Summer Residency Program (ESRP), 33
IHS Scholarships for Native Americans, 253
Intensive Summer Science Program (ISSP), 160
Introduction to Engineering and Science Summer Institute, 145
LULAC National Scholarship Fund, 254
Math and Science for Minority Students (MS²), 130
Minority Engineering Summer Research Program, 52
Minority Enrichment Seminar in Engineering Training (MESET), 54
Minority High School Student Research Apprenticeship Program, 182
Minority High School Students Research Apprentice Program, 30
Minority Scholars in Computer Science and Engineering, 42
MIT MITES—Minority Introduction to Engineering & Science, 133
MITE Programs, 31
NACME Incentive Grants Program, 254
National Society of Black Engineers Scholars Program, 258
Northeast Science Enrichment Program, 130
PREFACE, 38
Preface Program, 48
Recruitment into Engineering of High Ability Minority Students (REHAMS), 39
Research and Engineering Apprentice Program (REAP), 192
Research Apprentice Program in Veterinary

Medicine for Minority High School Students, 76

Saturday Academy, The (Bennett College), 216

Society of Hispanic Professional Engineers (SHPE) Educational Grants Program, 260

STRIVE for College and Careers in Science, Mathematics, and Engineering, 137

Summer Engineering Academy (SEA): Summer Apprenticeship Program (SAP), 43

Summer Minority Student Science Training Program, 104

Veterinary Enrichment Program, 79

Women

These programs are limited to females. Many other programs especially encourage applications from female students.

Access to Careers in the Sciences (ACES) Camps, 184

AT&T Engineering Scholarship Program, 249

Douglass Science Institute for High School Women in Math, Science, and Engineering, 149

Duke Action: A Science Camp for Young Women, 64

Engineering Summer Residency Program (ESRP), 33

Exploring Career Options in Engineering and Science (ECOES), 147

Math and Science Spectacles, 116

Preface Program, 48

Radcliffe Summer Program in Science, 134

Science Quest, 172

Smith Summer Science Program, 135

Society of Women Engineers Scholarship Program, 261

Summer Study in Engineering Program for High School Women, 41

WISE: Women Investigating Sciences and Environments, 147

Women in Engineering Program (Michigan), 45

Women in Engineering (WIE) Program (Ohio), 50

Women in Science and Engineering (WISE) Program, 118

Women in Science and Mathematics Workshop, 161

Women in the Sciences, 164